2/25/2017

Dear Aida Nevárez-La Torre,

It was a pleasure to meet you and hear about your research. Hope you find this book interesting and useful.

Best,
Debora Upegui
dupegui@gmail.com

The New Americans
Recent Immigration and American Society

Edited by
Steven J. Gold and Rubén G. Rumbaut

A Series from LFB Scholarly

Growing up Transnational
Colombian and Dominican Children of Immigrants in New York City

Débora Upegui-Hernández

LFB Scholarly Publishing LLC
El Paso 2014

Library of Congress Cataloging-in-Publication Data

Upegui-Hernández, Débora, 1975-
Growing up transnational : Colombian and Dominican children of immigrants in New York City / Débora Upegui-Hernández.
page cm
Includes bibliographical references and index.
ISBN 978-1-59332-617-3 (hardcover : alk. paper)
1. Children of immigrants--New York (State)--New York. 2. Colombian Americans--New York (State)--New York. 3. Dominican Americans--New York (State)--New York. 4. Cultural fusion--New York (State)--New York. I. Title.
JV6600.U64 2014
305.23089'68729307471--dc23
2014007868

ISBN 978-1-59332-617-3

Printed on acid-free 250-year-life paper.

Manufactured in the United States of America.

Table of Contents

List of Tables and Figures

Acknowledgements

> I belong to a land that is still unknown to herself.
> I write to help her reveal herself – to reveal, to rebel –
> And seeking her out I seek out myself,
> And with her, in her, I lose myself.
> (Galeano as cited by Fischlin & Nandorfy, 2002, p. 60)

As I ponder over the journey that writing this book has entailed, I am deeply grateful to Michelle Fine for believing in me from the start and, most of all, for helping me find my voice. Learning and doing Participatory Action Research deeply changed my understanding of social psychology and research and I thank you for that. I would like to thank Kay Deaux and Philip Kasinitz who so generously offered their time and support throughout this journey, as well as, Gary Winkel and Jennifer Ayala for their invaluable comments and support throughout this process. I am also grateful to Suzanne Ouellette, Roger Hart, Colette Daiute and Ethel Tobach.

I am deeply grateful to the Center for Urban Research at the CUNY Graduate, Mary Waters, John Mollenkopf, Jennifer Holdaway, Ervin Kosta and all the graduate students who were part of the ISGMNY project. This book would not have been possible without your work and generous access to the Immigrant Second Generation database.

The Center for Latin American, Caribbean, and Latino Studies (CLACLS) was an oasis of *cariño, confianza, y apoyo* which validated our shared experiences as Latinas/os in academia. I especially thank Laird Bergad for his intellectual and financial support throughout my work in this book.

Gracias a mi compañero, Rafael Torruella, por su apoyo incansable e incondicional. Gracias a mi mama Maritza, mi hermano Carlos. Le dedico este libro a mi Abuela Libia, por ser mi ancla y porque Colombia, para mí, eres tú. A mi familia en Colombia, a mis primas y primos, a mis tías y tíos, Edilma, Elvia, Libia, y Marleni, que siempre me hicieron sentir como si nunca hubiera partido. Su cariño y apoyo me sostuvieron en los momentos en que más sola me sentí desde la diáspora, y el regocijo del regreso siempre me llena el corazón de felicidad y me recuerda que mi pasado sigue siendo parte de mi presente y mi futuro. Este libro es en parte un tributo al amor que me han brindado y a lo importante que siempre han sido en mi vida. Finalmente este libro es para mis sobrinos, Isabela y Anthony, porque ustedes representan nuestro futuro y son nuestra esperanza, porque ustedes llevan sangre colombiana y puertorriqueña, y son la esperanza de un 'abrazo cultural', never let anyone tell you that you are not fully Colombian or not fully Puerto Rican. You are who you are, and we are better because you exist. I love you.

I would also like to thank my friends Marissel, Yesenia, Carmen Ana, Tere, Vikky, Carolina, Patricia, Valky, and Laura for our many conversations and keeping me sane. There are many friends who shared this journey with me and they may find their names in the pages of this book as a way to honor what I learned from their experiences.

Finally, I am in great debt to those Latin American thinkers that have inspired my desire to fight for social justice and represent my intellectual heritage: Ignacio Martín Baró, Paulo Freire, Franz Fanon, Orlando Fals Borda, Fernando Ortíz, Eduardo Galeano, Gabriel García Márquez, and Mercedes Sosa.

CHAPTER 1

Introduction and Literature Review

> , hearing,
> with half my soul at sea and half my soul on land,
> And with those two halves of soul I see the world.
> (Excerpt from a poem by Neruda in Arana, 2002)

This book explores how Colombian and Dominican children of immigrants living in New York City negotiate multiple, and often conflicting, identities, selves, and histories. In other words, children of immigrants may feel they are part of two, or more, nation-states/cultures and find meaning in these multiple national identities instead of being tied to a notion of loyalty to only one country. In many ways, the relationship between the country of origin and the country of settlement of an immigrant shapes the context in which immigrants and their children negotiate their social and personal identities. Bringing a transnational perspective to the psychological study of identity negotiation among children of immigrants is important in order to understand how maintaining transnational ties allows them to maintain continuity between their pasts and presents and to be able to forge a successful future. This study is designed to contribute to research about Colombian and Dominican second generation immigrants within the social sciences and the psychological study of migration from a transnational perspective.

For the purposes of this study, both 'second generation' and '1.5 generation' immigrants are considered 'children of immigrants', recognizing their common experiences of growing up and coming of age within the American school system and culture. Using a terminology based on generations seems problematic and reductive. Referring to children born in the United States as 'immigrants' overemphasizes their differences, contributing to a process of 'othering' and social distancing, which implies that children with immigrant backgrounds are not fully American and are not part of the in-group ("us"). "More important perhaps, they are not immigrants culturally. Having been raised in the United States, most of them accept norms of behavior, language, and gender roles that often create profound disconnect with the world of their parents" (Kasinitz, Mollenkopf, Waters, & Holdaway, 2008, p. 294). Therefore, I refer to respondents as children of immigrants throughout.

Social psychologists have emphasized the usefulness of levels of analysis for comprehending the diverse approaches to the study of social identity within and across disciplines (Verkuyten, 2005a). Given the transdisciplinarity that characterizes immigration research and my own academic experience, this book moves across levels of analysis in order contextualize and provide a comprehensive approach to the study of Dominican and Colombian children of immigrants' transnational practices and how such transnational experiences affect their personal and social identity negotiations. This approach serves to emphasize the importance of the intersection between the individual and her/his social and political context. I see the process of immigration and transnationalism as dynamic social processes that are shaped by social/structural forces (i.e. race, gender, social class, national policies) as well as by personal agency and choices.

I relied upon Deaux's definition of social identity as "including self-definition, language use, social and cultural habits, [family,] friendship [and social] networks, and other significant aspects of social and psychological life." (2006, p.7) As Verkeyten's noted:

> [W]hat is at stake [in social identity] is not that which distinguishes a person as an individual from other individuals, but that which is shared with others. The emphasis is not on what makes a person unique, but on similarities to some shared differences with others… These characteristics distinguish a person from people that do not have that characteristic and puts him or her together with those that do. (2005a, p. 42)

An important distinction should be made between social identity and sense of identity. The first is externally assigned by others in an effort to socially position an individual while the second refers to the subjective (psychological) experience of such categorization. In exploring the process of identity negotiation among children of immigrants, I share the assumption that "[i]dentity issues concern both personal interpretations and sociocultural constructions, and these issues cannot be reduced to one another" (Verkuyten, 2005b, p. 61).

My participation in the Immigrant Second Generation of Metropolitan New York (ISGMNY) study was the driving force in my decision to use a secondary analysis approach for this study. As I read and coded interviews for the ISGMNY study, I was inspired by respondents' narratives about their transnational practices and ties, and how natural they appeared to be in their lives, despite the skepticism with which immigration literature has discussed them. As a Colombian immigrant, I was initially inclined to investigate the transnational experiences and identity formation among Colombian immigrants. However, after reading interview transcripts of Chinese, Jewish Russian, Caribbean, and Latin American immigrants, I was impressed by how similar their experiences were in some domains, yet so different in others. I realized how important and useful a comparative approach among different Latino national groups would be.

This study focuses on Dominican and Colombian respondents in an effort to compare my findings to prior research about these two national groups. The existence of marked social class and race differences among these two immigrant groups' profiles in New York City and similarities in their migration histories and United States' political and military involvement in their home countries, contributed to my interest in these particular groups. I did not focus on Puerto Ricans as a group because of Puerto Rico's political status as an American territory, the fact that Puerto Ricans are U.S. citizens, and the island's colonial relationship to the United States. This means that Puerto Ricans are not usually considered immigrants in the same way as other Latin American national groups. Accordingly, Puerto Ricans do not have to deal with fear of deportation or the consequences of having undocumented status as do immigrants from other Latin American countries. Puerto Ricans do not feel that the experiences of Latin American immigrants relate to their own Puerto Rican experience. On the other hand, Ecuadorian and Peruvian immigrants in the United States share similar socio-economic profiles with Colombians, yet their racial make-up is marked by a much larger population of Amerindian descent and Mestizo individuals. Ecuadorian and Peruvian immigrants have a different history and experience with race formation processes in their countries than Colombians. Although I compare and use national groups as categories of distinction, I do not assume homogeneity within them. I acknowledge that, within immigrant national groups, there is enormous heterogeneity of experiences and social class backgrounds.

MIGRATION AND PSYCHOLOGY LITERATURES

The world has witnessed, in the last half of the twentieth century, an unprecedented intensification of movements of people, goods, companies, and capital (Basch, Glick-Schiller, & Szanton-Blanc, 1994; Levitt & Waters, 2002; M. M. Suárez-Orozco, 2002). Migration literatures have proliferated in an attempt to understand the processes and outcomes of these movements of people becoming more inter-disciplinary now than ever with contributions from sociologists, demographers, economists, anthropologists, legal scholars, post-colonialists, and epidemiologists (Bhatia & Ram, 2001a; M. M. Suárez-Orozco, 2002). Yet psychologists have not played as big a role as one would expect (Berry, 2001; Deaux, 2000; Mahalingam, 2006) in understanding the social and psychological effects of the phenomenon of human migration. This review explores how human migration and changes in the dynamics of incorporation of immigrants and their children create and transform individual and collective identities, subjectivities, longings, everyday practices, and relationships. These topics are well-suited for socio-psychological research. This literature review revisits social constructs such as national identity, diasporas, transnationalism, and transnational social fields usually addressed within the realm of political, sociological, and anthropological scientific writings, yet rarely visited by psychologists. My goal is to open a space for introducing the psychological back into the study of human migration without (re)inscribing individualism or reducing politics to individual lives. At the same time, this study brings a transnational perspective to the psychological study of immigrants and their children's lives.

The concepts of 'nation' and 'nation-states' are usually intertwined in our minds and in psychological research. In this time and age, it is hard to talk about nations without talking about nation-states. But this is not a coincidence. When one considers the concept of 'nations,' one almost immediately thinks of the governments and nation-states associated with them which reifies how successful nation-state building projects have been in rendering those ideas as 'taken for granted' and unquestionable. Wimmer and Glick-Schiller argued that the methodological nationalism of social sciences "assume[s] that countries are the natural units for comparative studies, equate society with nation-state, and conflate national interests with the purposes of social sciences"(2003, p. 578). Recent research on theories of transnationalism deconstructs these concepts within social sciences and migration research and has highlighted their social and political construction.

This literature review is organized in several sections that increasingly complicate the subject of identity negotiation within changing political entities and social spaces. It begins by describing how different disciplines in the social and behavioral sciences have approached the question of how immigrants are incorporated into the contexts where they chose to settle upon migration. I outline with broad strokes the main differences between theories of assimilation (sociology), acculturation (psychology and early anthropology), diaspora formation and transnationalism (anthropology and cultural psychology). I then introduce the concept of transnational social fields as a construct that extends what psychology and sociology have theorized as social fields and elaborates on how globalization and transnational border crossings constitute new transnational spaces where social relationships and lives are simultaneously affected by multiple geographical, economic, social, and political realities. I also explore the differences between the concepts of diaspora, diasporic identities/communities, and transnational identities/communities. Another section compares psychological definitions and research on ethnic and national identities and how they are challenged by transnational realities. This is followed by a discussion of work that has explored psychological concepts and processes affected by migration and transnational/cross border experiences of immigrants such as, theories of biculturalism, Bicultural Identity Integration, cultural frame switching. It also discusses how dialogical self theories account for identity development in the midst of multiple cultural frames. Following this section, I provide an overview of migration research focused on children of immigrants, more commonly known as 'second generation immigrants', and offer conclusions that have been made about the nature and extent of their involvement and attachment to their parents' home country. Research findings addressing the relationship of social variables such as race and gender, and the experiences of children of immigrants are also discussed. Finally, in order to contextualize the transnational experiences of Dominican and Colombian children of immigrants, I provide an overview of both groups' migration histories to the United States as a background for understanding how each group arrived in the United States with particular social, economic, and political characteristics.

THEORIZING THE INCORPORATION OF IMMIGRANTS ACROSS DISCIPLINES

Theories of assimilation have been advanced largely by sociologists and date to the beginning of the 20th century when the largest wave of immigration, mostly of European origins, entered the United States (M. M. Suárez-Orozco, 2002). The assumption then was that immigrants would eventually assimilate into American culture, leaving behind their old country views and attachments. Assimilation was understood as "a process of change that is directional- indeed unilinear- nonreversible, and continuous" (M. M. Suárez-Orozco, 2002, p. 24). Suaréz-Orozco (M. M. Suárez-Orozco, 2002) outlined three main assumptions in the dominant discourse about the assimilation of immigrants: the 'clean break', the 'homogeneity' and the 'progress' assumption. The first meant that immigrants were expected or understood to be moving from their home country to a host country without hopes or thoughts of returning. The second assumed that immigrants would, over generations, become part of mainstream American society. Finally, assimilation theory expected that later generations would do better than their immigrant parents and experience upward social mobility.

More recent waves of immigrants have challenged the assumptions behind assimilation theories (Kasinitz, Waters, Mollenkopf, & Anil, 2002; Portes & Rumbaut, 2001; Waldinger, 2004) and shown them to be problematic. First, more recent immigrants continue to arrive mainly from Asia (over 25%) and Latin America (50%) which makes it harder to assume that their children will be incorporated as 'white-ethnics' in the same way that third and fourth generation Irish and Italians were (M. M. Suárez-Orozco, 2002). Second, immigrants 'of color' are experiencing continued discrimination and racism which undermines the possibilities for later generations to be more successful than their immigrant parents (Farley & Alba, 2002). Third, more recent immigrants are maintaining social, economic, and political ties with their countries of origin with greater intensity and ease (Eckstein & Barberia, 2002; Hirsch, 2000).

Early theorizing of segmented assimilation by Portes and Zhou (1993) represented an effort to accommodate the realities of the new wave of Asian and Latin American immigrants by outlining different pathways to assimilation that permitted either upward or downward mobility depending on their contexts. Perhaps the most controversial aspects of that theorizing was the argument that those who were living along side marginalized groups were bound to become marginalized themselves and would assume a reactive position towards mainstream society. Another point of criticism was the emphasis on predicting which pathway immigrants would follow based on a number of variables which did not allow room for overcoming such contextual difficulties unless one lived in an 'ethnic enclave' which provided social capital and economic resources. Portes and colleagues (Portes, Fernandez-Kelly, & Haller, 2008, 2009) have recently refined their model of segmented assimilation and have moved from describing the different pathways of assimilation as *reactive, selective and symbolic assimilation* to *consonant, selective and dissonant acculturation.* One of the most useful contributions of segmented assimilation theory is the identification of three major 'exogenous' factors shaping immigrants' assimilation: immigrant parents' human capital, the social context of the host country, and the composition of the family, all of which are moderated by the presence of a prosperous co-ethnic community.

Although proponents of segmented assimilation coincide with much research that highlights racism and unfavorable labor markets as major barriers to social mobility among immigrants, their continued emphasis on the negative role of 'deviant lifestyles' and lack of consideration of social and structural processes behind them remains problematic. Recently Water and colleagues (2010) examined the fitness of segmented assimilation's acculturation typology based on data from the ISGMNY study. Their findings dispute the extent to which participating in ethnic enclaves and type of acculturation will have an effect on social mobility among children of immigrants. Their data showed that the above variables did not explain differences in social mobility among immigrant groups by nationality. Stepick and Stepick (2010) affirm that the use of segmented assimilation as a typology of acculturation remains controversial, as it emphasizes a framework of national group's perceived deficiencies rather that interrogate the social structures and processes that inhibit immigrant groups' social mobility and create a negative host context.

More recently, Alba and Nee (2003) and Alba (2009) proposed redefining assimilation as a process of boundary blurring rather than a process of losing one culture and taking up another. In part as a response to segmented assimilation, this 'new assimilation' theory focuses on the process by which people become assimilated or adapt to their host culture. It asserts that "privilege groups defend the boundaries that separate them from the less fortunate" (Alba, 2009, p. 15) and would continue to do so, if they feel their privileges are threatened by new groups. However, if immigrants are not perceived to be a threat to the mainstream's position of privilege, then assimilation and incorporation is possible through the blurring of boundaries. This perspective assumes that social mobility in the form of socio-economic ascent facilitates social proximity and porous borders. Alba (2005, 2009) defines blurred boundaries as "zones of ambiguity" that allow immigrants who are part of a minority group to belong or feel comfortable as part of the majority group even if it is only temporary" while bright boundaries are those aspects of social reality that are perceived as non-ambiguous such as skin-color. Finally, Itzigsohn (2009) offers what he calls, a theory of *stratified ethnoracial incorporation* that challenges both segmented assimilation and 'new assimilation' theories by emphasizing the intersection of racializing processes and socio-economic stratification. He emphasizes race and stratification as social processes, dynamic in nature, that occur within immigrant groups, which have usually been overlooked and have the potential to challenge dominant notions of race and social realities.

On the other hand, the acculturation perspective has received more attention within psychology (Bhatia & Ram, 2001a; Berry, 1997; Colic-Peisker & Walker, 2003; LaFromboise, Coleman, & Gerton, 1993). Berry used the concept of acculturation to describe the process whereby a cultural group experiences changes as it comes into contact with another cultural group. More specifically, psychological acculturation is understood as the changes a person undergoes as he/she comes into contact with members of another cultural group. Berry's model (1997) of psychological acculturation suggested four paths or outcomes for immigrants: integration, assimilation, separation/segregation, or marginalization. Inherent in his theorizing was the assumption that integration was the best possible outcome where "there is some degree of cultural integrity maintained, while at the same time seeking to participate as an integral part of the larger social network."(Berry, 1997, p. 9) Those who find themselves in other cells of the 2 x 2 matrix would experience psychological stress to varying degrees. Their emphasis is on psychological stress as a result of the process of acculturation. Despite acknowledging individual differences and diverse contexts, Berry and his colleagues assumed a universalist perspective to acculturation (Berry and Sam, 1997 as cited by Bhatia & Ram, 2001b).

Cross-cultural psychologists have used this perspective to understand what psychological changes occur in the process of immigration. In other words, they focus on how the individual adapts to a different society and culture as they migrate from one country to another. LaFromboise and colleagues (1993) argued that, to a great extent, the acculturation approach maintained assumptions similar to those held by the assimilation approach with regards to adopting the mainstream culture, the existence of a hierarchy among the different groups coming into contact, and understanding the process as a unidirectional one. However, acculturation differs from assimilation in so far as it allows for understanding that adapting to a new culture and context does not require that the immigrant group stop identifying with its culture and its country of origin.

Although the dilemmas encountered by immigrants since the late 19th century are still alive, the perspectives under which they are understood and examined have changed. The social context within which migration occurs has gone from 'assimilation' during the early part of the 20th century, through definitions of 'acculturation', 'melting-pot', 'pluralism', 'segmented-assimilation', and 'salad bowl' among others. These views rested on fixed definitions of 'home' and 'host' countries that serve as points of departure or arrival for the development of identity among immigrants and the maintenance of separate social spheres. However, what might a transnational perspective look like? "Contemporary immigrants are seen as maintaining familial, economic, cultural, and political ties across international borders, in effect, making the home and host society a single arena of social action" (Foner, 2001, p. 36).

Early research on transnationalism dealt with the need to undermine assimilation, acculturation, and incorporation theories' inadequacy to study the phenomenon of living across borders in an increasingly globalized society (Levitt & Glick-Schiller, 2004). First, they needed to open up a space for their theories of transnationalism to be considered seriously, as offering a different and important contribution to immigration theory. Then, they found the need to support their claims with empirical research and to convince scholars that this was a worthwhile approach for mainstream migration theorists to consider (Levitt, DeWind, & Vertovec, 2003). Although transnationalism is not in itself a new phenomenon, its use as an analytical lens in migration theory dates from the 1990s. As a theoretical perspective it continues to evolve and refine its conceptual and methodological premises as evidenced in the publication of special issues by *Ethnic and Racial Studies* in 1999 and by *International Migration Reviewin 2003* (See Levitt et al., 2003; See Portes, Guarnizo, & Landolt, 1999 and Vertovec, 2009 for an extended review of criticism and debates in the field).

A transnational perspective challenges a number of assumptions held by psychological theory and methods. First, it assumes that people have multiple social identities whether cultural, ethnic, or national. By having legal citizenship in more than one country, transmigrants may feel they are part of two different nation-states and find meaning in multiple ethno/national identities instead of being tied to a notion of loyalty to only one country. Second, policies of dual-citizenship and dual-nationality are changing the social representations of national loyalty and citizenship as mutually exclusive to one nation-state, changing the social representations of migrants in their home country and among co-nationals who have not migrated. Third, and most interesting for identity and social psychology theory, the existence of a 'transnational identity' that emerges in the experience of 'trans' (understood as crossing) national borders and territories as they navigate transnational social fields.

TRANSNATIONAL SOCIAL FIELDS

Carteau's definition of 'space as practiced place' where the process of creating stories about displacement "transforms places into spaces and spaces into places" (1988 cited by Sorensen, 1998, p. 244), helps us recognize how sharing a transnational space facilitates the perception of common characteristics among migrants who maintain transnational ties and relationships. Sharing a social and psychological space with family members and friends no longer requires geographical proximity or face-to-face interaction, which has traditionally been the focus of social networks, social support, and identity theorists (Vertovec, 2009). It also provides the basis for the formation of transnational social groups and diasporas. "They are here and there and in between" (Guarnizo, 1994 cited by Sorensen, 1998, p. 244). Suarez-Orozco echoes this understanding as he acknowledges "[i]mmigrants today are more likely to be at once here *and* there, articulating dual consciousness and dual identities, in the process, bridging increasingly unbounded national spaces" (2002, p. 27).

Nina N. Sorensen (1998) challenges the tradition of thinking in terms of fixed entities, dichotomies, and categories. She pushes open ethnic and national social categories, personal identity; and definitions of home and host countries as spaces that define identities by exploring the complexity inherent in the relationship between migration and identity. "[I]n this world, the Dominican cultural identity space is occupied by transnationals and locals whose lives and experiences are interweaved with the questions of *aquí?* or *allá?*, of here? and there?" (Sorensen, 1998, p. 243). Although she was trained in the field of anthropology, her subject of study – identity – transcends disciplinary boundaries. She contributes a different perspective to the psychological discussion of identity that has been called a "transnational perspective". By arguing the existence of a "transnational social space" that "encompasses the whole of what individual migrants have lived through and therefore bears the potential for bringing experiences from different times and different locations into one single field of analysis" (1998, p. 24), Sorensen theorizes the continued involvement of immigrants across borders and challenges theories of assimilation and acculturation.

Transmigrants create 'social fields' that cross national boundaries through their everyday lives and maintain personal, social, economic and political ties in more than one country/nation-state (Basch et al., 1994; Bhatia & Ram, 2001b; Eckstein & Barberia, 2002; Fouron & Glick-Schiller, 2002; Hirsch, 2000; Levitt, 2000; Mahler, 2001). The concept of 'transnational social fields' allows us to bring together into a single field of analysis immigrants' life experiences from different times (past, present, and future) and different locations (home-country, host-country, homeland, country of residence). Having one's transnational social space legitimized through dual-citizenship policies can have an empowering effect for personal, social, and political identities, as well as for social and political action both, in the home and host country (Levitt & Waters, 2002; Riccio, 2001; Vertovec, 1999). This would be especially true for transmigrants that may refuse naturalization or to become citizens of their host country for fear of losing their home-country's citizenship, a symbol of their national identity. It has been documented that when policies of dual-citizenship are implemented, naturalization rates increase (Faist, 2001) facilitating immigrants' access to health and social benefits only available to citizens in the United States. Thus, geographical borders alone no longer define citizenship. National governments are (re)defining notions of citizenship by granting double-citizenship to those who in other times would have been considered either expatriates or part of a national diaspora (Glick-Schiller & Fouron, 1998).

In 1994, Basch, Glick-Schiller, and Szanton Blanc used the term "transnational social fields" to describe the transnational social spaces. Their conception of transnational social fields is based on the concept of a social field as "an unbounded terrain of interlocking egocentric networks" (1999). By concentrating on the concept of social fields, they pushed beyond the scope of social networks which usually referred to social relationships among specific persons with whom one has contact with in one's immediate physical context. Transnational social fields encompass social spaces created by the existence of transnational social networks and affect migrants beyond specific social networks they may have in the country in which they have settled.

The concept of social fields has its origins in psychological field theory and has an interesting intellectual history. According to several accounts (Bargal, 2006; Lewin, 1997 [1948,1951]; J. L. Martin, 2003), Kurt Lewin introduced the concept of psychological and social space/field to the repertoire of social psychologists in his book *Field Theory in Social Science* (1951). Lewin's theorizing was influenced by

Gestalt theory and primarily developed the implications of field theory for understanding the psychological field/space of an individual. In the late 1960's, field theory reappeared in sociology in Pierre Bourdieu's work. According to Swartz (1997 as cited by J. L. Martin, 2003), Bourdieu credited Lewin's field theory for having a major role in his sociological theorizing of social spaces and field theory. Although Bourdieu did not hold in high regard the psychologists of his time (2008), his theorizing of social fields, *habitus* and different domains that define social spaces (such as economic, cultural, social and symbolic capital) have much in common with social psychological concepts and epistemologies. Despite criticisms, different postulations of field theory coincide on three aspects: first, a field represents an area of analysis with specific dimensions in which persons and institutions are positioned; second, a field is perceived as an organization of forces; and third, fields are sites of contestation, "a battlefield"(J. L. Martin, 2003). The most significant contribution of field theory, and psychological/social fields at the time, was that "psychological events are conceived as a consequence of the interaction between the person and the environment" (Bargal, 2006, p. 374) at a specific point in time and space highlighting the interdependence of individuals and groups (Allport's 1948 foreword to Lewin, 1997).

Transnational perspectives have been advanced mostly by anthropologists, sociologists, and some political scientists. They build on work about "diasporic communities" which are considered groups of people displaced or exiled from their countries of origin without the possibility of return but who maintained psychological, social, economic, and political ties with a common past and future that may or may not involve a nation-state or home country (Clifford, 1994). As Clifford puts it "the empowering paradox of a diaspora is that dwelling *here* assumes a solidarity and connection *there*. But *there* is not necessarily a single place or an exclusivist nation" (1994, p. 322 emphasis added). These diasporic communities were usually dispersed among a number of different locales i.e. the African diaspora, which includes people of African descent in the United States, the Caribbean, Central and South-America, or the Jewish diaspora. According to Safran, what defines a diaspora is "a history of dispersal, myths/memories of the homeland, alienation in the host (bad host?) country, desire for eventual return, ongoing support of the homeland, and a collective identity importantly defined by this relationship"

(1991, as cited by Clifford, 1994, p. 305). The histories of diasporas are intimately tied to histories of colonialism and post-colonialism, of power, oppression, and economic dependence.

More recently, diasporas have come to be understood as one type of transnational community (Levitt, 2000). There are a number of definitions given to the term transnational communities, but I will use Levitt's definition, which is rather comprehensive. She understands transnational communities as:

> ...rooted in particular, bounded sending- and receiving-country locales. Because they emerged from the social networks that precipitate migration, members tend to know one another personally or have family members or acquaintances in common during the early phases of community formation. They form organizations that express their identity as a transnational group. They exhibit some level of self-consciousness about belonging to a community spanning borders...Transnational communities include both migrants and non-migrants, though the nature of non-migrant participation varies considerably. (2000, p. 461)[1]

Diasporic and transnational perspectives acknowledge that immigrants participate both in their homelands/home countries while they incorporate into their host countries.

By focusing on transnational social fields, researchers (Basch et al., 1994; Fouron & Glick-Schiller, 2002; Glick-Schiller & Fouron, 1998, 1999; R. C. Smith, 2003; Sorensen, 1998) have been able to examine the processes by which immigrants maintain ties to the country they emigrated from, at the same time that they live and adapt to the countries where they settled. Despite the enormous potential for understanding and focusing on human interaction and interpersonal relationships inherent in the uses of transnational social fields as a concept, many of these researchers have focused instead on the kinds of activities that transmigrants carry out such as remittances, trips to home

---

[1] Levitt acknowledges that using the term 'community' does not imply that all members have a sense of affinity or solidarity with one another.

country, phone and e-mail communication, transnational business practices, social/human capital among others (Guarnizo, A. I. Sanchez, & Roach, 1999; Portes, 2003). Researchers have studied the outcomes of these behaviors on assimilation, acculturation, and/or incorporation, their effects on ethnic identity, and patterns of integration into the host-country (Portes, 1999). Others have focused on the impact of transnational activities in the political and economic development of sending-countries (Guarnizo & Díaz, 1999; R. C. Smith, 2003).[2] A few others have begun to question how transnational ties redefine our understanding of sociological constructs such as motherhood, parenting, citizenship, and loyalty among others (Hondagneu-Sotelo & Avila, 1997, 2003; Mahler, 2001).

While research on transnational ties is important for understanding the process of migration and transmigration, the psychological importance of transnational ties for immigrants and non-immigrants remains neglected. For example, identity is almost always mentioned as being affected by these processes yet there has been little discussion of how people understand their identities at a personal level beyond the group membership or psychological consequences of migration for their well-being (Bhatia & Ram, 2001a, 2001b; Berry, 2001; Mahalingam, 2006). In addition, there has been little room for discussing variation by nation, language, color, gender, class, or sexuality among immigrants' experiences. In a recent article, Vertovec (2004, also 2009) notes social science literature on transnationalism mainly focused on understanding the social organization, specific political and economic practices and institutions of transnationalism while questions about motivations, meanings, attitudes, feelings and people's agency in these transnational processes remained largely absent. Beyond that, transnational "dispositions and practices have substantial impact on individual and family life course and strategies, individuals' sense of self and collective belonging, the ordering of

[2] Although Smith (2003) makes an important discussion of how the political state through political decisions has contributed to changing the social representation of transmigrants, citizenship and migration in general. He also elaborates on how these changing social representation contribute to (re)shape peoples' identities and lives.

personal and group memories, patterns of consumption, collective socio-cultural practices, approaches to childrearing and other modes of cultural reproduction." (Vertovec, 2004, p. 977)

In contrast, the dialogical model of self presented by Hermans (2001) has theorized transnational contexts and their connection to personal, cultural and social identity processes by drawing on Bathkin's notions of polyphony and multiple voices inherent in each utterance or speech act. The dialogical approach to understanding identity construction and multiple identities has received greater attention from psychologists (Bhatia, 2002; Bhatia & Ram, 2001a, 2001b). A dialogical model of self illustrates how negotiating immigrants' identity involves multiple negotiations with larger sets of cultural, political, and historical contexts (Bhatia, 2007). Since "[t]he dialogical self is conceived as social; not in the sense that a self-contained individual enters into social interactions with other outside people, but in the sense that other people occupy positions in the multivoiced self..." (Hermans, Kempen, & Van Loon, 1992, p. 28), it allows us to consider the influence that social relationships in the home country would continue to exert on transmigrants' sense of self, social, and personal identity. Individuals who participate in an immigrants' transnational social space remain in constant dialogue with the immigrant, physically and/or psychologically, and are part of the social contexts that anchor the immigrants' identity. Interpersonal networks have been identified by Deaux and Martin (2003) as one of two levels of social context that can limit or support social identities by redefining their meaning and/or content. These social identities may or may not be incorporated by transmigrants as part of their personal and/or social identities. Pioneering research in cultural psychology, Murphy and Mahalingam (2004 cited by Murphy, 2006) designed a transnationalism scale which includes four domains: family ties, cultural ties, economic ties, and political ties. Family support and immigrants' cultural ties were found to be positively associated with social support, which in turn was positively related to life satisfaction. These findings suggest that there is more ground to uncover in the psychological implications of transnational social fields and ties.

CHALLENGING PSYCHOLOGICAL DEFINITIONS OF ETHNIC AND NATIONAL IDENTITIES

> …I came across a theory claiming that bilingualism can hurt you…, which claimed that in operating as two distinct personalities with distinct tongues, a bicultural person will be highly suspect to those who have only one culture. The bicultural person seems so thoroughly one way in one language, so thoroughly different in another. Only an impostor would hide that other half so well. A liar… The truth about biculturalism is more complicated. That others doubt you is not the point. (Arana, 2002, p. 280)

Transnationalism represents an emerging paradigm in the study of the process of immigration. This paradigm breaks away from what Andreas Wimmer and Nina Glick Schiller (2003) called "methodological nationalism" which has naturalized and equated society with nation-state territorial boundaries within the social sciences. This means that migration social scientists have traditionally reified the political and historical interests behind modern projects of nation-state building of the twentieth century. They pointed out mechanisms and moments at which point social scientists stopped questioning the validity of nation-state building projects and, in doing so, contributed to naturalizing the idea that 'culture' and 'society' could be equated with nation-states. In the process, populations that made up the nation-state were assumed to be homogeneous and immigrants could be viewed and labeled as threats to a nation's (society's) homogeneity.

Basch et al. points out that transmigrants may or may not use the language of transnationalism or transnational communities to describe their experiences of living in between worlds: "Living in a world in which discourses about identity continue to be framed in terms of loyalty to nations and nation-states, most transmigrants have neither fully conceptualized nor articulated a form of transnational identity."(1994, p. 8) Basch and colleagues note the discourse of "ethnic identity" used to describe and explain immigrants' efforts to hold on to their cultural roots and continue identifying themselves with their home countries, has served to advance the nationalistic project of the United States and other receiving countries. Using the conception of ethnic identity rather than that of national identity, immigrants' and minority claims to their home country cultures are usually perceived as posing a threat to the cohesion of the nation-state and to the meaning of "America" and being "American" (Clifford, 1994; Deaux et al., 2007).

Early psychological contributions to the field of immigration research can be grouped in two domains: acculturation and intergroup relations (Berry, 2001). Intergroup relations research appears to have been most productive and received more attention given the relatively large number of studies exploring and testing hypotheses about ethnic stereotypes, attitudes, and prejudice; their influences on self-esteem, well-being and discrimination at the personal level, and the influence of multicultural ideologies at the societal level. Some examples include Pettigrew's (2006) work on anti-immigrant prejudice and discrimination, Phinney and colleagues' (2001) work on the effect of attitudes and characteristics of immigrants on receiving countries' response to immigrants, work on stereotype threat, and perceived discrimination (Deaux et al., 2007), and ethnic identification (Verkuyten, 2005b; Verkuyten & deWolf, 2002) among others. In a recent article, Kay Deaux (2008) explored what it means to be an immigrant from a social psychological perspective, what is an American, and what it means to have a hyphenated American identity. She concluded that data showed having multiple identities, such as ethnic and national identities, does not entail mutual exclusivity of one over the other. She also asserted that assumptions about the meaning of national identity (i.e. ideas about patriotism and loyalty) and the incompatibility of multiple identities were behind society's uneasiness with multiple national and cultural origin identities. A comparative study among Colombian, Salvadorian, and Dominican immigrants found evidence that 'exposure to life in America' had positive effects on transnational behaviors and that higher levels of adaptation to life in the United States and longer time living in the United States facilitated transnational social, political, and economic exchanges among immigrants regardless of the country of origin. (Itzigsohn & Giorguli-Saucedo, 2005)

By using the discourse of 'ethnicity', cultural pluralists can "construct a U.S. nationality that incorporated, and yet kept subordinated, people of color."(Basch et al., 1994, p. 43) What in the immigrants' minds represents a national identity may be arbitrarily subordinated as an ethnic identity within the host country through the language of ethnicity. It also served to reify the fact that immigrants will never be fully understood as "Americans" but would have to remain hyphenised ethnics (Foster, 1991). Perhaps this is the reason why discourses of ethnicity seem to hold only as long as they are held within the nation-state in which they have been constructed (Clifford, 1994). As soon as one moves outside of a national frame of thinking, ethnic categories lose their meaning. Immigrants may be considered ethnics in their host country, but in their home country such labels may represent national identities and lose their meaning as categories of ethnicity, i.e. "Dominican" as an ethnic identity label vs. "Dominican" as a national identity label. Yet Riccio (2001) warns that simply replacing the label "ethnic group" with transnational would be a mistake and would fail to capture the multiple and complex ways in which immigrants and transmigrants live their lives and make sense of their identities.

The ethnicity of immigrants usually involves a different categorization within their home countries. Therefore we should reconsider whether the concept of 'ethnicity' needs to be reevaluated and understood in the context of transnational social fields that involve more than one nation-state as their point of reference (Itzigsohn, 2004; Itzigsohn, Giorguli, & Vazquez, 2005; Oboler, 1995; Portes & Rumbaut, 2001). Certainly, it points to the inadequacy of ethnic labels that double as national identity labels. The fact that immigrants identify with ethnic labels such as Dominican, Puerto-Rican, Mexican, Peruvian, Irish, does not mean that immigrants understand them to be ethnic identity labels. Immigrants may believe them to be national identity labels. What those who created the labels understand them to be is not necessarily the meaning they hold for those who respond to them. Calling oneself 'Mexican-American' does not necessarily mean that a person understands her/himself as part of an ethnic group. It may simply be one's understanding of self as both, a citizen of Mexico and a citizen of the United States.

Processes of nation-building and delimiting citizenship contribute to delineate how national identities are created and shaped. From this perspective, we can better understand Montero's (1984) definition of national identity. She defines national identity, from a liberation psychology perspective, as:

> *... el conjunto de significaciones y representaciones relativamente permanentes a través del tiempo que permiten a los miembros de un grupo social que comparten una* ***historia*** *y un* ***territorio común****, así como otros elementos socioculturales, tales como el lenguaje, una religión, costumbres e instituciones sociales, reconocerse como relacionados los unos con los otros biográficamente.*
> ... the group of meanings and representations relatively permanent through time that allow members of a social group that share a **history** and a **common territory**, as well as other socio-cultural elements, such as language, religion, customs, and social institutions, to recognize themselves as related to each other biographically. (cited by Martín-Baró & Cañas, 1990, p. 2 translation and emphasis are mine)

The history of a people and a common territory are essential in this definition of national identity, setting national identity apart from an ethnic identity.[3] In an earlier article, Martín-Baró (1986 as cited by Martín-Baró & Cañas, 1990) posited that Salvadorians understood themselves as Salvadorians to the extent that they assumed the Salvadorian national identity as the images that are related to their social group such as family, friends, neighbors, etc., their family's specific physical and social context, customs and lifestyle. Portes and Rumbaut (2001) also found that national and ethnic identity identifications were intimately tied to associations with the place of birth of one's parents and family. The strength of association of national and ethnic identities to one's family and parents may change over time. Young adults' sense of national and ethnic identity was less dependent on family characteristics than in their teenage years. Considering these social psychological definitions of national identity within the context of their political meanings, we can better understand how the socio-political changes taking place through the process of

---

[3] In reality these identities are sometimes harder to pull apart and differentiate. In many instances ethnic identity is taken to stand for national identities when the person doesn't live in the country of nationality. Still many immigrants understand their identities as national identities and not as ethnic identities.

globalization are changing the contexts in which people are creating, shaping, and (re)constructing their personal, social, and political identities (Basch et al., 1994; Faist, 2001; Foster, 1991). A transnational perspective pushes open identity definitions, encouraging their (re)evaluation in the context of lives that are lived across nation-states, in the 'here and there, and always in between' (Clifford, 1994).

From the beginning, transnational theorists affirmed that transnationalism was not mutually-exclusive of assimilation. In other words, they did not claim that immigrants who live transnational lives would not assimilate or incorporate into their host society. Still, assimilation theorists, like Portes (1999), pushed for a more decisive position on the relationship between an assimilation perspective and a transnational perspective. More recent research has made explicit and explored the ways in which these two perspectives actually relate to one another and the connections under which they reinforce or hinder each other (i.e. Portes, Escobar, & Radford, 2007). Levitt, DeWind, and Vertovec clearly state that researchers in the field share the assumption that "host-country incorporation and transnational practices can occur simultaneously" (2003, p. 571) and acknowledge that future research should racialize and gender transnational theory.

Psychological research on intergroup relations and cross-cultural psychology has begun to explore the relationships between ethnic and national identities among immigrants and how they relate to adaptation and psychological well-being. Phinney, Horenczyk, Liebkin, and Vedder (2001) suggested an interactional model to understand the interrelationship of ethnic and national identity. They reached the conclusion that although ethnic and national identity may be independent theoretically, empirically they are interrelated and are affected by the contextual circumstances of immigrants' place of settlement. Multicultural societies are more likely to allow space for the integration of multiple identities and reporting bicultural identities than societies that discourage the maintenance of immigrants' ethnic cultures. (Deaux, 2008; Phinney et al., 2001). Although there are few psychological studies examining the relationship between national and ethnic identities, most psychological researchers of acculturation and biculturalism agree that integration strategies have positive outcomes for immigrants' psychological well-being and self-esteem (Berry, 2001; Mahalingam, 2006; Phinney et al., 2001; Verkuyten, 2005a).

THE PSYCHOLOGY OF TRANSNATIONAL IDENTITIES

> Perhaps it is simply that a bridge depends on two sides to support it, **that it is a promise, a commitment to two**… I love to walk a bridge and feel that split second when I **am neither here nor there**, when I am **between going and coming**, when I am God's **being in transit,** suspended between ground and ground… Because I'm neither gringa nor Latina. Because I am not any one thing. The reality is I am a mongrel. **I live on bridges**; I've earned my place on them, stand comfortably when I'm on one, **content with betwixt and between**… I count both their cultures as my own. But I'm happy to be who I am, strung between identities, shuttling from one to another, switching from brain to brain. I am the product of two people who launched from one land to another, who slipped into other skins, lived other rules – **yet never put their cultures behind them… what they did put behind them were pasts.**
> (Arana, 2002, p. 301)

In 1906, Gino Speranza, secretary of the Society for the Protection of Italian Immigrants, affirmed "the conception of citizenship itself is rapidly changing and we may have to recognize a sort of world or international citizenship as more logical than the present peripatetic kind, which makes a man an American while here, and an Italian while in Italy…The old barriers are everywhere breaking down." (cited by Foner, 2001, p. 35) A contemporary of DuBois, Speranza recognized in the experiences of Italian immigrants what DuBois, describing the experiences of African-Americans, called *Double-Consciousness* (DuBois, 1903:1990). Immigrants also experienced the sense of "two-ness", of "two unreconciled strivings", "two-warring ideals" in one body. Since then, many researchers have made similar parallels (Anzaldúa, 1999, 2002; Glick-Schiller & Fouron, 1998; Hermans & Kempen, 1998; Hondagneu-Sotelo & Avila, 2003; Levitt, 2001a; M. M. Suárez-Orozco, 2002). For example, Sorensen believed this feeling of "two-ness" was part of the experiences of Dominican immigrants in the United States (1998).

Writers and researchers have discussed experiences of living in 'borderlands,' as having a foot in two or more cultures, whereby a person becomes a sort of hybrid. In her own words:

> At the confluence of two or more genetic streams, with chromosomes constantly 'crossing over', this mixture of races, rather than resulting in an inferior provides hybrid progeny, a mutable, more malleable species with a rich gene pool. From this racial, ideological, cultural and biological crosspollinization, an 'alien' consciousness is presently in the making- a new *mestiza* consciousness… It is a consciousness of the Borderlands. (Anzaldúa, 1999, p. 99)

Anzaldúa was talking about crossing the boundaries of race, ideology, culture, and biology that stirred from her experiences as a New Mestiza Chicana living/crossing the borders between Mexico and the United States, Spanish and English, Indian and Non-Indian, White and Colored, Mexican and Chicana, never fully feeling at home in a single culture. She spoke of a world where the future "lies in healing the split that originates in the very foundation of our lives, our culture, our languages, our thoughts" (Anzaldúa, 1999, p. 102). The domains of nationality and citizenship go beyond language and culture and also have very real meanings for immigrants, children of immigrants, sending and receiving countries. Immigrants and their children share a common experience of living in a state of border-crossing, whichever their countries of origin and/or residence are. They share a feeling of living their lives on a bridge and/or a 'third space'[4] between *here* and

[4] Gutierrez, et al. (1995) conceptualized the 'third space' as a social space where "…two scripts intersect, creating the potential for authentic interaction to occur". In their conception of a third space, the authors highlight three things: 1) the interlocutors involved get outside of their usual 'roles', 2) the script that develops should be responsive/collaborative as the result of tension and conflict as the parties interchange and listen to each other's perspectives, and 3) should occur a number of times in order to help change the dynamics of the interactions towards more dialogic interaction where knowledge is (co)constructed. I am suggesting in this paper the use of the notion of a 'third space' to understand the mental, psychological and internal process that might

there. A number of studies describe how immigrants used these metaphors and similar ones when they talk about their experiences (Sorensen, 1998; M. M. Suárez-Orozco, 2002; Vertovec, 2004).

From a psychological point of view, the concept of immigrants' 'bifocal' orientation to life is perhaps the most interesting. Vertovec uses the term 'bifocality' to refer to findings that describe how immigrants maintain a 'dual frame of reference' where they "constantly compare their situation in their 'home' society to their situation in the 'host' society abroad" (2004, p. 974 paraphrasing Guarnizo, 1997). This feeling of simultaneously being *here* and *there,* of *double belonging* is described by Golbert (2001) as a 'double-consciousness' that develops in maintaining and participating in transnational social fields and having a transnational conception of self. Many researchers have repeatedly mentioned the existence of such 'bifocality'/'double-consciousness' among immigrants. Some examples are Guarnizo's study of Dominicans (1997), Roger Rouse's study of migration between Michoacán and California (1992), Ruba Salih's research with Moroccan women in Italy (2003), and David Kyle's (2000) description of his Ecuadorian participants (see Vertovec, 2004 for reference). In an earlier article, Vertovec conceptualized his notion of 'bifocality' by stating that those living in diasporic communities experience a sort of 'diaspora consciousness' as a result of dual or multiple identifications to 'here and there':

> Compounding the awareness of multi-locality, the 'fractured memories' of diaspora consciousness produce a multiplicity of histories, 'communities' and selves- a refusal of fixity often serving as a valuable resource for resisting repressive local or global situations. (Vertovec, 1999, p. 451)[5]

---

occur within a person through her/his interaction with his/her context as she/he lives in a transnational social field.

[5] Transnationalism theories have been critized for overemphasizing the process as liberating, positive, grass-roots and based on individual's agency (Hondagneu-Sotelo & Avila, 2003). More recently, researchers have began to warn against some of the possible negative aspects of transnationalism like the reification of elite political systems across borders (R. C. Smith, 2003) and how

However he omitted any reference to DuBois' (1903:1990) conceptualization of 'double-consciousness' and his work about African American identity.

A second domain of immigration research that has received attention from psychologists (besides intergroup relations) relevant to experiences of double-consciousness, transnational experiences and bifocality is the study of acculturation strategies and immigrants' adaptation to their new environments. The domain of acculturation and cultural identity remain the focus of cross-cultural psychologists (Berry, 2001; Mahalingam, 2006). While social psychologists have focused on the psychological characteristics of ethnic identities, cross-cultural psychologists have mainly examined the role of cultural identities among immigrants and conceptualized bicultural identities as an example of the relationship between multiple identities. According to Berry's (2001) topology of acculturation research, cross-cultural psychologists are concerned with questions of intercultural contact and cultural maintenance. At the societal level, they have focused on acculturation attitudes, while targeting behavioral shifts and cultural identity at the individual level. Berry's acculturation model (1997, 2001; Sam & Berry, 2006) proposes that out of 4 possible outcomes (assimilation, separation, integration and marginalization), *integration* represents the most adaptive and psychologically healthy outcome for immigrants entering a new culture and society. Integration is defined as an adaptation strategy or outcome whereby immigrants maintain their culture at the same time that they adopt the culture of their new host country. Early research on multiple identities explored how biculturalism, defined as immersion in two or more cultures, affected psychological processes and outcomes. The term bicultural competence was used to describe the ability of individuals to be aware of and draw from diverse cultural norms (LaFromboise et al., 1993). In an effort to understand bicultural individuals' experiences, Hong and colleagues (Hong, M. W. Morris, Chiu, & Benet-Martinez, 2000; 2003) have more recently advocated for adopting a *dynamic constructivist*

---

in some cases, like Haiti, transnational nation states discourses use hegemonic nationalistic discourses to "channel energy and resources away from struggles for social and economic justice" (Glick-Schiller & Fouron, 1998, p. 358).

approach to the study of culture and social cognition, which they used to construct a theory of *cultural frame switching* in response to social and cognitive heuristic cues among bicultural individuals. More specifically cultural frame switching involves using different cultural interpretative frames to respond to diverse contexts and situations, which include changes in the meanings attached to each cultural frame (Pouliasi & Verkuyten, 2007)

Phinney and Devich-Navarro (1997) tested the existence of two types of bicultural individuals: *blended* and *alternating* biculturals, which differ to the extent that individuals perceive their cultures to be compatible or not. In the case of perceived incompatibility, *alternating biculturals* switch between cultures according to the social context. Building on this work and on the theorizing of cultural frame switching (Hong & Chiu, 2001; Hong et al., 2000; Hong et al., 2003), Benet-Martinez, Leu, Lee, and Morris (2002) present a model of Bicultural Identity Integration (BII) that isolates two components, cultural distance and cultural conflict, in the process of constructing a bicultural identity. Cultural distance pertains to the level of overlap or separateness between cultures as perceived by the person, while cultural conflict relates to the level of conflict/incompatibility or harmony between both cultures from the point of view of the individual. Recent studies suggest perceived cultural distance is closely related to personal performance and contextual variables (Nguyen, Huynh, & Benet-Martinez, 2009; Wiley & Deaux, 2010) while perceived cultural conflict may respond more to intra- and interpersonal processes. Tadmor, Tetlock and Peng (2009) recently proposed Acculturation Integrative Complexity (ACM), as an alternative model for understanding the acculturation process of immigrants until they eventually become bicultural. According to this model, becoming a bicultural immigrant increases the integrative complexity of one's identity compared to immigrants who chose to assimilate or adhere to the host culture only leaving behind their own home culture. However, this model may not be as helpful in understanding children of immigrants' identity process. In general, children of immigrants are more likely to be considered fully bicultural compared to their immigrant parents, who have a better fit with the framework of acculturation integrative complexity. Research on biculturalism, frame switching, bicultural identity integration and performance are useful in understanding transcultural individuals and exploring the psychological characteristics of a transnational identity. By engaging in transnational social fields, children of immigrants are in fact multi-cultural or bi-cultural at the very least. As such, transnational identity may be understood as a type of bi-cultural identity.

A common denominator among research on biculturalism, bicultural identity, frame switching, and bicultural identity integration has been the use of quantitative and hypothesis testing methodologies. A more qualitative and narrative inquiry line of cross-cultural psychology has taken a different approach to the study of multiple identities among immigrants using a post-colonial studies perspective and focusing on transmigration, border-crossing and diasporic identities (Bhatia, 2002; Bhatia & Ram, 2001b, 2001a; Hart & Lindegger, 2002; Tappan, 2005). Bathia (2002) considered the consequences that postcolonial relations and relations of economic dependence between 'First' and 'Third' world have on migration patterns and the subsequent formation of what he calls *diasporic identities* within transnational migration. In many ways, this line of narrative dialogical analysis of immigrant's experiences acknowledges the existence and role of transnational social spheres among immigrant communities. In order to carry out their analysis, Bathia & Ram (2001b, 2001a) conceived immigration as a dialogical process "that involves a constant moving back and forth between incompatible cultural positions"(Bhatia, 2002, p. 57). Their postcolonial critique of assimilation and acculturation strategies revolves around the belief that "acculturation is not a matter of individual strategy... Rather, the formation of immigrant identities in diasporic communities involves a constant process of negotiation, intervention and mediation that is shaped by issues of race, gender, sexuality and power" (Bhatia, 2002, p. 59). As Bathia argued:

> In contrast to the universal models of acculturation in cross-cultural psychology, the dialogical view of acculturation does not emphasize that the voices and cultural positions that are in conflict and disagree with each other need to be replaced by a set of voices that are integrated or harmonious with each other. Rather, ... [it] emphasizes that asymmetrical power relations between conflicting voices and *I* positions are very much part of the diasporic self... assumes that *I* positions are shaped by

> issues of race, colonization and power... It is... situated, negotiated, and contested... (2002, p. 73)

There are many parallels between the description of bicultural identity and frame switching processes and that of the dialogical self. According to Hart and Lindegger (2002), "there is evidence of multiple selves, with conflict in dialogue resolved by alternating dominant voices in different times and spaces and through the use of rhetorical devices allowing the co-existence of two potentially conflicting voices" (2002, p. 5), which seems congruent with the descriptions of *alternating biculturals*. There is a need to develop a "competence to act as part of the globalizing world [which] creates an unprecedented challenge to the relation between unity and multiplicity... The prospect is to achieve a unity of the self via its polyphonization." (Hermans, 2001, p. 363) A new conception of the self, that allows for understanding immigrants and their children find themselves at different points in the *continuity-discontinuity* continuum than non-migrants, would help change the discourse about migration and alter power asymmetries based on that discourse.

However, being able to achieve this "unity of the self via its polyphonization" requires certain psychological skills to manage different cultural-social positions effectively. It is the development of these skills, in addition to a history of family or personal migration from one country to another that makes up the psychological content of what might be called a "transnational identity". Hermans (2001) highlights four psychological skills that would allow a person to deal with multiple cultural positions and organize them in a productive manner. First, the person would have knowledge, experiential or not, of multiple cultures and their meanings without given priority to one of them at all times regardless of the situation. Second, she/he would be able to embody collective and personal positions with voice, in order to establish a dialogue with other personal or collective positions within her/him. Third, a person would have the ability to develop coalitions or combinations among positions in order to embrace complexity and uncertainty in specific situations. Fourth, she/he would be able to manage which social position is chosen to have a dominant role without diminishing or undermining the importance of other positions that may not be called for in that particular circumstance. And I would add a fifth skill, the ability to entertain and be at ease with uncertainty, complexity, multiplicity, and bridges. A conception of the self as dialogical activity between multiple personal and social voices allows us to move away from using dichotomies to understand "hyphenated" and "hybridized" identities (e.g. Mexican-American, Black-American, Arab-British). In other words, one could think of immigrants and their children as being in different places in the *continuity-discontinuity* continuum according to their life circumstances at the moment.

WHAT WE KNOW ABOUT CHILDREN OF IMMIGRANTS

This study focuses on second generation immigrants largely due to the growing concern and speculation about how the post-1965 second generation would fare in their adulthood years compared to the "success" stories of the earlier pre-1965 waves of migration by Irish, Italians, and Germans among others (Suarez-Orozco, 1995; Smith, 1994; Grasmuck and Pessar, 1993; Gans, 1992; Portes and Zhou, 1992, 1993). The importance and attention given to the second immigrant generation post-1965 has much to do with the demographic changes taking place in the United States. According to the 2010 American Community Survey (Grieco, Acosta, de la Cruz, Gambino, Gryn, Larsen, Trevelyan, & Walters, 2012), at least 24% of the United States population is 17 years old or younger. According to the 2011 Current Population Survey, Children of immigrants (17 years old or younger with at least 1 foreign born parent) make up 21% of all children and youth in the United States (U.S. Census Bureau, Current Population Survey, 2011). Only 3.3% of children under 17 years old were foreign-born and had migrated to the United States. It is worth noting that about 75% of children with at least 1 foreign-born parent are school age (5-19) (U.S. Census Bureau, Current Population Survey, 2011).

Early assimilation theories in sociology helped explain how European immigrants (i.e. Irish, Italian, Polish, and French) eventually became assimilated into what we know as 'American mainstream culture' Having the United States' borders virtually closed to immigration between the 1920's and 1960's, facilitated the process of assimilation of early European immigrants by eliminating access to the continued influx of new immigrants (Kasinitz et al., 2008). In addition, these early European immigrants and their children eventually were incorporated into the mainstream by becoming 'white ethnics' and contributed to viewing 'American culture' as synonym with 'being white'. Since immigration quotas were eliminated in 1965, the racial and ethnic distribution of immigrant backgrounds has changed dramatically (Deaux, 2006; Foner, 2001; Kasinitz, Mollenkopf, & Waters, 2004). Today's immigrants are coming mostly from Latin America and Asia which effectively makes them non-white 'racial others'. They are retaining their cultures aided by the constant influx of new immigrants. Recent immigrants are refusing to become monolingual English-speakers and are generally proud of being bilingual speakers (Berry, 2001; Deaux, 2006; Kasinitz et al., 2008; Portes & Rumbaut, 2001).

Recent immigrant groups have challenged straight-line assimilation theories that expected children of immigrants and subsequent generations to do better than previous generations. They have raised the question of how these new immigrants and their children will fare in the United States. Some have predicted that the post-1965 second generation is/will not do better than their parents (Gans, 1992, 1999). Others within sociological theory (Portes & Rumbaut, 2001; Rumbaut, 2008) have used the concept of segmented assimilation as a model for understanding the diverse modes of incorporation observed among today's second generation immigrants. This model predicts that second generation youth who identify with American minorities (i.e. African-Americans) will experience downward social mobility while those immigrant groups who decide to avoid 'American culture' and remain within their ethnic culture will enjoy upward social mobility. Within psychology, differential outcomes between immigrants and their children have been identified as the *immigrant paradox.* According to the immigrant paradox, U.S. born children of immigrants are more likely to do worse on a number of psychological, physical, educational, and social mobility outcomes than their parents or their immigrant counterparts (Fuligni & Pedersen, 2002; García-Coll & Marks, 2009; Hill & Torres, 2010; Portes & Rumbaut, 2001; C. Suárez-Orozco & M. M. Suárez-Orozco, 2001; C. Suárez-Orozco, Rhodes, & Milburn, 2009). Since 4 in 5 children of immigrants are in fact born in the United States (U.S. Census Bureau, American Community Survey, 2009a), understanding their experiences and how they view the world is extremely important in order to provide them with the opportunities and support they need to succeed.

The 2nd generation immigrants' debate has also spurred much interest about whether immigrant children and US-born children of immigrants will maintain transnational ties and for how long. The transnational behaviors of second generation immigrants have become a major topic of interest in the field of migration. Given that immigrant youth and US-born children of immigrants have become the fastest growing sector of the United States population under 18 years old (Levitt & Waters, 2002), many sociologists (i.e. Mary Waters, Phil Kasinitz, Alejandro Portes, Rubén Rumbaut) who were initially interested in studying 2nd generation youth have found it necessary to consider transnationalism and its consequences. This is evident in the appearance of several books exploring transnationalism among the 2nd generation such as *The Changing Face of Home: The Transnational Lives of the Second Generation* (Levitt & Waters, 2002), *Inheriting the City: The Children of Immigrants Come of Age* (Kasinitz et al., 2008), and *Legacies: The Story of the Second Generation* (Portes & Rumbaut, 2001).

Smith (2002) asserts that transnational practices, meanings, and experiences among the first generation may be different from those of the second generation and agues that "rather than squashing transnationalization, assimilative pressures actually foster it by giving the second generation a reason to want to redefine their Mexican-ness in a new context" (p.147). Rather than assimilate into the United States' ethno-racial hierarchy that places Mexicans (U.S. born as well as immigrant born) in a disadvantageous position in relation to Whites, Blacks, Asians and U.S. born Puerto Ricans in New York City, Mexican children of immigrants prefer to use other Mexicans as a point of social reference for constructing their identities. Fouron and Glick-Schiller (2001) echoed these findings in their analysis of interviews with Haitian-American youth who chose to identify as Haitian in order to avoid their racialization as Blacks in the United States. Dark-skinned Haitian-American youth reported experiences of direct discrimination at their jobs. According to Fouron and Glick-Schiller, "They (youth) said that they had learned that despite their citizenship and their fluency in English, the United States 'is not your country'" (p.67). This experience has also been encountered by second generation immigrants from different ethnic and national backgrounds (Levitt & Waters, 2002).

Although there is debate regarding how transnational the second generation is, there is evidence that immigrant children and US born-children of immigrants are caught between two worlds, that of their parents' and the world in which they grew up. Butterfield (2004) discusses how his West Indian second generation participants described feeling like they did not completely fit in their parents' immigrant world or an 'American' world. There is evidence of recognition of children of immigrants' transnational experiences in the publication of a book on the subject, *The Changing Face of Home: The Transnational Lives of the Second Generation* (2002) by Peggy Levitt and Mary Waters. In her contribution to the book, Levitt (2002) documents the experiences of three second generation individuals from different national-ethnic backgrounds (Dominican Republic, Ireland, and India). She interviewed participants in Boston as well as family members in their respective sending countries. She highlighted three factors as having an effect on transnational practices: institutional completeness, life-course, and socio-economic factors.

SOCIAL DIMENSIONS IN THE LIVES OF CHILDREN OF IMMIGRANTS

The intersections of race, gender, and social class are perhaps the variables that have most influence in shaping children of immigrants' experiences and social identities. Portes and Rumbaut (2001) affirm that parents' social class knowledge, social networks, family structures and type of school attended along with race, are the variables that most shape the ethnic identity of second generation youth. Although this is not an exhaustive review of evidence and research documenting how children of immigrants are affected by socially constructed structures such as gender, race, and social class, it provides an overview of important findings that have bearing on the research questions addressed in this book.

Race

A number of researchers have concluded that racism and discrimination on the basis of skin-color/ethnicity are some of the greatest challenges that children of immigrants must confront (Alba, 2009; Butterfield, 2004; Deaux, 2006; Jensen, Cohen, Toribio, Jong, & Rodríguez, 2006; Phinney, 2002; Sirin & Fine, 2007; Tormala & Deaux, 2006; Waters & Kasinitz, 2010). Unlike language and cultural differences that may diminish with subsequent years and generations, skin-color and race differences remain highly visible (Alba, 2005, 2009). The visibility of skin-color becomes a reminder of one's place in the social and racial hierarchy (Phinney, 2002; C. Suárez-Orozco & M. M. Suárez-Orozco, 2001). Butterfield (2004) suggests that children of immigrants learn about race and what '*blackness*' means in school and with their peers, both contexts which are highly dependent on neighborhood characteristics. As a consequence, some researchers have observed that children of immigrants may be more susceptible to stereotype threat (Deaux, 2006), negative social mirroring (C. Suárez-Orozco & M. M. Suárez-Orozco, 2001), residential segregation (Alba, 2005; Itzigsohn, 2009) and places immigrant youth with darker skin-color at risk for reactive and unsuccessful assimilation by blocking their access to social mobility (Portes et al., 2008, 2009; Portes & Zhou, 1993).

Growing up in transnational social fields, children of immigrants are more likely to experience at least two different racial stratifications and be aware that their different cultures circulate different discourses about race. For example, Itzigsohn (2004, 2009) argues that, for Latina and Latino youth, coming to terms with a black-white racialized social order is part of becoming 'American' and that, as a panethnic category, "Latino/a or Hispanic" hold an ambivalent position within the United States racial order. However there are differences among the racializing processes that are encountered by different immigrants even when they share a panethnicity. Waters and Kasinitz (2010) described how Latino immigrant youth from the Dominican Republic are racialized in a different way than South American immigrants. Dominicans reported being mistaken as African-American or Black, while South Americans in general were usually mistaken as Southern European (Italy, Greece, Portugal, and Spain). Experiences of ethnic misidentification provide an informal indicator of how immigrant youth are perceived racially by others based on their skin color. In order to escape negative stereotypes and discrimination related to being mistaken as Black or African American, it has been documented that dark Dominican (Itzigsohn, 2009; Itzigsohn et al., 2005) and Haitian (Waters, 1994) immigrants emphasized their ethnic origins through dress codes, behaviors and language use. Pursuing transnational ties and long distance nationalism among immigrants and their children has also been connected to the desire to escape and deal with discrimination and racism in the United States (Fouron, 2003; Fouron & Glick-Schiller, 2002).

Recent findings highlight the intersection of gender and race in the experiences of children of immigrants. Young men and women who are growing up in the United States with immigrant parents experience the consequences of racialization differently. López (2002, 2004, 2006) has highlighted the importance of examining the intersection of race and gender among children of immigrants and its effect on their educational opportunities and school experiences. Her findings document the differential treatment by school administrators, teachers, school guards, and security personnel received by Dominican boys and girls in a New York City high school. Girls' racializing process was marked by over sexualization in public spaces, while boys' were seen as trouble-makers and racial profiling by police officers and school security guards. Dominican boys were treated as suspect in and outside school while Dominican girls' bodies were the subject of control and surveillance. López points out that the different racialized and gendered treatment experienced by Dominican youth may be behind the differences in their behavior in the classrooms and their attitude towards schooling. López (2002) observed that girls were more likely to feel empowered in the classroom and feel that school was a source of hope and self-efficacy while young men were usually disengaged and were more skeptical of the opportunities that schooling offered them. Along the same lines, Kasinitz and colleagues (2004; 2008) and Waters and Kasinitz (2010) reported that dark-skinned young immigrant men were more likely to report incidents of discrimination, racism, and encounters with the police than dark-skinned young immigrant women.

Sirin and Fine (2007) found gender differences among Muslim children of immigrants and their experiences of discrimination. For men, greater exposure to discrimination was associated with lower levels of integration into 'American' culture, while among Muslim girls discrimination was associated with higher levels of anxiety. Muslim girls appeared to respond to discrimination with a more positive strategy, they felt it was up to them to educate others about their culture. On the contrary, boys reported having feelings of despair and defeat as a response to discrimination. A recent study of Latino youth in the Midwest found similar gender differences with respect to perceptions and effects of discrimination (Umana-Taylor & Guimond, 2010). Perceived discrimination was significantly association with higher levels of ethnic identity exploration and expression of less positive feeling about their ethnic group among male Latino youth, yet it had no significant effect on girls' ethnic identity. These findings testify to the importance of the intersection of race, gender, and national origin in shaping the experiences of children of immigrants.

Gender

How gender shapes transnational behavior and ties among children of immigrants remains understudied. However, some studies have explored how gender intersects with migration (Espín, 2006; Grasmuck & Pessar, 1991), acculturation (Kasinitz et al., 2008; López, 2004; Mahalingam & Haritatos, 2006), and the negotiation of hyphenated identities (Sirin & Fine, 2007). Kasinitz and colleagues (2002) found that women were more likely to have high levels of transnational behaviors than men. They noted that, although previous research (Smith, 2002) demonstrated that immigrant men have higher stakes in maintaining transnational ties, this was not the case among children of immigrants in their sample. They pointed out that gender roles and expectations about women's family obligations may in part explain such differences. Considering that gender roles and beliefs differ among cultures, gender is bound to become a site of contestation between the new culture immigrants are expected to adapt to and their own culture.

Women have usually been expected to be the bearers of culture, to transmit the group's cultural values and norms to the new generation, and do the cultural work (Dion, 2006; Mahalingam, Balan, & Haritatos, 2008; Umana-Taylor & Guimond, 2010). Mahalingam and Haritatos (2006) found gender differences in the meaning of what it meant to be 'a good daughter' and differential treatment in specific domains among their Indian-American participants. In others words, young Indian American women were expected to be 'a good daughter' and follow cultural rules to a higher degree than men. Aside from the gender division of housework, dating, marriage, and curfews were all enforced differently by immigrant parents. Girls were more restricted in their behavior and had to conform to stricter dating rules which may be tied to the beliefs that women are the transmitters of culture and family values. In her earlier work on immigrant women and sexuality, Espín (1997) observed that "during the acculturation process sexuality become the focus of parents' fears and the girls' desire". However, this process also presented opportunities for Latina young women to challenge gender roles as they negotiate between their experiences and their mothers,' all the while maintaining a deep respect for their mothers' strengths even as they remained critical of their strategies and gendering behaviors (Ayala, 2006).

Young woman actually had some advantages or easier access to educational opportunities as a result of differential treatment they received from teachers, school professionals, and police officers in schools. López's work (2002, 2004) documents how school administrators and staff treated young men and women differentially based on gendered assumptions about their behaviors. Young men were expected to be confrontational and were treated as threatening the social order while young women experienced a somewhat more open and trusting space where they could express themselves and aspire to succeed despite racialized stereotypes and low expectations of teachers. Young Dominican girls perceived more possibilities; felt empowered to voice their demands in the classroom, and believed in education as a tool for social mobility than their young male counterparts.

Race, gender, and social class intersect to shape children of immigrant's experience as they grow up in the United States. Although they share the experience of having immigrant parents, growing up and managing multiple cultural contexts, the color of their skin, whether they men or women, and their social position within socio-economic system determines the opportunities they have access to and how they are treated by the larger society. The following section delves into particular similarities and differences in migration histories among Dominican and Colombian immigrants.

DOMINICAN AND COLOMBIAN IMMIGRANTS IN THE UNITED STATES

Race, different migration waves, immigration status, social class, patterns of geographical concentration upon arrival in the United States and historical relationships of their home countries with the United States are some of the variables that differ among Colombian and Dominican immigrants. It has been recognized by now that immigration flows from the global south to the global north tend to follow well-established patterns of colonial and post-colonial relationships among former colonial/imperial powers and former colonies, as well neo-colonial relationships between imperial economic powers, such as the United States and England, and the countries they exert economic control over via free trade zones, International Monetary Fund and political watchdog policies (López, 2002). Padilla and Peixoto (2007) assert that former colonial subjects "tend to be overrepresented in flows to the countries that colonized them" (p. 1). Similarly, Alejandro Portes noted there was "a strong tendency for immigrants to come from countries where the United States had sponsored direct or indirect military incursions" (Lundquist & Massey, 2005, p. 53). These factors help create political and economic conditions that drive emigration. In turn, it is not surprising that a large portion of immigrants from Latin American and the Caribbean countries have found their way to the United States and Spain. Rumbaut adds:

> To be sure, transnational communities do not emerge ex nihilo; their formation and the movements of people crossing national borders that occasion them need to be placed and understood in concrete historical contexts. International migrations are rooted in historical relationships established between the sending and receiving countries – including colonialism, war, and military occupation, labor recruitment and economic interaction, and sociocultural exchanges. (2002, p. 45)

The landscape of Latino/Hispanic and Latin American immigrants in New York City has changed drastically in the last decade. Even though Dominicans still hold the second largest share of Latino/Hispanic/Latin American descent population (19.9% in 1990, 24.6% in 2000 and 25.3% in 2010) in New York City, it is no longer the fastest growing immigrant community of Latin American origin in the city (Bergad, 2009, 2011). Today, Mexicans are the fastest growing national group among immigrants of Latin American in New York City (3.3 in 1990, 8.4% in 2000, and 14.3% in 2010). In contrast, the percentage of Colombians among the Latino/Hispanic population in New York City has declined (from 5.2% in 1990 to 4.9% in 2000 and 4.2% in 2010). The proportion of Colombians and Dominicans living in New York City who were foreign born decreased from 77% in 2000 to 66% in 2010 for Colombians and from 69% in 2000 to 63% in 2010 for Dominicans. New York, Los Angeles, Miami and Chicago have been traditional recipients of Latin American immigrants, yet southern cities like Atlanta, Boston, and Phoenix are increasingly becoming "new immigrant destination cities" (Marrow, 2008). The following sections provide a brief overview of the migration histories of Colombian and Dominican migration to the United States, and highlight some points of convergence and divergence between them.

Dominicans

The history of Dominican migration is intimately tied to United States' intervention in the Dominican Republic and subsequent post-colonial relationships of economic dependence to the United States. A number of researchers have connected different periods of United States' military and political intervention in the island with the increase of migration flows from the Dominican Republic to the United States and Puerto Rico. The United States occupied the Dominican Republic militarily on at least three occasions in the past century - 1916, 1924 and 1965 - resulting in the exodus of Dominicans to the United States (Duany, 2005; Hernández, 2002; Kasinitz et al., 2008). During times of political turmoil, middle-class segments, political organizers, dissident professionals and university students are more likely to exile themselves as was the case between 1961 and 1970 after the Trujillo dictatorship and the U.S. Marine invasion of the Dominican Republic in 1965. In the Dominican Republic, the United States' embassy itself distributed visas to those who were considered political dissidents to prevent situation similar to that occurring in Cuba at the time (Duany, 2005). As a consequence, the first wave of sizeable Dominican migration to the United was mostly highly educated, professional, from middle –class backgrounds, and had high levels of political and cultural capital (Hernández, 2002; Itzigsohn, 2005). Grasmuck and Pessar (1991) also found evidence that migration from the Dominican Republic in 1970s and 1980s was a more middle class migration from urban areas or small towns. In contrast, during the early 1980s through the 1990s Dominican emigration was driven by economical distress as a result of economic measures instituted by Balaguer's government (1966-1978) through the implementation of import substitution industrialization (Itzigsohn, 2005).

Pioneering migration research by Grasmuck and Pessar (1991) documented a back and forth circulation of goods, social remittances, and people between the Dominican Republic and the United States as far back as the early 1980s. They concluded that out-migration contributed to bringing new ideas about gender roles and social class configuration to the island through family social networks, migrant's visits, and, occasionally, migrants returning to live in the island. In addition, they noted that in the 1980s, Dominican women migrants felt fortunate to find jobs, mostly as garment workers in New York City, which allowed them to alter gender role divisions within their households and changed their views about an eventual return (Grasmuck & Pessar, 1991; Pessar, 1987). Even women who didn't migrate benefitted from changes in the division of labor in households because non-migrant relatives in the Dominican Republic introduced gender role changes enjoyed by migrant women.

According to Puerto Rican census data, immigration from the Dominican Republic to Puerto Rico peaked every four years coinciding with presidential elections up until mid 1990s (Duany, 2005). The Northeast, including New Jersey, New York, Massachusetts, and Rhode Island, has traditionally served as the point of entry and settlement for the large majority of Dominican immigrants (Hernández, 2002). Many of these Dominican migrants' families were already part of a migration circuit between the United States and the island, similarly to other Caribbean islands like Puerto Rico and Jamaica. In 1994, the Dominican government approved legislation recognizing dual citizenship rights for Dominican immigrants living abroad. Duany (2005) has characterized Dominican migration to the United States and Puerto Rico as a transnational migration circuit and pointed out that Dominican immigrants in the continental United States are 6 times more likely to be documented than Dominican immigrants in Puerto Rico. Geographical proximity between the Dominican Republic and Puerto Rico facilitated the migration of Dominicans who were not able to secure authorization to enter the United States with the end result of having a greater proportion of undocumented Dominican immigrants who were more likely to come from rural backgrounds.

The Dominican Republic has had a troubled history of race relations with Haiti since the 1800s. In the nineteenth century, Dominican elites constructed Dominican identity in opposition to Haitian identity (Aparicio, 2006; Duany, 2005). Dominicans "were conditioned to understand that they were 'not Black' as Haitians were the true measure of Blackness" (Aparicio, 2006, p. 132). Rafael

Leonidas Trujillo's dictatorship scapegoated Haitians while he was in power and contributed to intensifying racism towards Haitians through the sponsorship of *antihaitianismo* as a state-sponsored ideology (Aparicio, 2006; Duany, 2005) which instigated the massacre of at least 15,000 Haitian immigrants in 1937 at the Haitian-Dominican border (Turits, 2002). In recent times, youth from Dominican backgrounds in New York City "develop identities around blackness within a context of racialization on two fronts" (Aparicio, 2006, p. 124) and have used them to organize around contemporary Dominican politics and in solidarity with other minority communities. Some examples of Dominican youth organizing around social and political issues of ethno-racial justice are AZABACHE, an organization of Puerto Rican, Black, and Dominican youth that organize around the Black and Latino experience in New York City, and the *Movimiento de Mujeres Dominico-Haitiana* (MUDHA) which works to promote solidarity and bring an end to racism and discrimination against Haitians in the Dominican Republic and among the Dominican community in the United States. Dominicans' experience with definitions of blackness in the Dominican Republic complicate their experiences of race and being racialized as black in the United States due to their darker hues and experiences of discrimination and racism (Hernández, 2002; Itzigsohn, 2004, 2005).

Another line of research on Dominican immigrants in the United States has dealt with how Dominicans self-identify and see themselves within the United States' ethno-racial hierarchy (Itzigsohn, 2004; Itzigsohn et al., 2005; Itzigsohn & Giorguli-Saucedo, 2005; Jensen et al., 2006; López, 2002; Waters & Kasinitz, 2010). Ricourt (2002) concluded that Dominicans in New York City exhibit one of three types of identities: a *new immigrant identity*, an *established immigrant identity* (combining aspect of both cultures and living between the Dominican Republic and New York City), or a *Dominican American* identity (identifying with the host culture and focusing on their lives in New York City). Her finding that immigrant women identified with the host country's culture at a more rapid pace than men and that men were more likely to express desires to return to the island, mirrored psychological findings about gender differences in immigrants' desire to return to their home countries. Ricourt's work suggests that panethnicity could occur at 4 different levels, without superseding or eliminating Dominican national origin identification: *everyday cooperation* (solidarity without embracing a discourse of Latino/Hispanic identity), *categorical* (identifying and using the panethnic label to describe oneself), *institutional* (getting involved in organizations and collective action with different ethnic groups as a result of embracing a panethnic discourse), and *ideological* (adopting the discourse of panethnic identity to mobilize behind it). These four levels seemed to differ on the level of strength and importance given to the panethnic label at the personal level, the level of action, and elicited behaviors.

The transnational experiences of Dominican immigrants and their children were discussed early on by researchers (Grasmuck & Pessar, 1991) and fiction writers (Álvarez, 1991). Julia Álvarez's memoir is an example of how transnational social fields permeate the everyday life of both migrants and non-migrant in both host and home countries. Despite having emigrated with her family at the age of 10 to escape the Trujillo dictatorship, she has focused a large part of her creative production such as, *In the time of the butterflies* (Álvarez, 2010) and *Before we were free* (Álvarez, 2004) on reconstructing from her conversations and relationships with relatives in the Dominican Republic what life was like for those who remained and lived through the dictatorship. Another example of research about the transnational experiences of Dominican immigrants is Peggy Levitt's work (2001b). Her book was not only transnational in content, but was also methodologically designed as a transnational ethnography of a small village, Miraflores in the Dominican Republic and Jamaica Heights in Boston, MA. Aside from the methodological implications of her work, Levitt's findings provided evidence that ideas and information about gender relations were circulated between Miraflores and Jamaica Heights. Furthermore, gender relations in the island were modeled to a great extent on Dominican immigrant women's experiences in the United States. In addition, she highlighted that the exchange of transnational knowledge circulates within family networks and sets a dynamic of class division based on who has access to transnational social networks (immigrant relatives) or not.

Colombians

Although there is far less research about Colombian immigrants and their migration than about Dominican immigrants, researchers of

Colombian migration have identified three waves of intense migration to the United States: a first wave between late 1940s through 1960s, a second wave late 1970s through 1980s and a third wave in the mid 1990s (Bermúdez Torres, 2005; Collier & Gamarra, 2003; Escobar, 2004; Guarnizo & Díaz, 1999; Guarnizo et al., 1999; Meyer et al., 1997). According to the American Community Survey, the influx of Colombians immigrants to the United States seems to have reached a plateau in the last decade (Bergad, 2009) that may be related to a relative perception of political and economic stability due to the presidential election of Alvaro Uribe in 2002 and 2006. Before the 1960s, there was a relatively small flow of immigration to the United States, mostly instigated by political violence and civil conflict related to the period known as *La Violencia* (1948-1962). Most of these earlier immigrants were relatively well-educated, from lower and middle-class backgrounds fleeing political violence in the main urban centers of Bogota, Medellín and Calí. The second wave of Colombian migration to the United States is associated with the advent of the internationalization of the drug market and the emergence of the United States as a major drug consumer of Colombian cocaine in the 1970s. Drug related migration involved a mix of lower-middle and working class individuals (Collier & Gamarra, 2003; Guarnizo & Díaz, 1999; Guarnizo et al., 1999). During the 1970s and 1980s, working class and lower middle class immigrants went to the United States to work in developing industries in Chicago and New York City. Collier and Gamarra (2003) pointed out that Colombia did not go through the deep economic crisis that other Latin American countries did, perhaps as a result of booming cash flow from illegal drug market. During these years, it was relatively easy for Colombians to obtain visas for work in the growing industrial centers of the United States and many did.

A third wave of migration from Colombia to the United States started in the 1990s until mid 2000s as a result of an increase in the political and economic crisis generated by the armed civil conflict. As is usual with political violence, this new wave of immigrants was composed of more middle, upper-middle and upper class families and professionals (Collier & Gamarra, 2003; Escobar, 2004; Guarnizo & Díaz, 1999; Guarnizo et al., 1999). Although the armed conflict created a difficult economic situation, it was nearly impossible for working class and lower middle class individuals to fulfill the strict visa requirements to enter the United States. Travel restrictions imposed on Colombian citizens worsened as part of the United States' "War on Drugs" initiated by the Reagan administration during the 1980s. Therefore, tourist or student visas became the only viable legal way to enter the United States which required applicants to document substantial economic resources and prove that they were not planning to overstay their visas by showing they had large real estate and capital investments in Colombia.[6] These immigrants were more likely to settle in Miami, FL and were better-off economically than immigrants from previous waves (Collier & Gamarra, 2003; Guarnizo & Díaz, 1999). Few working class people attempted to enter illegally by crossing the Mexican-U.S. border. As a result, most undocumented Colombian immigrants entered the U.S. legally and have overstayed their visas.

Aside from these waves of increased migration, a number of Colombian immigrants have entered the United States through family reunification and this yields a more diverse combination of social class and educational backgrounds. A study of Colombian immigrants commissioned by the Colombian consulate in New York City found that Colombians in New York and New Jersey tended to have higher levels of education and be better off economically than other Latino immigrant groups (A. Hoffman & Escala, 1999). Guarnizo and colleagues (1999) reached a similar conclusion and added that the location of Colombian immigrants' settlements (ethnic enclaves) in the United States was related to social class differences. Los Angeles and Miami were populated by more affluent, middle-class and upper-class Colombians while Chicago and New York/New Jersey had a more working and lower-middle class profile. Guarnizo and colleagues (Guarnizo et al., 1999) also reported high levels of transnational behavior such as remittances among Colombians and feelings that their emotional needs would be better met in Colombia. Meyer and

---

[6] This is particularly important because it gives Colombian undocumented immigrants an added advantage to regularize their legal status. A requirement for legalizing one' status (by marriage, etc) is to have entered the country legally. If a person cannot demonstrate that they entered legally, they must request a pardon, leave the country and wait at least 10 years before they began any regularization process. If one entered legally but overstayed, one must simply pay a penalty.

colleagues (1997) discussed how technological projects were introduced by government initiatives to utilize the educational capital of Colombians abroad and promoted transnational involvement and transfer of knowledge of exiled professionals.

Another line of research about Colombian immigrants comes from sociological work on transnational political involvement and participation. For example, Cristina Escobar (2004) looked at the transnational political participation of Colombians in the United States and Colombian politics as a result of dual-citizenship policies adopted by the 1991 Colombian constitution. Naturalization rates among Colombians who were U.S. legal residents actually doubled during 1992-1994 and have remained stable since, because of dual-citizenship implementation (Escobar, 2004). Research on the transnational political participation of Colombians has also identified mistrust and social fragmentation among Colombian immigrant communities in Canada, United States, Britain and Spain, which represents a paradox for migration literature that assumes ethnic solidarity among immigrants from the same country of origin. Collier and Gamarri (2003) reported low social capital and social trust among the Colombian community they studied in Florida. Social trust and solidarity was restricted to family and friends while social ties with other Colombians and with other ethnic/national origin groups were weak. They argued that this mistrust accounted for the lack of political participation locally despite large amounts of human and social capital. Colombian immigrants appeared to formulate their identities around family, friends, social class, and region rather than as an association with Colombia as a country. Another reason for the lack of social ties among Colombians was attributed to a need to disassociate from stereotypes about drug trafficking and to avoid any involvement with Colombians of 'dubious' origins (i.e. drug or guerilla related). A number of researchers have identified similar reasons (i.e. violence, criminality and drug stereotypes) behind the social mistrust among Colombian immigrants in the United States (Guarnizo & Díaz, 1999; Guarnizo et al., 1999), in London (Bermúdez Torres, 2003) and Spain (Bermúdez Torres, 2006; Riaño-Alcalá & Goldring, 2007) Among Colombian immigrants, social class appears to trump ethnic/national origin group identities as the basis for delimiting in-group boundaries and solidarity (Guarnizo & Díaz, 1999). Riaño-Alcalá & Goldring also found "Colombians maintaining social and economic ties with family… without challenging the socio-political status quo" (2007, p. 8) in Canada. Colombian immigrants also appear to be content to be racially and ethnically non-identifiable which might contribute to their patterns of relative spatial dispersion, with the exception of Jackson Heights, Queens.[7]

The particular relationship between political violence, mass migration of political and economic elites with high levels of human capital, and foreign military or economic intervention has already been documented in the history of Nicaraguan (Lundquist & Massey, 2005) and Dominican migration (Duany, 2005; Hernández, 2002; Itzigsohn, 2005) to name a few. Nicaragua represents a similar situation of armed conflict and a paradoxical relationship of United States interventions that was tied to the mass exodus of better-off urban dwellers. Just as in Colombia, rural dwellers migrated to urban cities or neighboring countries in response to economic hardships in Nicaragua. However in times of mounting political violence, on the heels of United States' covert military intervention, Nicaraguan urban dwellers migrated to the United States instead of neighboring countries (Lundquist & Massey, 2005). In Colombia, economic hardships were more likely to result in migration to neighboring countries like Ecuador and Venezuela, or even Spain (while it did not require a visa for Colombian travelers). In contrast, the escalation of political violence facilitated an exodus to the United States. According to Lundquist and Massey, increased political, economic, and military intervention by the United States created a space for migration networks to develop. Although the United States has not militarily intervened in Colombia on a large scale, it has provided massive military funding, training, and equipment since the implementation of Plan Colombia by the Clinton administration. In 2007-2008, Colombia received 520 million dollars in aid from the United States (the majority of which was destined for military purposes) as part of the 'War on Drugs', which made it the 6th largest recipient of aid from the United States. The only countries that received more money from the United States were Iraq, Afghanistan,

---

[7] However, Jackson Heights in Queens and Union City in New Jersey are perceived as a drug market hub by many more affluent Colombians, especially by third wave Colombian immigrants.

Sudan ($779 million), Egypt ($684 million) and Ethiopia ($592 million) (*Development aid at a glance 2010: Statistics by region*, 2010). At one point, Colombia was the third largest recipient of United States aid.

To Group or Not to Group

As Latin Americans continue to migrate to United States, Latinos have become the largest minority groups according to national census data (*Statistical portrait of Hispanics in the United States, 2008*, 2010). It is common practice among United States citizens and government agencies to refer to them as Latinos/Hispanics depending on the specific government agency and particular political views (see Oboler, 1995 for a historical review). The U.S. census continues to ask about Hispanic/Latino origin data as ethnic background/ethnicity despite evidence that Latinos/Hispanics have become racialized. Whether the panethnic label Latino/Hispanic represents a race or an ethnicity has produced much debate and continues to challenge black and white racial conceptualizations which have historically characterized American race relations (Itzigsohn, 2004, 2009; Jensen et al., 2006; Oboler, 1995). The phenotypical composition of people in Latin America covers the full spectrum of skin-color. Latinos/Hispanics have found it relatively easy to assume and appropriate the label in order to denote their common cultural, linguistic, and historical roots regardless of skin-color. Latino immigrants from different national origins have rallied behind their common Latino/Hispanic ancestry in order to organize and galvanize for social justice and access to services, social and political power (Itzigsohn, 2009). The 1st of May Immigrant marches, organized all over the country since 2005 to demand immigrant reform, are but one example of the power that panethnic labels and identities offer.

For researchers as well, it offers the opportunity to demonstrate stronger significant results where otherwise small sample sizes of national origin groups would jeopardize or undermine the importance and significance of results. Although Dominican and Colombian immigrants have different migration histories and experiences with/in the United States, researchers have usually grouped them together as part of a larger panethnic Latino/Hispanic/Latin American immigrant group. Having a Latin American background, Dominicans and

Colombians have a number of communalities such as language and cultural traditions which largely developed as a result of colonization by Spain until the 1800s. Yet the socio-structural differences among them are many. A review of their migration histories shows a shared history of economic and military involvement by the United States in their respective countries of origin, a belief in an ideology of *mestizaje* as racial mixture, and selective migration waves that correlate with periods of either economic or political problems that determined the socio-economic characteristics, level of human and cultural capital of those migrating. In many ways the experiences of Dominicans and Colombians migrating and incorporating as Latin American/Latino or Hispanic immigrants into the United States society are very similar. They also differ in particular ways that may produce differential outcomes for both national groups.

However the process of grouping together different Latino national groups also obscures important differences such as structural problems specific to the experiences of particular national groups. For example, focusing on Latinas/os access to health care and education as a panethnic group highlights their disadvantages versus other racial groups, namely as Asians, Blacks and Whites, yet it obscures the role of socio-economic status and skin-color in isolating and socially excluding Puerto Ricans and Dominicans from other national origin groups such as South Americans (Alba, 2005, 2009; Frank, Akresh, & Lu, 2010; Waters & Kasinitz, 2010). In fact, a more accurate picture is that immigrants with high level of human capital and lighter skin color are escaping marginalization at the bottom of the social and racial hierarchy while Puerto Ricans and Dominicans see their chances for social mobility and better opportunities slip away. As Portes and colleagues (Portes et al., 2009) argue, processes of racialization create contexts in which some groups have access while others are blocked, in fact reifying race as a 'bright boundary' (Alba, 2005) among Latino immigrant groups. It is important to compare the experiences of Latino national groups in order to understand how they are differently affected by social, economic, and political structures.

Colombian and Dominican immigrants have different racial profiles which have consequences for theirs and their children's life chances and experiences in the United States. There is evidence that, in the United States, most Dominican immigrants are perceived to be racially black and are all categorized as Latinos (Itzigsohn, 2009). In a study of Dominican immigrants in New York, Jensen and colleagues (2006) found that only 15.4% of participants described their skin color as light while the remaining 84.6% chose some gradation of brown to describe their skincolor: 49.2% chose light brown, 26.7% medium brown, and 7.7% described themselves as being dark brown. Their findings demonstrate that Dominican immigrants are aware of being darker and being perceived as blacks in the United States. These numbers coincide with the racial profiles of Dominicans in the Dominican Republic. Central Intelligence Agency World Fact Book (2010) reports racial stratification of the Dominican Republic as white 16%, mixed 73%, and black 11%. On the other hand, Colombian racial stratification is reported as mestizo 58% (white-Amerindian mixed), white 20%, mulatto 14% (white-black mixed), black 4%, mixed black-Amerindian 3%, and Amerindian 1% (*CIA - The world factbook*, 2010). Therefore, Colombian immigrants are more likely to have lighter skin color than Dominican immigrants.

Although there is not much information about how Colombians self-identify or describe their skincolor, there is evidence that, at least among children of immigrants, Dominicans and Puerto Ricans are more likely to be misidentified as black or African American while South Americans report being misidentified as white or Southern Europeans such as Greek, Italian, Spanish or Portuguese (Waters & Kasinitz, 2010). Several researchers have pointed out the negative effects of racial stratification of immigrants on residential segregation. Darker Latino/Hispanics live in poorer neighborhoods than lighter Latino/Hispanics even after controlling for socio-economic status, language, and education (Alba, 2005, 2009). More recently, a study analyzing data from the 2003 New Immigrant Survey documented Latino legal residents who were darker earned $2,500 less than those who were lighter skinned after controlling for all other measures (Frank et al., 2010). At this point, there is consensus among migration researchers that skincolor and race have enormous consequences for the incorporation of immigrants. Race has been characterized as a bright boundary with enduring and long lasting effects in the quality of life and opportunities for social mobility among immigrants (Alba, 2009).

Linguistic details such as accents, pronunciations, and word/vocabulary choices are used to make assumptions about a person's regional and class origin usually contributing to discrimination and social exclusion (Zentella, 2005, 2008). Dominicans and other

Caribbean Spanish speaking groups, among Latin American immigrants, have been stigmatized for their accents and language use. Part of this process has occurred because such linguistic features have been associated with darker skin and poorer backgrounds for Dominicans, and have been used as a way to demarcate racial and class differences among Latinos in the United States. Zentella (2008) found that Colombians were more likely to consider 'speaking like other Colombians' as a compliment (only 3% did not), while 15% of Dominicans felt that being told they spoke like other Dominicans would be offensive. Such responses denote awareness among Dominicans that they way Dominicans as a group spoke was stigmatized and was perceived as a negative. In order to understand how groups with different Latin American national origins relate to each other, it is important to explore their experiences within the panethnic label.

As an immigrant group, Dominicans have received relatively more attention by researchers than Colombians for a number of reasons: first, they are a more established immigrant group; second, Dominicans were, until recently, the second largest group of immigrants from a Latin American background in the U.S. after Mexicans; and third, traditionally they have a longer history of migration to the United States. For example, Kasinitz and colleagues (2008) sampled Dominicans in their study of children of immigrants because they were the largest Latin American immigrant group in New York City and grouped together Colombians, Peruvians and Ecuadorians as a South American group because individually their numbers were too small to make a sound statistical comparison.

Another study (Portes et al., 2007) comparing immigrant transnational organizations among Colombian, Dominican, and Mexican immigrants found differences between Colombian and Dominican immigrant communities in the types of migration, main cities of destination, and demographic characteristics. Colombians were found to be mostly legal immigrants with increasing numbers of unauthorized immigrants and political asylees compared with Dominicans who were characterized by a combination of legal and unauthorized immigration. The majority of Colombian immigrants were found in Miami, New York City, and New Jersey while Dominicans were highly concentrated in the Northeast – New York City, Bergen and Passaic counties of New Jersey, and, more recently, in

Boston and Providence. A major finding was that transnational organizations and the behaviors associated with them took different forms depending on the nationality of the immigrant community. Transnational involvement was focused on political and professional activities for Dominicans, participation in hometown associations from largely rural communities for Mexicans, and philanthropic and cultural activities for Colombians.

Although not exhaustive, the research reviewed reveals important differences in migration histories and group characteristics among Colombian and Dominican immigrants which have had significant effects in shaping the experiences and trajectories of Dominican and Colombian children of immigrants. Colombia and the Dominican Republic have experienced economic and military interventions yet they have occurred at difference historical moments. Therefore, their patterns of migration waves, although similar, have not coincided in time periods. While early migration waves from the Dominican Republic came from middle- and upper-middle class, early migration from Colombian was primarily an economic migration of working class people. More recent migrants from Colombia have been primarily from urban, upper- and middle-class origins compared to working-class and rural backgrounds for migrants from the Dominican Republic. As a result, Dominican and Colombian immigrant communities in New York City have different social class and educational backgrounds. Dominican transnationalism has been largely involved in political and economic participation across borders compared to a lack of transnational political interest and involvement among Colombians. Social class divisions among Colombian immigrants defined their relationships with other Latino national groups as well. Although both groups shared in the belief of racial stratification as *mestizaje*, the Dominican Republic has a more complicated relationship to ideas and experiences of 'blackness,' as well as, a larger share of population who are dark-skinned compared to Colombians, who in general are lighter-skinned and have a small phenotypically black population. These differences make a comparison between Colombian and Dominican children of immigrants' experiences a worthwhile and valuable addition to research about Latino immigrants' experiences in the United States, and even more for the psychological literature which has not paid much attention to these two groups.

RESCUING THE HUMANITY OF CHILDREN OF IMMIGRANTS: RESEARCH QUESTIONS

Examining children of immigrants' life experiences from a transnational perspective implies understanding "the new collectivities and identities that are reshaping our world, and the ways in which these challenge our sense of who we are, and what are our rights and obligations to the collective good should be." (Levitt, 2001a, p. 2) Moreover, it calls into question much of the psychological research that has focused on predicting and assimilating immigrants into the mainstream society. In this book, I highlight the implications that asking psychological questions from a transnational perspective has, as well as, knowledge that has eluded psychologists through the omission of the transnational realities of many immigrants and their children from psychological inquiry. Suffice it to say that, although not all children of immigrants live deeply transnational lives, most of them have - at one point or another - participated in transnational activities or have themselves been affected by coming into contact/interacting with other transmigrants. We cannot continue to overlook this reality if we want to understand migration processes, transnational experiences, and the lives affected by it.

This book adds to the psychological and migration literatures in a number of ways. First, it brings a transnational lens to the psychological study of identity formation and explores qualitatively how children of immigrants develop identities within transnational social fields and make sense of them. Second, it contributes to highlight the interconnectedness and intersectionality between national, ethnic, racial, and transnational social identity processes and the inadequacy of traditional ethnic identity and racial identity models within psychology. Third, it adds to our knowledge of children of immigrants experiences in the United States by exploring the psychological implications of transnational ties and relationships as well as the psychological content of transnational identities formed in the multiplicity of transnational life. Fourth, it adds to the literature about Colombian and Dominican immigrants by exploring the effects of class and race differences within and across national groups. Finally, this study highlights the importance of viewing the experiences of immigrants and their children as part of a larger life project that rests on the continuity and connection between pasts, presents, and futures, between memories, goals, and hopes that nurture their motivation, resiliency, and humanity.

The research questions guiding this book were designed to address different levels of analysis. Pettigrew's model of levels of analysis in the social psychological study of immigration argues that social and personal phenomena can be approached from three different levels of analysis: macro, meso, and micro (as cited by Deaux, 2006). By focusing on different levels of analysis, one can move from the social/political context to the individual while acknowledging that they are parts of a person's whole experience, which constantly reinforce each other. According to Deaux (2006), most social psychological work is done at the meso level of analysis which focuses on immigrants' social interactions and contains concepts such as stereotypes, social networks, behaviors, and attitudes among groups. Verkuyten's (2005b) model of level of analysis for the study of social identity formation and maintenance processes serves to understand how social structures, interpersonal relationships, and subjective experience are interconnected in the process of identity negotiation. I analyzed the responses of Dominican and Colombian children of immigrants in order to document their similarities, as well as their diverse experiences as a result of the differences among both immigrant groups in terms of race, migration histories, social, and cultural capital of their parents and characteristics of their respective immigrant communities in New York City.

Accordingly, this book compares Dominican and Colombian respondents in order to explore what experiences they share and in what ways they differ from each other. The research questions examined in this book represent an effort to engage different levels of analysis in order to contextualize the experiences of Dominican and Colombian children of immigrants in New York City who participate in transnational social spaces. The research questions guiding this project were:

- What implications does their parents' home country have on the negotiation of social identities among Colombian and Dominican children of immigrants?

- To what extent do Colombian and Dominican children of immigrants maintain emotional, social, political, and economic ties to their parents' home country? What affects their willingness, and ability to maintain transnational ties with their family, friends, community and other members of their transnational social field?

- How do gender, race, and social class shape the life experiences of Colombian and Dominican children of immigrants in the United States?

By exploring the transnational experiences of children of immigrants and their effect on identity negotiation, psychologists can expand their understanding of immigrants' and their children's identity processes within a perspective of continuity of life. An approach based on the assumption of continuity of migration and identity processes moves away from using a lens of rupture/displacement/loss that imposes a "before/after migration" dichotomy; one that does not "congeal into a conceptual refusal to recognize settlement, opting instead for models of arrivals, second generations, [and] hybrids" (Hutnyk, 2005, p. 95). It also emphasizes the dynamic character of such processes and the possibilities for social change and challenging the status quo behind traditional views of migration and assimilation/acculturation processes. We should remember that the process of incorporating into a new society does not necessarily require leaving behind past lives. Immigrants maintain and remember those past lives as they continue to forge new lives. Migration then becomes a new process of transition and change in the lives of immigrants and is transmitted, as such, to their children.

The following chapters lay out the process by which I analyzed the data and arrived at my conclusions. Chapter 2 provides a roadmap for how this research project was designed, outlines the process used to analyze the data and provides an overview of major findings. Chapters 3, 4, and 5 develop in more detail findings that relate to each of the research questions described above. Each chapter addresses a specific level of analysis. Chapter 3 focuses on the individual and psychological experience of identity negotiation among children of immigrants. Chapter 4 explores findings about social and interpersonal relationships by documenting transnational practices of respondents and discussing the social and psychological implications of transnational ties for children of immigrants and their identity negotiation. Chapter 5 covers findings about Dominican and Colombian respondents' interaction with social structures and institutions and how immigrants and their children respond to them by making decisions within constrained circumstances. Finally, chapter 6 provides some concluding thoughts and discusses implications of these findings.

CHAPTER 2

Methods and Analysis

In this study I used a mixed-methods (Grasmuck & Pessar, 1991) design to explore the *Immigrant Second Generation of Metropolitan New York* (ISGMNY) data set qualitatively and quantitatively. Researchers have mainly examined transnational practices and the negotiation of identities among immigrants and children of immigrants either through qualitative (i.e. in-depth interviews) or quantitative (i.e. large sample surveys) methods and few scholars have combined both. In fact, this consideration weighed heavily in choosing a design for the ISGMNY study (Kasinitz et al., 2008). For example, Fouron and Glick-Schiller (2002) used "lengthy" interviews with college seniors who were born in Haiti; Graham (2001) based her analysis on ethnographic fieldwork and in-depth interviews both in the Dominican Republic and New York City along with archival data from publications and official documents from both countries; Duany (2005) compared the transnational practices of Dominicans who migrated to United States with those who migrated to Puerto Rico by using data from the U.S. Census and the Immigration and Nationalization Services (INS); Rumbaut (2002) compared the first and second immigrant generation pre- and post-1960 by analyzing the Current Population Survey (CPS) by the U.S. Census. Rather than using one methodology or approach, this project combines both qualitative and quantitative methods to present a more complicated picture of how second generation immigrants negotiate their multiple, often conflicting identities, their participation in transnational social fields, and how this process is shaped by factors like gender, national origin, immigration status, social class, race, perceived discrimination, and ethno-racial identity.

Researchers have used quantitative data to ascertain the extent to which immigrants maintain (or not) transnational ties (i.e. how often they travel, talk to family, send money to home country), the strength and density of ties across national borders and the types of activities and domains that are represented in such interactions (Foner, 2002; Fouron & Glick-Schiller, 2002; Itzigsohn et al., 2005; Kasinitz et al., 2008; Murphy & Mahalingam, 2004; Valentine, 2006; Rumbaut, 2002). On the other hand, qualitative researchers have focused mainly in qualifying what transnational ties look like, how they are narrated by immigrants, or the social and political institutions they are a part of (Kibria, 2002; Levitt, 2002; Rivera Sánchez, 2008; R. C. Smith, 2002; Sorensen, 2005; Vickerman, 2002) In other words, they illustrate the social construction of transnational social fields and networks. By using both qualitative and quantitative data, I strived to bring these two methodological frameworks together in order to address critiques and shortcomings attributed to particular methodological approaches.

SAMPLE AND DATA

This research project analyzes data collected by the *Immigrant Second Generation of Metropolitan New York* study (ISGMNY) carried out from 1998-2000 by John Mollenkopf, Philip Kasinitz, and Mary Waters[8] conducted by the Center for Urban Research at the CUNY Graduate Center. The research design involved secondary analysis of both qualitative and quantitative data collected on Dominican and Colombian young adult children of immigrants (ages 18-32). All participants were classified as, "second generation" immigrants (those born in the U.S. to parents who immigrated after 1965), "1.5 generation" immigrants (those born abroad who arrived by age 12 and grew up in the United States and had at least one parent who was born outside of the United States) or "1.25 generation" immigrants (those who arrived in the U.S by age 6 and had completed most of their formal education in the U.S. school system). In the ISGMNY sample, at least

[8] The ethnographies collected as part of the ISGMNY study where compiled in the 2004 book *Becoming New Yorkers: Ethnographies of the New Second Generation*, edited by Philip Kasinitz, John Mollenkopf, and Mary Waters.

fifty eight percent of Colombian and sixty-one percent of Dominican respondents were classified as "2nd generation immigrants"; twenty-one percent of Colombians and twenty four percent of Dominicans were classified as"1.5 generation immigrants"; and at least twenty percent of Colombian and fifteen percent of Dominican respondents were classified as "1.25 generation" who arrived in the U.S by age 6 and had completed most of their formal education in the U.S.'s school system (see table 1). For the purpose of this study, I decided to forgo the classification of respondents using the 2nd, 1.5 or 1.25 generation terms. Instead, I chose to refer to these young adults as "children of immigrants" in recognition that, despite differences in their ages upon arrival in the United States, immigrants from 1.25 and 1.5 generations were both mainly raised in the United States and attended New York City schools. In addition, early on in the research process, it became apparent that respondents, regardless of being born in the United States or arriving as young children, felt identified with the United States as the country where they were raised and where they felt at home.

Table 1. Phone Survey Respondents by Immigrant Generation

Immigrant Generation	Colombians	Dominicans
2nd Generation (Born in the US)	58.4 %	61.0 %
1.5 Generation (7-12 years old)	21.1 %	23.7 %
1.25 Generation (1-6 years old)	20.5 %	15.3 %

The data I analyzed consist of quantitative phone interviews with Dominican immigrants (393) and Colombian immigrants (169) as well as follow-up qualitative in-depth interviews with Dominican (25) and Colombian respondents (18). The ratio of female to male participants was about equal as depicted in table 2. Both phone (close-ended questionnaire) and in-depth semi-structured (open-ended questionnaire) interviews asked participants about their current immigration status, school, work, family, social identity, and their perceptions regarding experiences with social disadvantage, discrimination, and inter-group competition. Participants' age ranged between 18 and 32 years old (M= 23.78). About a third of the sample of Colombian and Dominican respondents were between 18 and 21 years of age; a third were between 21 and 25 years old; and the remaining third were between 25 and 32 years of age.

Table 2. Phone Survey Respondents by Gender

		Female	Male	Total
In-depth interviews	Colombians	11 (61.0%)	7 (39.0%)	18
	Dominicans	11 (43.5%)	14 (56.5%)	25
Phone Survey	Colombians	89 (52.6%)	80 (47.3%)	169
	Dominicans	231 (58.7%)	162 (41.2%)	393

The majority of Colombian respondents lived in Queens (73%) during most of their school years, while Dominican respondents mostly lived in Manhattan (28.5%) followed by Queens (23.4%) and Brooklyn (22.4) during their school years (see table 3). Although the residential patterns of Colombian and Dominican participants in this study was similar to the overall residential patterns of Colombians and Dominicans in New York City in 2000, they do not reflect the changes in residential distribution among Dominicans as of 2010. There was almost no difference among Colombian residential patterns in New York City between 2000 and 2010 (Bergad, 2009, 2011). The majority of Colombians in New York City lived in Queens in 2000 (76%) and continued to live there in 2010 (70%). However, there was a shift in the residential patterns of Dominicans. In 2000, Manhattan was home to 34% of Dominicans and the Bronx was home to 33% of Dominicans in the city. By 2010, there seemed to be an exodus of Dominicans from Manhattan (27%) to the Bronx (41%) (Bergad, 2009, 2011).

Table 3. Respondents' Longest Place of Residence during School Years

Place lived longest 6-18 years old (school age)	Colombians	Dominicans
Bronx	5.4 %	17.6 %
Brooklyn	9.0 %	22.4 %
Manhattan	1.2 %	28.5 %
Queens	72.9 %	23.4 %
NJ Metro	6.0 %	5.3 %

The majority of U.S.-born Colombian respondents were born in Queens while U.S.-born Dominican respondents were largely born in Manhattan (see table 4). These data indicate that a large number of participants were probably still living in the boroughs where they were born.

Table 4. Respondents' Place of Birth

Place of birth	Colombians	Dominicans
Bronx	1.8 %	5.6 %
Brooklyn	10.2 %	14 %
Manhattan	4.8 %	24.9 %
Queens	34.7 %	10.4 %
NJ Suburbs	2.4 %	2.8 %
Abroad	42.5 %	39.9 %

Survey Data

The ISGMNY study included Dominicans, Chinese, West Indians, South Americans (Colombians, Peruvians and Ecuadorians were grouped together), and Russian Jewish children of immigrants between 18-32 years of age. The comparison groups included U.S. born African-American, White, and U.S.-born Puerto Ricans (as opposed to island-born) without an immigrant background. A total of 3,426 phone interviews were conducted through a random digit dialing procedure in order to select 3,300 target interviews. I obtained permission from the

principal investigators to carry out secondary analysis on a subset of data that included only Dominican and Colombian respondents.
After carefully reviewing the phone survey, questions that were related to the themes and research questions of this project were selected. A second review of the selected questions helped determine how they might be related to each other and what concepts or constructs they could be considered a measure of. A later reading of the selected questions considered whether some of them could be grouped together as indices or factors. The final variables selected for further analysis are listed below (for a full description of each of the variables see AppendixA).

Micro Level Variables = Age, Immigrant Generation, Respondents' Educational Attainment, Number of Children, Language Behavior

Meso Level Variables = Parents' Country of Origin, Parents' Educational Attainment Prior to Migration, Parents' Relationship Stability, Number of Siblings, Transnational Practices.

Macro Level Variables = Social Class in U.S., Home Ownership, Race, Neighborhood Social Characteristics, Quality and type of Schools.

In-depth Interviews

The follow-up in-person interviews were conducted by 16 interviewers from the different ethno-racial groups in the original study. An effort was made to match interviewer and interviewee according to the ethno-racial group to which they belonged even though the interviewers themselves were not necessarily second-generation immigrants. The interviews followed a semi-structured format and the themes were organized in a way which was similar to the phone survey. They were designed to cover the same general areas of the questions in the phone interview but in greater detail. The in-depth semi-structured interviews lasted 2 to 4 hours and were audio-taped, transcribed, and organized digitally using Atlas TI software. A sub-sample of interviewees from the initial pool of the telephone survey respondents (10 %) were subsequently interviewed in-depth in the original study. The sample of in-depth interviews I analyzed consists of 25 interviews with

Dominican participants (11 women and 14 men) and 18 with Colombian participants (11 women and 7 men, see table 2).

ANALYZING THE DATA

In an effort to understand what it was like for children of immigrants to negotiate multiples identities among transnational social fields, each research question was examined using both qualitative and quantitative data. I approached the quantitative data to explain how prevalent the phenomenon of transnational ties was among this group of Dominican and Colombian second generation immigrants. The qualitative data added stories and narratives to the statistical results helping to understand how these data translated into respondents' lives. I used both types of data to keep my assumptions in check and to provide triangulation validity to my analysis. Having both sources of data helped me examine complex patterns and avoid making overgeneralizations.

The phone interview data was analyzed using the Statistical Package for the Social Sciences (SPSS). After cleaning the data and replacing missing data via the Missing Values Analysis module in SPSS, I produced descriptive statistics for all variables such as frequencies, means, and standard deviations. At this point, those variables that were not normally distributed were transformed. The variables were divided between psychological constructs and sociological constructs. In the end, the psychological variables were eliminated due to lack of valid responses. I carried out correlation tests among the remaining variables. However, since they were mostly categorical variables and measured sociological factors that did not necessarily add information about the psychological experiences of participants, I do not discuss them in this book. The purpose of this research project did not merit further inferential statistical analysis. The results of Chi-square tables have been inserted in the text along with data from the qualitative interviews in an effort to emphasize the iterative process of the analysis. All the tables included in the text obtained Chi-Square values that were significant at either $p=0.01$ or $p=0.05$.

As a coder for the ISGMNY study, I carried out preliminary analysis of the interview data coding references to "transnationalism" or "transnational behaviors." Subsequently for this book, I approached the interviews for a second reading with a narrative analysis perspective and a third reading with a thematic analysis perspective. The thematic and narrative analyses were based on a grounded theory (Charmaz, 2000; Glasser & Strauss, 1967) approach. Since this is a secondary analysis of in-depth interviews and phone surveys which I did not collect myself, I felt it necessary to approach the interviews individually as narratives before identifying any themes across them. This was extremely helpful in bringing to life and attempting to reconstruct the context and dynamics of the interview in itself, the entire story the interviewee presented in the course of the interview, and the quality of rapport between the interviewer and the interviewee. After reading a number of interviews, I was able to distinguish between styles of interviewing among different interviewers and to piece together short life narratives for each interviewee. The latter was facilitated by the fact that the interview protocol questions followed a chronological order and covered the interviewee's life experience from childhood through the present.

In order to be systematic in my analysis and to facilitate the identification of differences and similarities across groups and within them, I read the interviews of the women first followed by the men's. Within each gender group, I analyzed the interviews of Dominicans first, followed by those of Colombian participants. The logic behind this ordering was to help me think in terms of ethnic/racial/national group differences as well as gender differences. After creating small narratives of each interviewee's life story, I proceeded to code each interview by selecting passages that spoke to selected themes guided by the quantitative findings and my original research questions: Identity, Family, Transnationalism, Race, Gender, Discrimination and Social Class. Doing so helped me organize the interview material in a way that was not necessarily chronological. Eventually these themes became the basis for the results chapters that are presented in this book. As part of the analysis of the interviews, I organized demographic and educational history information about each interviewee in tables (See Appendix B). These tables help infer some patterns between and across the participants and groups, which I then explored by going back to the interviews or the survey data for insight.

Table 5. Research Questions, Variables and Themes

Research Question	Quantitative Variables	Qualitative Themes
1) What are implications of their parents' home country for the negotiation of identities among Colombian and Dominican children of immigrants?	*Age,* *Respondents' Educational Attainment,* *Number of Children,* *Language Behavior*	*Being the child of immigrants,* *Being "American",* *Contending with different worldviews,* *Social comparisons*
2) To what extent do Colombian and Dominican children of immigrants maintain emotional, social and economic ties to their parents' home country? What affects their willingness and ability to maintain transnational ties with their family, friends, community and other members of their transnational social field?	*Parent's Country of Origin,* *Number of Siblings,* *Parents' Educational Attainment Prior to Migration,* *Parent's English Skills,* *Parents' Relationship Stability,* *Transnational Practices*	*Family as anchor for transnational experiences,* *Transnational ties Language- site of connection and membership,* *Life Cycle*
3) How do gender, race, and social class shape the life experiences of Colombian and Dominican children of immigrants in the United States?	*Personal Gross Income,* *Respondent's and - Parents Level of Education,* *Neighborhood,* *Social Characteristics,* *Quality and type of Schools,* *Respondent's Number of Children,* *Race and Marriage patterns*	*Schools and Neighborhoods,* *Parents' cultural capital - Urban vs. Rural background,* *Finding one's place in society,* *Rites of Incorporation- Marriage as social/racial positioning & negotiation*

OVERVIEW OF FINDINGS

> The New *mestiza* copes by developing a tolerance for contradictions, a tolerance for ambiguity. She learns to be an Indian in Mexican culture, to be Mexican from an Anglo point of view. She learns to juggle cultures. She has a plural personality, she operates in a pluralistic mode – nothing is throughst out, the good the bad and the ugly, nothing rejected, nothing abandoned. Not only does she sustain contradictions, she turns the ambivalence into something else...
> That focal point or fulcrum, that juncture where the *mestiza* stands, is where phenomena tend to collide. It is where the possibility of uniting all that is separate occurs. This assembly is not one where severed or separated pieces merely come together. Nor is it a balancing of opposing powers. In attempting to work out synthesis, the self has added a third element which is greater than the sum of its severed parts. That third element is a consciousness –a *mestiza* consciousness – and though it is a source of intense pain, its energy comes from continual creative motion that keeps breaking down the unitary aspect of each new paradigm. (Anzaldúa, 1999, p. 102)

> "That's one thing that I always appreciate. Always remember where you come from, -where you came from, teaches you how to go forward". (George, Dominican)

A number of immigration scholars (Espiritu & T. Tran, 2002; Fouron & Glick-Schiller, 2002; R. C. Smith, 2002; Vickerman, 2002; Wolf, 2002) have taken up the task of comparing the immigration and transnational experiences of different groups and their children through anthropological and sociological accounts of individual immigrant groups. These researchers have emphasized how immigrant groups differ on a number of outcome and demographic variables. Across these studies (Espiritu & T. Tran, 2002; Fouron & Glick-Schiller, 2002; R. C. Smith, 2002; Vickerman, 2002; Wolf, 2002), there is evidence that some children of immigrants maintain transnational ties. Young children of immigrants use their parents' home country as a social referent as they navigate transnational lives and negotiate multiple social identities. The interviews and phone surveys revealed deep similarities among Dominican and Colombian children of immigrants, especially in their psycho-social experiences growing up in New York City and negotiating ethnic/racial/national identities. Despite these similarities, the data revealed significant differences between Dominican and Colombian respondents attributable to differences in social class, cultural capital, skin-tone, gender, schools and neighborhoods.

Through the readings of the in-depth interviews it became apparent that the way in which participants described their experiences of developing and becoming aware of their ethnic/racial/trans/national identity resonated with Bronfenbrenner's ecological model of human and child development:

> [H]uman development takes place through a process of progressively more complex interaction between an active child and the persons, objects and symbols in its immediate environment. To be effective, the interaction must occur on a fairly regular basis over extended periods of *time*. Such enduring forms of interaction in the immediate environment are referred to as *proximal processes*. (Bronfenbrenner & Morris, 1998, p.996 as cited by Tudge, Mokrova, Hatfield, & Karnik, 2009, p. 200, italics in the original)

In other words, Colombian and Dominican respondents related stories about how their ethnic/racial/trans/national identities became relatively important in different stages in their lives and to different degrees. Those changes coincided with Bronfenbrenner's (Bronfenbrenner & P. A. Morris, 1998) model of development. In his model, the child is at the center and her/his development is affected by her/his interactions with her/his immediate surroundings and social groups as she/he grows up, such as family, school, friends, work etc where the child spends her/his time. In this scenario, the immediate family constitutes the first and most important emotional social group in the child's learning who she/he is and her/his place in society. From there, pre-school and primary school experiences as well as interactions with playmates become the child's first interactions with the larger society around her/him. As they continue their lives, school and family become substantial factors that shape their social environment. As they become adolescents, dating and finding a partner are added to the set of socially important and emotional events in their lives. In their young adult life, college and the workplace become the stage of identity negotiation. And for those who are young parents already, having children brings to the front identity and cultural heritage questions as they ponder how they want to educate their children. To such extent, children of immigrants are no different than most non-migrant children in the United States and elsewhere. However, what differentiates children of immigrants from children without an immigrant background is that they are raised simultaneously among different ethnic/national cultures that span (trans)national borders and are adept at navigating them. Figure 1 (below) depicts an adaptation of the Bronfrenbenner's model of ecological development that includes the transnational social spheres in which children of immigrants are embedded. In order to emphasize that relationships between spheres in the individual's system change when they have children who themselves are embedded in their own circles and will develop their own systems, I have added a circle that is attached to the individual's interlocking context.

Analysis of the interviews and phone surveys revealed substantial social-psychological overlap for the children of Dominican and Colombian immigrants, particularly with respect to identity negotiation. Yet, their institutional and interpersonal experiences of engaging with others differed remarkably. In other words, these children of immigrants understood themselves subjectively in much the same way, as being both a member of a national immigrant group and an 'American' citizen. They grew up amidst two or more different socio-cultural spaces: the intimate culture of their national immigrant groups re-created by their families and the socio-cultural reality of growing up in the United States, especially in New York City. These Dominican and Colombian respondents contended with two or more cultures within a transnational social space, the culture of their parents' home country and the culture of the country where they were born and/or raised, the U.S. Yet as these young people confronted public institutions and interacted with class, race, and political hierarchies, they were treated differently and granted differential access to opportunities according to their social and racial standing in United States' society. Such differential access and treatment placed Dominican and Colombian participants on life trajectories which were different from each other.

Figure 1. A Transnational Ecological Model of Child/Human Development

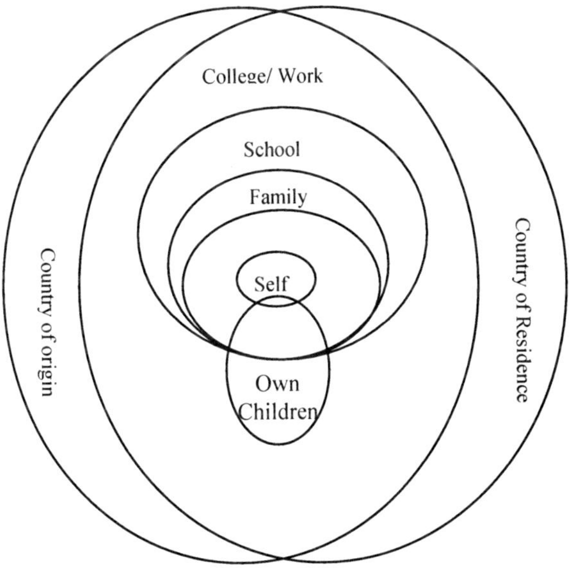

Source: Adapted from Bronfenbrenner's Model of Ecological Development

Bronfenbrenner's ecological model of human and child development (Bronfenbrenner & P. A. Morris, 1998, 2006) and Verkuyten's levels of analysis of social identity processes (2005a) served to organize the presentation of findings in the following chapters. In his model, the child sits at the center where he or she interacts and spends time in different contexts and environments which shape her/his development. The development of the child is most affected by the interpersonal interactions with different persons, groups and cultures as she/he grows up. For that reason, I present my findings focusing on the order in which this process of identity negotiation took place within the ecological environment of these Dominican and Colombian children of immigrants. The chapter "*Negotiating Self and Identity*" discusses the most intimate processes of identity negotiation that occur within the respondents' (trans)national psychological space.

It illustrates how their lived experiences growing up as children of immigrants created the potential for the encounter of cultures (their parents' and the host country's) within their psychological space and their transnational social fields. The chapter also explores the meaning that being "American" takes for these respondents under such circumstances. Finally it, presents a discussion of how these Colombian and Dominican children of immigrants viewed and dealt with the contradictions, conflict, and ambiguity inherent in negotiating different cultural norms, values, expectations, and beliefs. The chapter "*Maintaining Transnational Relationships*" analyzes the role that (trans)national ties occupies in the lives of these Colombian and Dominican children of immigrants. The chapter develops how the Family becomes the anchor for (trans)national practices, ties, and desires. Family relationships across borders mediated motivations to visit the home country of the respondents' parents as well as decisions about sending money or not to relatives beyond national borders. It also discusses the importance that language assumes by enabling communication and relationship building. Life cycle and stages emerged as a particularly useful framework for understanding what particular (trans)national practices respondents engaged in or not. The chapter "*Encountering Social Structures*" highlights some of the factors that contribute to placing Dominican and Colombian respondents on different trajectories that reproduce racial and socio-economic inequalities across national borders. The chapter focuses on transition moments that afforded some level of decision-making and agency to respondents amidst limited circumstances and racial/social/economical constrains. Choosing the right neighborhood, deciding to finish high school, avoiding pregnancy, and deciding who to marry were all transitional moments in the lives of these young people. However, how they acted upon their options (or lack of) was shaped by their multiple identities and the cultural and (trans)national social worlds they inhabited. The conclusions and discussion chapter develops some implications that these findings have for theorizing cultural encounters and identity negotiation, proposes a new framework of 'trans'-culturation as an ethics of radical interconnectedness rooted in a cultural embrace, and discusses methodological implications for psychological theory and practice.

CHAPTER 3

Negotiating Self and Identity as a Child of Immigrants

The first theme to emerge among these two groups of interviewees from Dominican and Colombian immigrant backgrounds was the importance of their experiences as *children of immigrants* as a decisive and constituting aspect of their process of identity negotiation. Most of the respondents did not see themselves as immigrants. Though perfectly understandable among those born in the United States, even those born in another country who arrived as children felt that the United States embodied the meaning of "home" for them. Many would not consider moving to another country to live because they felt that the United States was their home. However, they were aware that their experiences growing up were marked by the fact that their parents were immigrants. This meant that they were used to participating in a culture at home and switching to a different culture in school or with friends who did not have immigrant parents.

What united respondents born in the United States and abroad, from Colombian or Dominican backgrounds, and made their experiences carry over to other ethnic/racial/national groups with immigrant backgrounds, was the fact that, as children of immigrants, they have had the common the experience of juggling different cultural norms, values, and expectations, that of their parents and the mainstream society they live in. Diana, a Colombian young woman, alluded to these common experiences as she described her relationship with her boyfriend who is the child of Ecuadorian parents and was born in the United States.

I: What do you like most about the relationship?

Diana: (repeats question) Maybe that we share the same the same ideas, like, children of migrant families, we both share the idea that we want to go beyond what our parents did. You know, usually, children of immigrants achieve higher levels of education and just financial situation over-all than their parents. But basically, you know, our goals are to retire and to be well. (Colombian, 26 years old)

Colombian and Dominican respondents referred to this issue regardless of their ethnic/racial/national group, social class, race, or gender. Being a child of immigrants marked the respondents' life experiences and how they understood their social reality. Regardless of the national group, gender, social class, or race, many spoke about how their experience of 'growing up' was different from others because their parents were immigrants. Their parents were raised in a different country and had a different culture, values, and expectations about how to raise children properly and what is acceptable behavior. Although their parents had gradually adapted to living in New York City and in most cases settled definitely in the United States, they did not wholly embrace what was perceived as "American culture" or the "American way of raising children"[9]. Stephanie, a Colombian woman, used an agricultural metaphor to describe it.

Stephanie: It's like growing apples in the banana fields. It really is. The method of raising is very different.

---

[9] This is the terminology used by the respondents and the interviewers. Additional use of these terms will indicate that it is the language used by the respondents or interviewers, and not my own.

I: I never heard that before - growing apples —

Stephanie: — that's what I always used to say to my mother. It's like you're raising me Colombian style and we're in the USA. It's like raising apples in a banana field. (Colombian, 32 years old)[10]

Differences in the immigrants' beliefs about raising children, referred to by Anibal as "old school fashion," were compared to the United States' mainstream beliefs about raising children. Anibal felt that the behavior of his parents, especially his father, was attributable to their cultural "old fashioned Hispanic" way of doing things. Their positions appeared to be conflicting because his parents continue to treat him like a child while Anibal expected greater independence and acknowledgment that he was a grown man. Anibal seemed to attribute these conflicting views to cultural differences between his parents' cultural expectations as a Hispanic family and his own experiences living in the United States where children are given independence at an earlier age. This Dominican male echoed the divide between parents' and children's views expressed by Stephanie.

I: How has it been to live with your parents the past 3 years? You've been living with them all throughout but how has that changed? How is that going?

Anibal: Pretty difficult.

I: Really?

Anibal: My parents haven't realized the fact that you're no longer a little kid. I have a kid. And old

[10] Through the rest of the paper I will use the initial "I" as an abbreviation for Interviewer. It should not be confused with the subject "I", since I did not conduct any of the interviews analyzed in this document.

fashioned. My father really is very old fashioned so it's been mainly a struggle dealing with him in the household. He's a stereotypical old fashioned Hispanic man.

I: Old school Dominican?

Anibal: Yes. It's crazy. It's quite crazy. We just got into it literally yesterday or the day before that. He just doesn't feel, I guess, the old school fashion of raising your child is like I don't have to have respect for you, you're my child. And it's like hold on a second, I'm a man now. Yes, I am your child but I'm a man. I'm no longer a child. I'm your son, yes, but I'm no longer a child. And I guess it's hard for them to deal with the fact that you are no longer a child. You are on your own. You have your own set of standards by which you feel you should be treated by and they don't know that. At times they need to recognize that. They feel that you are beneath them, because you are their offspring, I guess, so to speak. (Dominican, 28 years old)

Cultural views, expectations, and values transmitted through family became incorporated into participants' cultural/personal repertoire and became part of these young people's internal dialogue. Hong & Chiu (2001) propose that communication and interpersonal exchanges between speakers and listeners are essential to the construction and maintenance of cultural knowledge. Cultural theories represent social positions that enter the person's repertoire and can at any point be called upon to form part of a particular social position with regards to a specific event or situation in time and space (Hermans, 1999, 2001). María identified what she thought was the origin of her doubts about her own ability to do a particular job and tied it back to her relationship with her mother and dad. Her mother and father's voices, telling her the limits of what she could do as a woman, represent collective cultural views and expectations. In her own internal dialogue, those positions were embodied by her parents' voices. Yet she did not blame her parents. She expressed a sense of agency in the choices she made. She defended her mother by saying that 'she did a good job' and that she would want to do the same for her own daughter.

I: How have those experiences influenced your adult life and your identity?

María: I think in a sense it did affect me. When I was telling you about when I found the high income for that job intimidated me, especially being a female. I felt like that was too much competition for me or something like that. And I think even though I am stubborn, but there's a certain part of me that does allow myself to be intimidated because I'm a female and I think in that sense there's a voice that sounds like my mom and my dad reminding me that I'm a woman and there are certain...

I: That traditional voice seeps in and it's still in you?

María: Yeah. I don't agree and I think it's something I should have gone for that job. And when I think of why I didn't, that's when it hits me where I've made the choices I've made sometimes. And in that sense it is affecting me. But my mother's way of raising us has affected me as far as I think the way that she did a good job. And I admire what she did so I think I want to do that for my daughter. (Dominican, 26 years old)

'REMOORING IDENTITY' – APPROPRIATING FAMILY TRADITIONS AS CULTURAL PRACTICES

As the following respondents discussed, being part of the family social group, its customs and norms were natural to them. Culture was transmitted through everyday interactions and rituals (Bourdieu, 1984; Bronfenbrenner & P. A. Morris, 1998, 2006; Hong & Chiu, 2001; Hong et al., 2000). By extension, their national origin heritage was transmitted in the way their families did things. As Verkuyten explains, "Culture is tacit, lived, and physically felt rather than realized and verbalized. It is the un-reflexive part of mundane practices (2005a, p. 79)." The fact that a group of families have similar traditions reinforces a sense of sharing a definite common culture and being part of a cultural national group.

I: What was it like growing up in an immigrant family?

María: To me it was just the way it was. I guess there was always reference back to the Dominican Republic and how things are done there. [...]. For me it was normal. (Dominican, 26 years old)

While another respondent added,

I: When you were growing up, in what ways like did your parents teach you about your background and your history? Like, your ethnic background history? Like, did you celebrate holidays, or was it the language, was it?

Lina: Well, the language definitely. I mean, I don't think- It's not like they sat down with me and you know, showed me something or an encyclopedia. It was more like an experience I had, because I was brought up with my parents and my grandmother. My grandmother spoke absolutely no English, so all we spoke in the house was Spanish and that was basically it.

I: Did you feel like a lot of- Like the food, like you mentioned, like the food you were eating, did you find that you were still cooking like your mom and your grandmother were still cooking like traditional homemade meals.

Lina: Yeah, but you know, it's always rice. Yeah. There was always a pot of rice being cooked.

I: I used to think that was normal.

Lina: Me too.

I: Like, doesn't everyone eat rice every day?

Lina: [laughter][laughter] It's like rice without a meal just isn't a meal. (Colombian, 34 years old)

When the participants spoke about their experiences and interactions with other Latinos (non Colombian or Dominican), they described certain information and ways of being as given and self-understood as common experiences and shared knowledge. Most of these similarities stemmed from being raised by immigrant parents from Latin American or Hispanic Caribbean countries. Some of these qualities (e.g. speaking Spanish, food and musical traditions) are esteemed, at least in the United States, because they originate from a shared language and history. The most recognized cultural or ethnic/racial anchor is sharing Spanish as a language although each national and ethnic group within Latin American countries has its own dialect/variety of Spanish or Portuguese. Other customs and cultural anchors that support the idea of a seemingly homogeneous Latino background are dietary choices common to many Latin American countries such as rice, beans, corn, and similarities in musical taste and folklore such as African-infused rhythms like *Salsa* (Puerto Rican origin), *Bachata* (Dominican origin), *Merengue* (Dominican origin) and

Cumbia (Colombian origin). These cultural practices contribute to creating a context for 'remooring' (Deaux, 2000; Deaux & Ethier, 1998; Ethier & Deaux, 1994). In other words, such practices and behaviors served to support and link respondents' cultural and national group identities.

I: What kind of food did you eat growing up?

Jorge: Oh my God, so many rice and beans. So many plantains. Let's see, a lot of meat. Very Dominican fare at home. To be fair, my mother had some variety, pasta dishes and such. It wasn't all like you know, *aguacate* and *platanos* (avocado and plantains - like big bananas) but that was always the substrate. Just about everything came with a side of rice and beans. So, it was never far from that background.

I: How about now, what do you eat?

Jorge: A little bit of everything. Sushi, some Italian, I've been eating a Lot more healthy lately. Partly - I owe that to my fiancée. Which is good, because I was coming to resemble the letter "B" in profile so I mean, that's good that I'm exercising a little more restraint. There's always a green vegetable. It's really just so varied, it's not really possible to classify. Not a whole lot of Dominican food, though, occasionally, yeah. (Dominican, 32 years old)

Bourdieu (1984) used the concept of *habitus* to refer to subjective dispositions that produce behaviors and perceptions as one interacts with each other in one's everyday life. This definition allowed him to explain the process by which our everyday actions and interactions with others were subjectively embodied and constitute part of our cultural reference system. The notion of I-positions and positioning described in theories of *dialogical self* (Hermans & Kempen, 1998; Hermans, 1999) seemed to develop through a similar process called *appropriation* (Tappan, 2005). In other words, one becomes identified with a particular ideology or cultural practice by appropriating that knowledge as a cultural tool available for use at any moment. According to Tappan (2005), there are at least two dimensions to this process: a sense of mastery ('knowing how to use) and a sense of ownership ('making it one's own). Using this framework, it is possible to see how Andrea ran down a list of meanings, practices and symbols that were contained in her ideology of Colombian culture to illustrate her mastery of the content of Colombian culture. She further emphasized her sense of ownership of Colombian taste in food through ordering at restaurants, even though she did not actually cook.

I: What kind of customs or traditions did you practice from your background?

Andrea: The nativity set for Christmas. I love that. The symbols from the *Chibchas* - which are basically the same thing. I have a lot from that. The history from Colombia, I'm passionate about that. I'm passionate about the people in my city, the department and the State that I come from. The food. I don't know how to cook, but I know how to buy it and enjoy it and I know how to request what I want, and how I want it.

I: So what kind of --

Andrea: *Arroz* (rice) *Frijoles* -beans, *coraeipa*. Cheese, *asopao de harina, tamalejos, nopuelos*, patties, *empanadas, cocala, manzana colombiana*, the apple drinks, all the weird juices that you can get in the restaurant, I love them all. The passion fruit. (Colombian, 27 years old)

In the following excerpt, José, a Dominican man, described how his taste in music changed over the years and was influenced by changes in music taste in the Dominican Republic as well. His account shows recognition that culture in the home country of his parents is subject to change as well. This perspective differs from typical immigrants' nostalgic views of culture that hold on to cultural expressions as they remember them subscribing to a static conception of ethnic/national culture among recent immigrants. José's experiences represent an example of how participating in a transnational context provides expanded opportunities for 'remooring' beyond the national borders of the United States. In addition it may contribute to understanding culture as changing social reality rather than as static, fossilized expressions.

I: Has your Dominican self-identity changed over time - since you left high school and went to college over here and became an adult and all that - how did your Dominican self-identity change over time?

José: To be honest with you, it changed like, in the early 90's, it changed because I remember that I would, you know, I would listen to *Merengue* like crazy. And all of a sudden, I wouldn't listen to *Merengue, salsa*, nothin', it was strictly Hip Hop and R &B and all of that, and you know, that's why, when people, - when I used to speak Spanish, people used to be shocked, because you would never tell –

I: -- They wouldn't put one and one together.

José: Exactly. So then, you know, like right now, you come to my house, and it's like probably like five CDs are *Merengue*, and five are *Salsa*, But - I listen to them but I put on the radio station *La Mega* or *Latino Mix* and I know every song that's there. But it's not because, you know, I don't know. It's like that part changed right there about listening to a lot of Spanish music in general, see, 'cause like salsa, I was into salsa but - I like to listen to old school salsa. I mean, I'm not saying I don't like the new stuff but give me *Gran Combo* and I'm there. Like with *Merengue*,

> the same thing. Like now, they have this *Merengue* what they call *Mambo*, and that dance shit - you know, you're just dancing like crazy. The words don't mean shit, but you're dancing, you know what I'm saying? Back in the day, Mito Yalona [not sure] or these people, his lyrics and some Music in there. You can relate to the letters he's talking about, the lyrics and all that. But then, you know, when I was there in D.R., it was it was mixed, because I would listen to *Merengue, salsa*, whatever Spanish, and here, I was saying to my cousin, "Yo send me some music," and he would send me some Hip Hop. Some R&B, whatever, so I had a mix. Then all my friends over there, you know, were into Hip Hop or R&B, even if they didn't understand the words, but they were like into the music music. (Dominican, 31 years old)

EMPHASIZING FAMILY COHESION – YEARNING FOR CONNECTION AND RECIPROCITY

Most of the respondents, Colombian and Dominican, were very proud of having what they described as close-knit relationships with their families. They appreciated and valued extended family. When speaking about their views of their ethnic/national/racial group, be it as Latinos/Hispanics or as Colombians/Dominicans, they held their group in high positive regard. When comparing their families to their American friends' families, they described Latinos as being more 'family oriented'. According to their accounts, we can infer that most of the youth in the project had social networks that extended beyond their immediate family members (parents, siblings). They usually spoke of their grandparents and aunts or uncles, their cousins, and other family members. One apparent difference was that Dominicans had more family members living within the United States and usually in their same neighborhoods compared with Colombians who seemed to have fewer family members living in the United States.

I: What was the best part about growing up in your family?

María: What do you mean? There were so many people at one point that there was always something to do, somewhere to go for something. There was always somebody cooking something, always something to go to. That's what I can remember.

I: And the worst part?

María: That there were so many people. (laughter) And also, as you get older, you realize there were so many problems. A lot of them. So the more people, the more problems.

I: You mentioned your grandmother as you were growing up. Were there any other family members around that were really close to you while you were growing up?

María: My godfather, my mother's brother. Mostly, I guess my mother's side of the family were the ones we were more closer to. And one of my father's brothers. My uncle on my father's side. (Dominican, 26 years old)

Deyanira's description of what she liked the most about Dominicans suggests that family cohesion and support were important for her self-esteem and was a source of positive regard for her family and ethnic/national group. Social embeddedness is an essential element of social and ethnic identity by "providing a context in which a person has easy access to others who are similar and who can validate one's identity and membership in the group" (Deaux, 2006, p. 108) The experiences narrated by respondents in this study helps advance the concept of social embeddedness by including transnational relationships as part of the individuals' social field, so one might talk about 'transnational social embeddedness". Her concept of family included not only close family members like parents and siblings but also her extended family, i.e. grandparents, cousins, aunts, and uncles. Maintaining close relationships with them, by going to parties and doing things together, was highlighted as having great importance as well.

I: What are the characteristics of Dominicans that you like the most?

Deyanira: The fact that we take—I know what I want to say, I just have to find the wording—we have more values than most Latino, Hispanic families; like we respect our parents and our grandparents a little more than others do. You know, I have Puerto Rican friends that they love their grandparents and all that, but they don't do all the little parties and masses and stuff that we do, and their families aren't as big as ours, you know, have all these kids and get together all these times and support each other, so it's like our family values, we take those more important than other races do. We work harder, I think, like I think I said before, you see us working at a young age, and working in the house more than anybody else, and cooking and all that. And the thing about the family, there aren't that many single-parent Dominican families that I've seen, not as much as in other ethnicities and other races. They're more two-parent families, and that's cool. (Dominican, 30 years old)

For María, having an extended family was something to look forward to, but as she grew up, she was able to appreciate the difficulties associated with having a large family. María was able to be both appreciative and critical of her family. In the interview, she acknowledged that there were more problems among her family than she knew at the time. Yet she did not have an unrealistic perception of her family; she was able to contend with the tension of understanding that extended families could be both, a blessing and a challenge.

I: How is it still to live with your mom?

María: It's fine.

I: What are the best things about it?

María: ???? like when sometimes I would be moving away. I guess it's like a cultural thing, but she didn't see why. Especially at that point, it was just me. And I wasn't with anyone and I didn't have a child.

I: When you went to the Bronx?

María: No, after I came back home from the Bronx and I told her... we were just talking about the future and I was telling her, "I want to get my own place." And she was, "Why?" (laughter) And I was, "Because it just seemed like the thing to do. It's the next step." But I guess with her, she doesn't... it's not just a, it seems like it's more of an American issue. Once you're 18, you've got to go. And she doesn't see things that way. So as far as me and her, how we mesh? We mesh fine. Yeah, there are times when I think she thinks I'm still 2 but I think that is going to happen regardless. Even when I was away at school, she called me every day and every time I came home she had 3 shopping bags of food to take back.

I: I bet that's the good part of it.

María: She's going to take care of me no matter what so it's fine. It has it's... but I think that is going to happen with anybody you live with. There are going to be times when you think, "You know, you are really getting on my nerves today."

I: Is she going to Florida with you or is she staying?

María: No, everybody is going to Florida. (Dominican, 26 years old)

Another common experience of these immigrant children concerned the large number of hours their parents work in order to make a living in the United States. Both Colombian and Dominican respondents wished their parents did not have to work so much. They missed having their mothers at home taking care of them and getting involved in their school work. With limited language skills, immigrant parents often worked long hours in low-paying jobs. Usually both parents worked outside the home and had less time to spend with their children on a daily basis. In some cases, a mother could work taking care of someone else's child, while her own child remained at home cared for by a nanny, a family member, or was left alone. These young people described growing up with a feeling of being on their own although they knew their parents were working hard to support and provide for their needs. Unfortunately, they found themselves having to care for their psychological needs on their own, e.g. going to school by themselves, coming back from school to an empty house, preparing dinner for siblings and doing their homework in the absence of other deeply caring adults. We can infer in Lina's words, a feeling of not having had the adequate attention she needed while growing up. Feeling deprived of psychological and emotional attention she wanted, she described a sense of envy that others had their mothers at home while she didn't. Lina was determined to avoid repeating this pattern with her own children.

Lina: I wish that she would have been more… I wish that she didn't have to work. I wish that she could've been home when I got home from school, because back then when I was growing up, the woman usually stayed home from work. I mean, you know, she would stay home and the kids would come home from school, and mom was there, you know, with a nice snack and all this stuff, whereas I didn't have that. And, I

> remember always feeling so envious. Like, you know, "You're so lucky your mother's here." And, so I would definitely have changed that and I wish that she was home you know, to maybe have taken better care of me, and made sure that, "How is your schoolwork going? Are you doing your homework? Let me help you with this? Are you having a problem in this area? Let's work on it". You know, I wish she had been more attentive with that and then also with food, you know, there was always like soda in the house. And I think that's terrible. Like, if I ever had kids there would never be any soda in my house. It's just so bad! (Colombian, 34 years old)

In the following exchange, Andrea demonstrated the ability to be both critical and understanding of her mother's actions. Although she regrets not being close to her mom while she was growing up because her mother was working, she realized that her mom had limited choices in the matter. Having to work after divorcing her dad, Andrea's mother could not provide the emotional attention and time Andrea longed for. Andrea made an effort to understand her mother's dilemma and puts the blame on an external social problem - "lack of money". This allows her to continue to love her mother and appreciate her for what she was able to do for her, even though she felt it was not enough to fulfill her psychological and social needs at the time.

Andrea: My mom, my mom had a really hard time, because once they separated, she had to go out and find a job, and she had never done that.

I: She didn't work before.

Andrea: She didn't work before, and she had No - she was working in a new place, with a different language, and no skills, or the skills that she had were no good - she didn't have the English to do it, and it was really hard for her. And it was really hard for her to see me grow up without her. And it became bad, and sad and horrible, and too many fights.

I: Did you have anybody else who could take care of you while they were working, like a neighbor or friend?

Andrea: No. My mom wasn't that mentality because she doesn't like to be friendly with neighbors. So we didn't have that. We didn't have family, relatives, here in the U.S.A.

I: Would you like anything to have changed the way you were raised, or growing up?

Andrea: Yeah. I wish there wasn't an issue with money. And other than that, I wish I had family- cousins, aunts, grandparents, and that community. That sense of community. (Colombian, 27 years old)

Few respondents had a stay-at-home mom who could watch over them, be there when they came back from school, and help them with their homework. Usually, this situation was not without conflict, especially for the mothers. For some mothers, staying at home meant forgoing opportunities to work and be more independent in order to care for their children full-time. Sometimes it was a personal decision and in other cases it was expected by their husbands and families. Colombian mothers were more likely to be at-home-mothers than were Dominican mothers among this group of interviewees. However one thing was clear, these young people preferred to be babysat or watched over by family members, be it grandparents, uncles, or even family friends, than by strangers. Some respondents like Jessica, preferred to have their moms at home or be taken care of by family members instead of having extra money.

I: Who took care of you while she worked?

Jessica: I know I had a babysitter when I lived in Queens. I don't remember her. And there's another one

> that she spoke about that lives here in the Bronx; I don't remember her either. Because after I reached junior high school I basically went to school by myself, came home by myself, had my own keys, whatever, and in the third or fourth grade my school was right down the block, so she was home by the time I got back. So I had a babysitter when I was really young, but after the third grade I didn't need one. (Dominican, 21 years old)

Some of the strategies used by Colombian mothers to deal with having to work but avoid leaving their children with babysitters involved working from home in jobs such as sewing or babysitting other children in their own homes.[11] Once the children were older, they were given the responsibility to come home by themselves and wait for their parents or they would be expected to go to a relative's home until it was time for their parents to arrive from work. Such was the case at Diana and Lina's homes:

> I: How was their working when you were growing up? Did you see them a lot?
>
> Diana: My dad, I would see him in the afternoons. My mom, when I was born, she took off, like she stayed at home, but she worked. She took care of children. She took care of six kids, and she would do her sewing work on the side, but doing the sewing work then was not samples, it was

[11] The reason why some Colombian mothers resorted to working from home is hard to establish. Lack of language and marketable skills or having undocumented status could account for the need to find ways to do some kind of paid work in their homes. At the time of the interview, most respondents reported that their parents had at least legal residency in the United States. Even if a number of the parents were initially undocumented, most would have qualified for amnesty under 1986 Immigration Reform and Control Act.

production work. Like they would give her two hundred dresses - take it home, bring it back in a week. (I: Wow) So she would get the pieces (talk over) the tops (talk over) like they would send her everything cut already. If it was dresses, she would get fifty pairs of sleeves and the rest and she had to put it together, and she had kids in her living room she had to take care of.

I: So did your mother usually take care of you when you were growing up? She didn't leave you with friends.

Diana: When I started, when I got like nine or ten, that they gave me my own key. I would get home - you know, get off the bus- it would drop me off right at the corner and I would walk from the corner to the building and just come inside and do my homework, watch TV. (Colombian, 26 years old)

While Lina described staying home with family members while her mom was working.

I: So did anyone take care of you then, when you were after school, were they home already by the time you got home from school?

Lina: No. Mm mm. My grandmother, when she would come from Colombia, she would be upstairs. My sister and her husband and my nephew were upstairs and my grandmother was upstairs also, and then we had the downstairs. So then after school I would be with my grandmother.

I: Oh, I see. So, you would be with family. (Colombian, 34 years old)

LIVING IN-BETWEEN – (RE)NEGOTIATING MULTIPLE SOCIAL IDENTITIES

These young people described lives lived as "Contact Zones" (Pratt, 1991), "Third Space" (Gutierrez et al., 1995), as a "Bridge" (Moraga & Anzaldúa, 1984), between two or more ethnic/racial/national cultures. Their life experiences are the product of two or more cultures, ways of being, valuing and behaving, coming into contact within their physical, social, and psychological worlds. Their lives are an example of the ever-changing, non-static quality of culture. They are constantly "becoming", finding and creating their place in society, negating the comfortable and constricting identity dichotomies (Hermans & Kempen, 1998) that societies want to perpetuate. Their identity negotiation represents a "trans" identity as in 'trans-gressive or trans-cendent'; one that goes beyond the pre-established identity narratives and categories by pushing and breaking away from boundaries. In the same spirit of Gloria Anzaldúa, I reclaimed this in-between space as *Nepantla*:

> And I now called it *Nepantla*, which is a Nahuatl word for the space between two bodies of water, the space between two worlds. It is a limited space, a space where you are not this or that but where you are changing. You haven't got into the new identity yet and haven't left the old identity behind either – you are in a kind of transition. And that is what *Nepantla* stands for. (1999, p. 237)

Both Colombian and Dominican respondents reported feeling that they were living between different worlds and cultures, their parents' culture anchored by the home country and the culture of the United States. They understood the expectations, values and norms that each culture was intent on transmitting to them. They discussed how the things they did as a family at home were different from the way families without an immigrant background did them. For example, respondents mentioned how gender roles in their parents' home country were stricter and more patriarchal than they perceived them to be in the United States. They also mentioned that race was dealt with differently in the United States than either in Colombia or the Dominican Republic. Some respondents commented that they felt the school system in the home country of their parents was more comprehensive and that students were more engaged at school compared to the United States. Even though they felt at home in the United States vs. their parents' home country, they reported that they did not feel fully "American" because they had different customs and values than their "White-American" friends and were always presumed to be "not-American" by others. On the other hand, when they visited Colombia or the Dominican Republic, they were not seen as "fully Colombian" or "fully Dominican" by their transnational families[12] and friends. At the same time, being abroad often made salient how "American" their beliefs and values about some issues were, i.e. gender roles and race. Butterfield described that a similar "feeling of not belonging in either an immigrant world or an American world was common" among her respondents, children of West Indian immigrants (2004, p. 300). Deyanira eloquently expressed how respondents felt like they were neither from here nor from there, but somewhere in between.

> Deyanira: I think that just being educated here versus somewhere else had a big influence and being a ??? because you are exposed to the main stream culture through education. I think having a strong family life and having a close knit family made it a lot easier to sort of see both worlds, view both worlds. Pick and choose what was part of me and what I was comfortable with. I think that.

> I: Any other questions you would add? Do you ever feel there was a time when your being an American and being Dominican was in conflict?

> Deyanira: No. And the reason I say no is because it isn't something that came overnight. Like one day I

---

[12] Here I am using Nina Glick-Schiller's definition of transnational that involves everyone who participates within transnational social fields and is affected by it, even they themselves have not travel across borders.

> woke up, "Hey, I'm this Dominican American." I set a process where through my entire life I've been exposed to what it is to be Dominican, what it is to be American, what it is. So it's sort of like something you learn by bits and pieces. That you sort of integrate in your personality. That if I would have moved here, migrated here from the Dominican Republic, it would have been a completely different process whereas being raised here it made it a lot easier. It wasn't such a foreign thing to be from both cultures. (Dominican, 30 years old)

It was common for respondents to compare and contrast situations, cultural norms, values, and ways of doing things between/across what they perceived as different ethno/cultural, national or racial groups. In some situations, the respondents preferred United States' values and norms while in other situations they voiced a preference for the values and norms of their parents' ethnic/national/racial group. Internal processes of dialogue between the host country's culture (United States) and the culture of their parents (Colombian or Dominican) produced feelings of affinity or repulsion, agreement or disagreement that determined which cultural rules, values, or norms were deemed more appropriate or favorable in particular moments. For example, Jessica (below) felt that it was not desirable to be "money-cautious and scared to spend"; that they no longer lived in her mother's or grandmother's time when they were less financially stable. Jessica believed this was an unrealistic preoccupation that had psychological and social costs for her and her mother.

I: How do you feel about that?

Jessica: Well, you know, there's anger there, because basically I can't really be angry at her because she thought she was doing right by us by getting a job and bringing more money into the house when really we needed her there. But I can't really blame her because that's what she was used to; that's what my grandmother did, and I

> guess it's a cycle. So I'm not—I don't want to do it to my kids, you know. It's really too bad that she passed on to us being money-cautious and scared to spend, you know, because that's really not healthy to be like that. Yeah, I'm angry a little bit, but I can't really blame her. (Dominican, 21 years old)

In another example, Jeremy compared the way women were raised in Dominican Republic and Puerto Rico versus the way they were raised in New York City. These valuations were the result of dialogue between the different collective voices of their parents' culture and the culture of the country where they were born. They represent positioning and re-positioning of the self whereby after considering both cultural positions (how Dominican women viewed themselves in the United States compared to women in the Dominican Republic), he decided to assume a different personal and social position than that of his immediate context

I: You said there's a difference between the ones that are raised over there and the ones that are raised over here?

Jeremy: Like I said, the women that are raised here, not all Dominican women but a lot of them around here and Puerto Rican also, they don't give much value to themselves. And Dominican women that I seen over there, Santo Domingo and when I was over there and my mother always talks about them when she goes over there, they have a little bit more respect or whatever. (Dominican, 21 years old)

Perhaps one of the most useful cognitive tools that living in *Nepantla* (between worlds) afforded respondents was the ability to find cracks/fissures in cultural discourses, which allowed them to be reflective of their realities. They were able to entertain different perspectives about the same issue, envisioned things as they might/should be and did not feel bound by the way things were.

Colombian and Dominican participants appreciated aspects of their parents' culture even as they were critical of others. Most respondents acknowledged that even though there were differences between their parents' "old ways" and their own way of doing things, not everything was negative. Even though María called her mother "old fashioned and traditional", she recognized that there were positive outcomes related to the extra attention and care she received because of her mother's traditional values (see excerpt in page 97). Paula's account provides another example of how respondents took stock of aspects and values from both cultures and decided what cultural norms and traditions they valued or not.

I: What characteristics of Colombians or Hispanic people do you like the most?

Paula: Sense of humor, their generosity, their openness, just the warm hospitality feeling that there is when you go into a Hispanic home. There is that sense of community or family. Even if you're not part of the family, you don't understand the language, "Come, we'll show you. Sit down, have a drink." That.

I: What characteristics do you like the least?

Paula: The flip side of that is the clichiness. The tendency to maybe not step out and venture into other groups. For whatever reasons, fear, ignorance, I do not know but that I don't like. You see a lot of that. They'll live in the same neighborhoods… I don't know. Open up a little. (Colombian, 30 years old)

EMBODYING COMPLEXITY – EMBRACING AMBIGUITY

Respondents seemed to be able to compare and contrast different cultures and systems that might at times appear irreconcilable and move beyond oppositional dichotomies (good vs. bad; desirable vs.

undesirable) towards a more integrative stance that would rescue the useful and desirable components of the conflict and disregard the not so useful or dated components. Using a "frame-switching" perspective, one can describe respondents' experiences as moving between different cultural frames for anchoring behavior in accordance to their context. As Verkuyten & Wolf (2002) pointed out, negotiating different cultures does not intrinsically evoke psychological stress. Rather, respondents' answers suggested that they derived a feeling of agency from being able to have access to more than one cultural repertoire/cultural frame. In the language of dialogical self theory, this state of being entails a constant process of negotiating between positions called 'innovations' about the established social identity discourses available in society (Sirin & Fine, 2007; Wiley, 2005). These innovations represent encounters between different social positions that could result in a number of outcomes: embracing a new social position, retaining the existing/original social position or the creation of a "coalition between opposites" according to changes in the situation and time. In other words, this would enable participants to critically evaluate their context and discern which social positions might be appropriate for their new context and what to leave out of their repertoires.

However, the work at the hyphen (Anzaldúa, 1999; Deaux, 2008; Sirin & Fine, 2007) does not occur in a vacuum. Historical, economic, physical, social, and cultural realities constrain the context in which this dynamic identity negotiation takes place. Power relations in the form of privilege, i.e. status, social class, gender, and race, give priority to certain dominant discourses over others. Therefore, stress and psychological suffering are more likely to be the result of inequality in power relations, what is valued by society vs. what is not, who is included vs. who is excluded. "... [It is not always a harmonious multiplicity. It is a multiplicity that can be contradictory even uncomfortable, because of the forces that try *to splinter it*, and stratify the pieces according to dominant power relationships." (Moraga and Anzaldúa, 1981 paraphrased by J. Ayala, 2005) In relationships where there are unequal power relations, finding a balance can be difficult, even alienating (Zaal, Salah, & Fine, 2007). For example, Andrea's interview excerpt illustrates how it can be difficult to create a balance between what parents feel is right and what their children see as the 'American' way of life:

I: Why do you think you had so much trouble in high school?

Andrea: The teenage years, and growing up, and in a new culture and trying to deal with that and my mother's ways of being were completely different to the living, I mean, she wanted to raise us girls to live in New York City, but the Colombian[13] way, and it was just not working. She wanted to be just as strict, she wanted us to follow the same guidelines and it was not working, and I became a rebel. I was a rebel. (Colombian, 27 years old)

Relationships between immigrant parents and their children were not always marked by conflict, frustration, and misunderstandings. As residents of *Nepantla*, respondents often times functioned as cultural translators for their parents and families, which gave them a sense of pride and recognition. Helping their parents navigate a new system and culture altered in some ways the power dynamics within the respondents' families. Also, different transitions as part of a person's life cycle and life changing events, brought about (un)expected changes in the way respondents viewed the relationship between their multiple cultures and cultural scripts. For example, these Dominican and Colombian respondents agreed that they would probably not change many things in their up-bringing. They often expressed that even though they might not have agreed with the strictness of their parents; there were positive differences between how their parents raised them

[13] In the transcript, the transcriber wrote "Columbia". It is a common mistake in the United States to write Colombia as if "Columbia" was an English translation of it. The fact that there is a province called "British Columbia" and "Columbia University", people might assume that the country's name is supposed to be written in the same way. Because there were several transcribers, some used "Columbia" and others used "Colombia". I will replace with "Colombia" wherever it is necessary because Colombians do not recognize the spelling of their country's name as "Columbia".

versus how some of their "American" peers, without an immigrant background, were raised.

I:	What was it like growing up in an immigrant family?
María:	To me it was just the way it was. I guess there was always reference back to the Dominican Republic and how things are done there. ??? staying in the household. For me it was normal.
I:	Did it create much of a generation gap between you and your parents?
María:	Yes. Right. ??? Probably more so for my brother than me. There were differences. Because my mother is a little more old fashion with me. She has certain views about how you should be???? But probably more so when I was a teenager. It became a big deal because that's when I wanted to establish my identity and it wasn't necessarily going with my mother's or father's view of how I should be or what I should aspire to learn. And that's when it was tough. But at the same time, I think my mother acknowledged that I was very stubborn and she said once that she trusts my ??? so even though she may not have agreed with some of the things that I said, that she trusted me.
I:	So the most negative or toughest part was the difference between your mom being very traditional and you creating your identity. What was the most positive thing?
María:	The most positive thing, I think even though she was old fashioned and traditional, I think the level of the attention, even though sometimes she was over protective the level of attention that she

> gave to us kept us from being involved in bad elements. Especially living in this neighborhood. (Dominican, 26 years old)

Respondents were conscious that particular situations are bound by time and space. By contextualizing circumstances and decisions, they were able to appropriate or reject specific cultural positions without entirely disregarding either culture. They were able to avoid attributing negative outcomes to individuals involved in the dialogue and were more likely to look at the context for answers. In other words, if they did not agree with their parents' perspective on an issue, they did not disregard their parents' advice on other issues. Instead of ignoring their parents completely, they understood that their parents' behavior was congruent with the culture in which their parents grew up. They maintained communication between their cultures open and were open to learning from all of them. They understood that embracing one culture at a specific time and place did not mean rejecting others forever. For example, they were more likely to consider attenuating circumstances on a person's behavior, and less likely to refer to individual personality traits as explanations for behavior. They were less likely to use essentializing arguments in making decisions about their *positioning*. "The 'clash of voices' between the overlapping and differently positioned/powered cultural frameworks living inside [them] produces a tolerance for ambiguity." (Torre & J. Ayala, 2009, p. 388) Respondents exhibited a capacity to embrace uncertainty, conflict, unanswered questions, and difference; felt excited about the prospect of learning from difference and were open to change.

I: Do you think anything is making it easier or harder for people your age to get along and get ahead compared to people your parents' age?

Anibal: Yeah, education. Just educating people on the differences and realizes that these differences aren't threatening in any way. They are just plain old Differences, cultural differences that you will have. And they are not there to intimidate anyone. That's it's just how this culture tends to be. They are not trying to imply anything Negative by it. They are not trying to... like I said not trying to do anything negative, in a sense. This is how they are. And you have to realize who they are and the fact that they don't mean it in any negative manner. They don't mean it to be aggressive. That just happens to be the way they go about their business.

I: You don't have to take everything personally.

Anibal: Exactly. Yeah. Education and also exposure to people. Exposure to different types and races and ethnicities so you can understand the differences and what they are. (Dominican, 28 years old)

The participants re-positioned themselves vis-à-vis different aspects of their multiple cultures on issues related to gender roles, appropriate forms of punishment for minors, definitions of identity and racism. In the end, they seemed to strive for establishing a balance between their many cultures and worlds that might integrate the most positive aspects of each. They were open to learning from others, crossing cultural boundaries and embracing new ways of doing things. By being critical of their immigrant parents' view of the world and the 'mainstream' culture in which they grew up, these young adults are contributing to a process of "deprovincialization" which acknowledges that "in-group norms, customs, and lifestyles are not the only acceptable ways to manage the social world (Pettigrew, 1997, cited by Schmid, Hewstone, Tausch, Cairns, & Hughes, 2009, p. 1087)." For example, Isabel and Jessica echoed other respondents in critiquing their parents' belief about gender roles and unequal gender relationships in their households.

I: Can you talk about some of those characteristics that you like the least?

Isabel: Of Colombian culture, I would say sometimes I think there is too much of a strain on women. I know that there is some type of need of discipline when they are young and to have them to know how to take care of the house, how to take care of their husband but I think there should be a more… less thought that they are inferior. Less thought that that is where they belong. It's fine, teach them that but teach them if they want they have the ability to go to other places and do other things.

[…]

I: Have there been specific times when you feel you've benefited from being Colombian?

Isabel: I think I have benefited from being Colombian. From being Hispanic because I love the fact that I know another language. I love the fact of being able to... The best of two worlds. You know the expression? Like being able to still keep and appreciate those things in my culture that I enjoy and that I think are beautiful and at the same time being able to change those things which I think machistic [machista][14], like with the dominating. Other things. Or the lack of independence with the women sometimes. So I get to take those things which I want and I adore and someone else might not know of these other ones because they never lived in a different culture or had within a different field. (Colombian, 23 years old)

Proponents of "bicultural identity integration" have delineated two sets of conditions of encounter of cultural frameworks, one among cultures that appear compatible and another between cultures that seem incompatible. When two cultures meeting in a 'contact zone'/*Nepantla*

---

[14] I believe she was referring to the noun "machista" which is defined as male chauvinist or full of machismo.

are seemingly compatible with overlapping cultural theories, i.e. a Latino cultural framework meets a Latin American cultural framework, there is low expectancy of conflict between the two cultures given the overlapping content of their cultural referents. In this case, such a person might exhibit a *Blended bicultural* identity 'in the absence of threat' (Wiley & Deaux, 2010) as opposed to an *Alternating bicultural* identity characterized by a perception of conflict or irreconcilable differences between cultures, e.g. a person struggling with Muslim and American cultures. For example, for respondents, especially among Dominican respondents, the cultural positions of their parents' vs. 'American' views with respect to gender roles and expectations were perceived as dissimilar and conflicting. They did not agree with what they perceived to be patriarchal gender roles and unequal gender relationships in their households, and often mention it as a discouraging factor in considering the possibility of living in their parents' home country. Yet it doesn't prevent them from loving their parents and being appreciative of other positive things from their culture.

I: What do you like the least about Dominicans?

Jessica: Some of the women are, like their self-esteem isn't that high; they depend on the man a lot. I don't want to sound like a major feminist or anything, I'm just like that because of how my father was, and I don't like the way some of the men act towards the women, and how they feel their seniority over…

I: Trust me, I understand.

Jessica: You know, they feel they're better than a lot of people, their egos are very high, and they're like above human standards. It sounds very harsh, but it's true; you wouldn't believe how these men feel like they're above everybody. Basically, their egos and the way they treat their women, I don't like it that much.

I: So how do they treat their women?

Jessica: I think I mentioned it before—"Your place is in the kitchen, you don't have to be working to take care of my kids, I don't want to give you money, you don't need my money as long as I pay the bills," you know, stuff like that. Money will always come into it, even though it's probably not good that it does. (Dominican, 21 years old)

MAKING SOCIAL COMPARISONS

Social psychologists have often studied ethnic identity or ethnicity in relationship to issues of group formation and group boundaries within national/local borders (Deaux, 2000; Tajfel, 1981; Verkuyten, 2005b) Outside of those borders ethnic identity labels lose their meaning (Triandafyllidou & Wodak, 2003). In the United States, ethnic labels serve to distinguish a social group as ethnically different from other social groups such as White or African-Americans. The labels used for social identification by these Colombian and Dominican children of immigrants responded to a context-situated interpretation of their surroundings and the people with whom they were interacting. Respondents attributed meanings to the labels they used (be it ethnic, racial, cultural or national origin) according to their interpretation of the context, domain, and audience. The interviewees read their social context and interlocutors, and made *social comparisons* that varied accordingly (Hong & Chiu, 2001; Hong et al., 2000; Wiley & Deaux, 2010). The variety and multiplicity of answers given to the phone survey and interview questions about race, ethnicity, or background do not represent identity confusion or conflict. Rather, this diversity of answers demonstrates that they have multiple and complex repertoires for social comparisons and are skilled at reading the expectations of their interlocutors and audiences (Deaux, 2000; Hong & Chiu, 2001; Hong et al., 2000; Wiley & Deaux, 2010). The labels are simply part of the story of who they are. How it is presented or packaged for others depends on who the other is: an in-group member, an out-group member, a majority/minority group member, a stranger, a friend, etc, as well as where they are in time and space.

Social and personal identities among these children of immigrants acquired meaning and took center stage in their positioning depending on the context and the situation in which they found themselves

(Verkuyten & deWolf, 2002). How they identified in terms of ethnicity, race, or national group varied according to who was asking the question as well. When asked by the interviewers how they would identify themselves, over 90% of respondents (in-depth interview sample) from both groups picked the national group label that denoted the country of origin of their parents. This actually mirrored a similar response among Latino youth nationally where 94% (ages 16-25) had used the national origin label and 87% had used the "Latino" or "Hispanic" label; 52% actually preferred the national origin label over labels "Latino or Hispanic" or "American" (Pew Hispanic Center, 2009)[15]. Although they used the national origin group label to name their historical and cultural background, they did not necessarily make a claim to citizenship of that country. Therefore, there was a significant difference in what the label "Dominican" meant to these children of immigrants compared to what it meant for their parents. For their parents, it meant the country where they were born, while for their children it meant the country where their parents were born and the cultural background of their family.

When asked in the phone survey how respondents' identified in terms of ethnicity or race, responses were extremely varied and complexed (see table 6). The label used most to describe themselves was "Hispanic", chosen by 34.4 % of Colombians and 35.9% of Dominicans, followed by the national group labels "Colombian" (12.3%) and "Dominican" (14.6%). In a study of Dominican immigrants, Jensen, et. al. (2006) found that lighter skinned Dominicans were less likely to chose a pan-ethnic label such as Latino and more likely to self-identify by the national origin label "Dominican". About a quarter of both Colombians and Dominicans answered the question using the labels "White" and "Black/African American" which are usually understood as racial categories. At least 1/3 of the Dominican respondents who chose a racial category (White, Black/African American or Some other race) selected "Black/African American". Only 1/10 of Colombians who chose a racial category selected "Black/African American" (see table 6). Besides the racial

[15] These percentages do not add to 100% because they represent responses to different questions.

implications of these numbers, they revealed the complexity and ambiguity associated with the labels "Latino", "Hispanic", "Spanish", "Hispanic-American" that can be used to mean an ethnic, racial, and/or cultural group. Adding to the ambiguity and complexity, national origin labels such as "Dominican" and "Colombian" may come to represent an ethnic, racial, cultural or national origin group or nationality.

It should be noted that although academics and activists tend to rely on the more politically correct term "Latino" to refer to United States citizens with a Latin American background, the term "Hispanic" was preferred in the phone survey by both Dominican and Colombian respondents. There are a number of factors that could influence this choice of labels. Researchers have documented that newly arrived immigrant groups in the United States and immigrant groups who have settled in the Northeastern coast prefer to use the term "Hispanic" to identify themselves (Itzigsohn, 2004; Itzigsohn et al., 2005; Oboler, 1995). It is also the more commonly used term in government forms and government agencies. There was a remarkable overlap among both Colombian and Dominican respondents' choice of identifying labels, which emphasizes that their common experiences as children of immigrants, including cohort experiences of being 1.5 or 2nd generation, have shaped their perception of the ethnic/racial/national hierarchy in the United States.

Table 6. Race/Ethnicity of Respondents

Race	Colombians	Dominicans
hite	26.0 %	12.9 %
Black, African American	3.9 %	12.9 %
Asian	0.6 %	0.9 %
American Indian	0.0 %	1.4 %
American	1.9 %	0.8 %
Spanish	7.1 %	4.5 %
Hispanic	34.4 %	35.9 %
Latino	5.8 %	4.5 %
Colombian	12.3 %	0.0 %
Dominican	0.0 %	14.6 %
Latino/Spanish/Hispanic-American	2.6 %	1.4 %
Some other race	3.2 %	9.2 %

There was great complexity of meanings attached to the different labels by respondents. This can be appreciated in the following dialogue. Anibal used several referents for social comparison to decide whether the ethnic/racial/national labels applied to his sense of identity or not.

> I: In the survey you didn't tell us what you consider your race to be. You told us your ethnicity was Dominican?
>
> Anibal: Yeah. It's confusing because race and ethnicity... they could almost be interchangeable. If you just hear them. But of course, they have different definitions and I know that. Right now, I'm confused. I'm not sure because it's been so long since I even got into it. I guess my race, you could say, would be Hispanic. And my ethnicity would be Dominican.
>
> I: Do you ever identify as Hispanic or Latino?
>
> Anibal: I wouldn't say Latino, because I'm not from Latin America. And I wouldn't say Spanish because I'm not from Spain. So I would say Hispanic because that basically covers almost the whole thing. And not for nothing, the whole island of Dominican Republic is Hispañola. I rounded it off. I have my own little way of working it out there. (laughter)
>
> I: Do you ever identify as African American?
>
> Anibal: No. I'm not African American. I do believe that I do have some in me. Way, way, way, back in the roots of course. But no, I wouldn't say I'm African American. (Dominican, 28 years old)

He acknowledged at least 7 different reference groups: non-Hispanics, non-Dominican Hispanics, Latin Americans, Spaniards (or

'Spanish'), Haitians and Dominicans from the island, African-Americans and Afro-Dominicans. These reference groups and social comparisons denote a deep and complex knowledge of the social, political and cultural context he lives in, which does not restrict itself to United States' borders and extends to the island of Hispañola, including both the Dominican Republic and Haiti. By distinguishing the subtle differences behind each term, Anibal demonstrated awareness of how he was perceived not only by the majority group, but also by other groups and subgroups that he came into contact with in the United States. He understood where he was positioned within each one of these groups, and how the groups positioned him in the ethnic/racial/national hierarchy. Yet, he decided which of those labels agreed with him or not. In addition, Anibal knew that the social hierarchies used in the United States were not replicated in the Dominican Republic and so he had his "own little way of working it out there". It is clear that he was aware and adept at working the ethnic, racial, cultural and national discourses both in the United States and in the Dominican Republic, which anchored his transnational social fields.

Respondents made decisions about how to identify themselves in relationship to where they were, who they were speaking to, how the question was asked and what the available answers were. They may be construed as *performing a bicultural identity* (Wiley & Deaux, 2010). Since different methods were used (phone survey and in-person interviews), there is evidence to suggest the way in which the question was presented influenced their responses. The survey itself presented race and then ethnicity within the same question, which might have primed respondents to think first in racial terms followed by ethnicity. Phone surveyors provided a limited amount of labels which did not include "Hispanic, Latino nor Spanish" among them. It is possible that respondents assumed the phone surveyors were members of an out-group such as non-Latino/Hispanic. Such assumptions would have had the effect of limiting the amount of information or complexity given in their answers. This coincides with research documenting the differences in the rapport between the interviewees and insider vs. outsider interviewers. Respondents reported occasions in which the phone surveyor changed the answer given in order to fit the categories provided, i.e. Hispanic became White.

I: Do you consider your race to be white?

Sandra: Hispanic. Cause I think I remember when she gave me the choices, mine wasn't a choice. I said, "Hispanic." And she goes, "Well, that's white." "Oh, okay."

[...]

I: Do you ever identify as Latina?

Sandra: Yeah.

I: When do you say one and when do you say the other?

Sandra: I don't really say Latina at all. But if I see the word, I recognize it and maybe see myself in it. But I never really use the word. (Colombian, 28 years old)

The in-depth interviews provided an opportunity to probe respondents about the answers they gave on the phone survey. Respondents were reminded of their answers to the phone survey and were asked their reasoning behind it. Interviewers followed up by asking respondents how they identified at the time of the interview. The interviewers were matched with the respondents in terms of ethnicity and when possible by gender as well. In effect, the interview created a context where two in-group members discussed their identity negotiation. Under such circumstances, it is probable respondents inferred more points of cultural/ethnic/racial commonality between themselves and their interviewers facilitating more nuanced discussions of their experiences identifying with different ethnic/racial/national terms that was not possible in the phone survey.

I: In the survey they asked you how you would, they asked you 'what is your race, what is your ethnicity'. And they gave you certain options and in the race option you chose 'other.'

Andres: I did? I don't remember. What were the other options? I should have chosen Hispanic or Latin. But there's a difference between Hispanic and Latin, and I don't necessarily see the difference but that's - I must have chosen that because they didn't have the right option. I think.

I: The thing is they don't give Hispanic or Latin for race. They gave - Black white, and a few others.

Andres: Hispanics are considered white?

I: I don't know how you feel about that.

Andres: Not 'white ' in the classic sense or the traditional sense. We're lighter skinned but we're not 'white' I don't think so. You look white but you have a Hispanic last name, I believe it sounds Hispanic. I think you're Hispanic also are you? Ok.

I: So the way they asked you -Other and Colombian which is based on- again they have a strict set of questions. What race would you consider yourself?

Andres: Hispanic or Latin, whatever it is. She told me there was a difference between Latin and Hispanic and I don't remember. Hispanic tends to be, oh no, there was Latin-American she said. And then Hispanic would be what, maybe from Spain, I'm not sure. So. Whatever would be from Latin America. I was born here though, so I guess I'd be a Colombian-American I guess, whatever.

I: So you usually identify as –

Andres: Hispanic, yeah.

I: Did you always identify that way?

Andres: Yeah.

I: And did that mean anything to you?

Andres: Yeah, I'm not Black, and I'm not white, so I would always say Hispanic. I'm proud. I never try to hide that. (Colombian, 18 years old)

How respondents answered the identification question did not only depend on their own social comparison to other groups. Their answers, like Anthony's, were tailored to the situation and the person who was asking the question (interlocutor) and to what kind information they were looking for (cognitive and emotive content):

I: In the survey you said that you considered your race to be white and your ethnicity to be Dominican is that correct? (A- (sound - neither affirmative or negative) Why do you consider your race to be white and your ethnicity to be Dominican?

Anthony: 'cause he, that's what he asked me and the way he asked me. (Dominican, 23 years old)

In the following excerpt we can appreciate that Yohana's choice of terms "Puerto Rican" or "Spanish" responded to a decision about how much information she wanted to reveal about herself and her complex experiences regarding culture, race, and ethnicity. This response implies a cognitive reading of the other's assumptions and expectations beyond the literal question, and necessitates an affective reading about how much the other cares and is to be trusted.

I: What would you consider your race to be?

Yohana: I'm Spanish. Puerto Rican Spanish.

I: And your ethnicity?

Yohana: Spanish? What do you mean?

I: Well, it's kind of tricky but I would ask you to make a distinction between what you consider your race to be and what you consider your ethnicity. Ethnicity is more like culture.

Yohana: Spanish.

I: In general do you identify as Puerto Rican or Spanish?

Yohana: I say I'm Puerto Rican, because it's easier than to get into everything else that I am.

I: To sort of not have to explain?

Yohana: Yeah, eventually, if I meet someone and we get to talking and stuff like that, then I'll say, "Oh, you know, my mother's Colombian and my father's Dominican." But basically, if someone says to me, "Where are you from?" Or "What are you?" I'll say, "Puerto Rico." (Colombian, 32 years old)

Among these Colombian and Dominican children of immigrants, discussions about identifying with an ethnic, racial, or national group were not viewed as critically important. As *Sharina* exclaimed "what is the big deal?" (see below). Yet, they admitted it was a common occurrence in their lives, especially when meeting new people or interacting with strangers. Many of the respondents reported that the assumption behind the question if asked by a non-Latino/Hispanic person was that the respondent had to be something other than "American." If they simply replied "I am American", it was dismissed and further probed for a different answer. So the use of different labels revolved around a need to explain who they are to others, and the underlying assumption that they do not belong to the "American" community.

Danilo: So sometimes people ask me 'where are you from?" I'm American, 'cause I guess when you say you're Hispanic - oh you're not -he's different so I'm American. I was born here. I tell them straight up. My parents are Dominican- I'm Dominican so I just say - that's what I say when they ask me where I'm from- what's my ethnic background, whatever. I say I'm Dominican but I always mess with them and say I'm American. 'Cause I Am American'. I'm an American citizen. Still Dominican. (Dominican, 20 years old)

The purposeful and deliberate use of different labels/social identities according to the time, place and audience revealed how respondents exercised agency in their relationship with others. Some of the respondents chose to "play with" which ethnic/racial/national labels they assumed in response to inquirers. In other words, they might say they belong to a group to see people's reactions to unexpected or seemingly incongruent ethnic/racial/national identifications. The respondents did not give an intrinsic value to social identities or group membership; rather they exhibited an understanding that identity categories are artificial, non- mutually exclusive and socially constructed. By virtue of growing up as children of immigrants and moving between national and transnational borders and spaces, they understood that social identity hierarchies and categories were subject to change and may be challenged.

I: Do you think that's race or ethnicity or more language or both?

Sharina: It's just the way they format the question. "You're Puerto Rican?" "You're Dominican?" *"You're something Spanish, right?" Or whatever.*

I: Are they ever surprised by the answer you give?

Sharina: Sometimes I lie just to see people's reaction.

I: Like what? This is interesting, this is getting good. (laughter)

Sharina: Sometimes I lie because I am, "What is the big deal I'm Spanish American, that's it." I don't know. I remember one time I went to a youth conference and I was, "I'm half Hawaiian and half Puerto Rican." (laughter) And the guy was, "What? How did that end up happening?" My friend is Dominican Chinese so I'll be, "I'm half Italian, half Puerto Rico." I'll just lie to see. It doesn't even make a different. If I'm a non-Spanish... if I'm mixed with a non-Spanish culture, is it a shock to them. I don't know. I just lie to see. But I eventually say, "no, I'm Latino." But I lie.

I: What do you say?

Sharina: It depends on their reaction. If they are, "Get out of here!!" I say, "Is that better than Dominican or Puerto Rican?" I'm a little hostile when it comes to that. (Dominican, 18 years old)

Sharina's statements expressed a critical view of the role of social hierarchies based on national origin. She questioned the validity and usefulness of being so preoccupied by people's national heritage. The question evoked a highly emotional response: hostility.

BEING AND DOING "AMERICAN" IDENTITY

As children of immigrants, these Colombian and Dominican youth considered themselves "American" because they were born or raised in the United States. Despite constantly being questioned about where they were from and their background, they continued to assert that they were "American". Being "American" however, became salient when their identities were questioned by others like when they visited their parents' country or when asked "where are you from?" by non-Latinos. In the following exchange, Andrea described her experience of realizing what it meant to be "American" or "Gringa" (term used in Latin America to refer to United States citizens) when she visited her parents' home country in Colombia.

I:	You were saying people called you 'gringa' sometimes when you were there? So do you think they see you as an American?
Andrea:	(Affirmative) They do.
I:	And what do they mean by that? What is the difference between an American and a Colombian?
Andrea:	I'm not lady like, I have a big mouth, as I was saying. I think too much. I speak too much. I move around too much. I move crowds.
I:	And those are things that a Colombian female shouldn't do.
Andrea	Right. Oh, God forbid!
I:	And how has that made you feel? (Soft)
Andrea:	How does that make me feel? (CB: Yeah) I think it's funny, 'cause it's more so than that, they want to label it because I'm an American and they know it's more than that. It's because I've got an education. That's (emphasis) what makes the difference. (Colombian, 27 years old)

For respondents being "American" meant embracing the civic principles and responsibilities expected of every citizen of the United States. Some of those principles mentioned referred to the United States' ideology of democracy and the responsibility of citizens to vote, pay taxes, and exercise their freedom of speech. These responses are very similar with those given by college students at Yale University in a study by Devos and Banaji (2005, cited by Deaux, 2008). These behaviors represent what Verkuyten and deWolf (2002) might called "doing identity". They cherished their civic freedoms and the economic, political, and social opportunities the United States offered them that were not available in their parents' home country, as both Deyanira and Sandra discussed in the following excerpts:

I: Do you feel like an American?

Deyanira: Yeah, I do but I do feel like a Dominican American.

I: What do you think it means to be an American?

Deyanira: I think it means living in a country where you're free to choose. Choose where you want to live. Choose you want to vote for, which president. So choose to speak our opinions and not be arrested for them so I think that's what it means to be an American and a Dominican American. (Domnican, 30 years old)

And

I: What do you think it means to be an American?

Sandra: To me, I consider myself, even by not being an U.S. citizen, I'm still an American because South America is also America, which a lot of people kind of miss that. But I just think to be an American is to have opportunities and be free to be what you can be and whatever you want to be. (Colombian, 28 years old)

In general, Dominican and Colombian respondents equated being "American" to their experiences of living in New York City. Kasinitz et.al. (2008) discussed in their book *Becoming New Yorker*, how the children of immigrants held New York City as a reference point for measuring and thinking about the United States as a whole. For them, New York City as a city of immigrants with enormous diversity of cultures served as a social representation of the entire United States. However, most respondents had not been to other parts of the United States even if they had already visited their parents' home country. Some respondents highlighted that to be "American" meant that they were born or raised in New York City.

I: What do you think it means to be an American?

George: For me, personally? To be born here.

I: You say you consider yourself an American.

George: If you're born here, yes. Because I have a right to vote and all that.

I: And when you were having those discussions with your parents and they're saying "You're Dominican, You're Dominican, - I'm American too.' what did you mean at that time?

George: Well, they were saying that this country stinks and this country is no good, what else? That they'd rather be in the homeland because in the homeland they could do this? Yeah, but you do that, you see what happens. They used to do that and they would screw up the country. Look how we are? We're not in perfect shape, but trust me, I would rather my sons to be here because God forbid something happens, in some way, somehow, there will be help. (Dominican, 28 years old)

The respondents truly valued '*being different*' as an integral part of being "American" and derived self-regard and esteem from it. In their opinion, it would be really difficult to live in a country or context that was not as diverse as New York City. Diversity was one of the things they missed the most when they visited or lived in their parent's country of origin. However, feeling "American" did not prevent them from being critical of United States' social problems and its international politics.

I: What do you think it means to be American?

Mario: I guess being born here, 'cause I have certain points of view about being American, like as - like I would never serve in the Armed Forces here in the United States.

I: Why not?

Mario: Because, just because of the way politics in the country, and stuff like that. I wouldn't want to - what's the word I'm looking for- people haven't asked me that question in a while like being an American is like serve your country, being patriotic, stuff like that. I love the United States, don't get me wrong but there's other problems in the United States that need to be addressed, you know, before I would want to like help out in that - let's say in the Armed Forces or something like that. Just some of the things that the United States goes about- you know- what they do, I don't agree with all the time. But - what was it again, feeling American or what makes me American?

I: What do you think it means to be -

Mario: Loving your country, working, you know, being a law-abiding citizen. Being a law-abiding citizen, loving your country, I guess. Paying your taxes. Things like that. I'm not too sure. (Colombian, 23 years old)

SUMMARY

This chapter has focused on how children of Dominican and Colombian immigrants negotiate their personal and social identities. An important finding highlights how being children of immigrants unites their psychological experiences of growing up in the United States. The similarities in their description of what it means for them to have immigrant parents and be raised in-between their parents' and 'American' culture were remarkable. Their sense of ethnic/racial/national identities was based on the cultural traditions they learned by participating in their family's everyday practices and ways of doing things. For them, culture was a way of doing things, therefore dynamic and open to change. The role of family and family cohesion in the cultural repertoire and belief system of Colombian and Dominican children of immigrants was paramount in establishing a difference between them and their non-immigrant 'American' friends. Having a social network that extends beyond national boundaries was a source of comfort and pride for respondents, especially when their parents' migration story meant not having access to family members geographically close-by.

Respondents dealt with their multiple cultural realities and transnational social spheres by comparing and contrasting situations, cultural norms and ways of doing things, and made decisions based on what they deemed most appropriate for the circumstances at hand. Sometimes they preferred their parents' cultural norms; other times they found them lacking and preferred their 'American' way of doing things; yet other times they combined them both. The possibilities for combining, changing, and challenging traditional social and cultural discourses are many. Despite much theorizing in acculturation models about psychological stress as a consequence of embracing social identity complexity, these children of immigrants were remarkably comfortable with navigating multiple worlds. It was simply the only way of life they knew; it was the natural state of things for them. Complexity, frame switching, positioning, and balancing opposites are what define and gives meaning to their lives. The process of social identification of these immigrant youth was based on mechanisms of social comparison and reading their audience very much in line with a social identity performance framework. The following chapter delves with more detail into the nature of transnational ties and relationships of respondents' as well as their significance for respondents' social identity negotiation and subjective experience.

CHAPTER 4

Maintaining Transnational Relationships

FAMILY AS ANCHOR OF TRANSNATIONAL TIES

Throughout the interviews, family emerged as key in maintaining contact and establishing social, economic, and interpersonal ties with the home country of the respondents' parents for both Colombians and Dominicans. There were a number of specific reasons and circumstances why respondents visited or continued to maintain contact with their parent's home country. Yet the explanations always revolved around family, either by reconnecting with or meeting new family members, helping relatives or sharing child-rearing responsibilities with extended family in the home country. Although researchers have been interested in the reasons why immigrants or their descendents might maintain attachments to their home country socially, economically, or politically (Deaux, 2006), they have not paid much attention to the role of family, both primary and extended. The findings in this study indicate that the family, as a social network and a source of interpersonal, social, and psychological relationships, serves as an anchor for the socialization of individuals into the culture of a national group and prolongs their connection with their parent's home country. In effect, it acts as a 'remooring' (Deaux & Ethier, 1998; Ethier & Deaux, 1994) context for their social identities based on the culture of the national group they had been socialized into.

Rather than an abstract cultural or social group, the family unit becomes the main referent for the children's understanding of what it means to be members of a particular social group that differs from the mainstream in norms, values, and customs (Mahalingam & Haritatos, 2006; Martín-Baró & Cañas, 1990; Pedraza, 2006). Their understanding of family included nuclear and extended family, even distant relatives beyond national borders. As such, parents, siblings and grandparents became some of the more important figures in this process of negotiating identity and maintaining transnational ties. In their work, Hong & Chiu (2001) outlined the importance of communication and interpersonal relationships among members as they participate in symbolic and cultural practices that transmit, reproduce, and change cultural theories. In this case, such exchange occurs across transnational borders as well. As Deaux describes "[t]he embeddedness of West Indian immigrants appears to be primarily with the family, though with a family that may be widely dispersed, including relatives in Canada or Great Britain (2006, p. 190)", which contribute to "preserve a more specific country identification". Further, Deaux suggests that having close family members in their home country may be a good predictor of strong ethnic identity and transnational involvement.

Two measures often used as evidence of the maintenance of transnational ties are whether or not a respondent has visited the home country of their parents and the frequency of those visits. It is important to point out that, in the larger study of which my respondents were a sub-sample, the children of Dominican and the South American immigrants had stronger transnational ties than their Chinese, West Indians, or Russian Jewish counterparts (Kasinitz et al., 2008; Kasinitz et al., 2002). At least 87.2% of Colombian and 89.3% of Dominicans had visited their parents' home country once in their lives. If we considered 4-9 visits to one's parents' home country as evidence of prolonged relationship and involvement, then almost half of the respondents would be defined as such. Forty three percent (42.8%) of Colombians and forty eight percent (48.2%) of Dominican respondents reported having visited their parent's home country more than 4 times in their lives (see table 7).

Transnational ties were initiated early on by their parents. Respondents were not involved in the decision making regarding such trips until they were much older. Usually, their first trips to Colombia or the Dominican Republic occurred as young children with their parents. Most of the time, the parents went to their home country to visit their own parents and relatives and would bring their children along so the children could meet their grandparents, uncles, aunts, and cousins. As Fischlin & Nandorfy (2002) firmly assert "[b]efore being shared, the past must be recuperated from keepers of official stories, witnessed together through all the stories that circulate in fragments, half-forgotten, forbidden, but alive" in spite of geographical, economic, and political boundaries.

Table 7. Number of Times Respondents Visited Parents' Home Country

Times Visited Parent's Home country	Colombians	Dominicans
Never	12.8 %	10.7 %
1-3 Times	44.5 %	41.1 %
4-9 Times	28.0 %	27.1 %
More than 10 Times	14.6 %	21.1 %

For some respondents, visits to their parents' home country turned into longer stays ranging from 6 months to a few years. This was more common among Dominican (28.3%) than Colombian (19.6%) families (see table 8). Parents' decisions to send their child or children to live with relatives, often grandparents or siblings, for an extended period of time to the Dominican Republic or Colombia, came about as a strategy to address extreme misbehavior or to protect their children from a "dangerous" environment.

Table 8. Respondents who Lived in their Parents' Home Country for 6 Months or More

Lived in Home Country for longer than 6 months	Colombians	Dominicans
Yes	19.6 %	28.3 %
No	80.4 %	71.7 %

Table 9. Reasons Respondents Moved to Parents' Home Country for More than 6 Months[16]

Reasons moved to parents home country	Colombians	Dominicans
Better Schools	11.5 %	9.6 %
Childcare	-	6.4 %
Visit/Vacation	3.8 %	8.5 %
Parents/Family related trip	38.5 %	21.3 %
Education Related	11.5 %	10.6 %

The interviews revealed that when parents could not deal with the situation affecting their children's behavior, some immigrant parents recruited the help of extended family members who happened to live in another country. Kasinitz and colleagues (2008) also documented this parenting strategy, which they called a 'transnational solution,' mostly among Latino/Hispanic families in their interviews and in the survey data of the larger ISGMNY study. For example, if a child were suspended from school, 'American parents' might decide to send them to their grandparents' house in another state or city, but since these immigrant parents often did not have other relatives living in the United States, let alone New York City, they resorted to sending them to their home country. In fact, "Parents/Family related trip" was identified as the most common reason respondents moved to their parents' home country (see table 9).

Usually young children were sent by themselves to live with relatives while the parents remained in New York City to work and visited in the holidays, if at all possible. These arrangements were usually difficult for the children because it meant psychological and physical separation from their parents for long periods of time, learning to live with relatives they barely knew, and having to constantly adapt to new environments. Although it was hard emotionally, a number of respondents agreed with José's comments (see below). They recognized some positive outcomes as a result of change in their physical and social context. Once the transition period passed, they

[16] Column values do not add to 100% due to missing data.

came to feel comfortable with their surroundings. This parenting strategy was part of everyday life and the family dynamics in José's family. He seemed to have come to expect such events. In the following excerpt, José narrated how he was sent away by his mother to live with his aunt because he was misbehaving in school.

José: Exactly, yeah. See, because I don't know that it was a conspiracy, that the grownups had with us, because all the cousins- they were sent over there, like when they was young, you know what I'm saying? Well, not - not all of them actually, when they were young. But it was like I've got two of them that they sent them over there, and it was like - because over here they was really, you know, getting out of control. Some one of them, they told him, " Go for a vacation," and all of this. They took him over there, took away the passport- anything that's possible that he could use to come back- they took away.

I: Was it kind of something to straighten him out? Or –

José: -- Yes. To straighten him out. Yeah. Then, you know, at the beginning, like for the first five months, oh, forget it. That brother was throwing fits, but then he calmed down, he got a job over there. And then once he grew up, you know, he got sent back to New York. He came back, and you know, he's cool. Like all of us, they did that to all of us. They sent us over there, and only like, four, like five of us had to go to school, like that transition, had to go through the transition and stuff. Only like five of us, because the other ones, they were like already grown up, so either they didn't finish going to high school or, you know, they wasn't gonna go, period. So, you know. That was basically that. (Dominican, 32 years old)

Dominican families were mostly living in neighborhoods with low-performing and overcrowded schools compared with Colombian families (López, 2004). Therefore, Dominican children were more likely to experience behavioral problems or act out at school than Colombian children. Additional factors that made Dominican families more susceptible to this situation were higher crime rates and the prevalence of illegal drug trade in their neighborhood streets. Such neighborhood characteristics were corroborated by López's (2004) ethnography of Dominican men in Washington Heights and Trillo's (2004) ethnography of second generation Latino students in El Barrio. These two ethnographies are particularly pertinent as they were commissioned to contextualize the data obtained by Kasinitz et.al.(2008). As a whole, Colombian families lived in safer neighborhoods, so the safety of their children was not necessarily a major concern. Dominican respondents were twice as likely as Colombians to report that the use and sale of drugs in their neighborhood were major problems while growing up. Only thirty two percent of Dominican respondents felt that drugs were not a problem in their neighborhood compared to 50% of Colombians (see table 10).

Carolina's story represents another example of the influence that family and parents have in immersing their children in transnational social spaces and networks that create the conditions for transnational ties and relationships. As Josselson proposes "[p]arental control is often explicitly in terms of group identity… Those with whom we live, who are our primary caretakers, define what we are in the larger social world… (1992, p. 188)." Carolina explains that decisions about traveling to Colombia and where to settle were made by her parents. She didn't really have any input in the matter until she was about 16 years old even though the outcome was not what she had hoped for.

Carolina: Most of my life there, then after seven, back and forth, back and forth. It was, my parents kept going back and forth, back and forth to where it would be better to raise a child. Then eventually, at age 16 they decided we were going to settle here. (Colombian, 29 years old)

Table 10. Respondents Who Reported Drug Use and Dealing in their Neighborhood as a Problem

"People Using or Dealing Openly in the Street while Growing Up"	Colombians	Dominicans
Big Problem	17.0 %	40.7 %
Somewhat of a Problem	32.1 %	27.4 %
Not a Problem	50.9 %	32.0 %

In most of the interviews where participants and their parents lived or went to the home country during vacation trips, the decision was determined by the parents. For the immigrant parents "... in their new "home," this communication [and exchange] with their families back in their old "home" represents the foundation of their emotional and economic well-being" (Pedraza, 2006). However, having limited freedom and being constrained to their parents' decisions was probably the reason why most respondents reported that their trips as children were sometimes boring or frustrating compared to the freedom they experienced when they decided to visit on their own as young adults. Unfortunately for some, their experiences as children marked their memories of their parents' home country and many decided that there was not much reason to visit again.

There were, however, some examples where the decision to move to their parents' home country was the respondents' decision. One such story was narrated by Paula, a Colombian woman who moved to Colombia at the age of 18 in order to cope with a difficult relationship break up. Moving to another place far from her ex-boyfriend and where she felt she would be safe amidst the love and affection of her extended family, she decided to live with her aunt in Colombia.

I: Have you been back to Colombia?

Paula: Me? Oh yeah. I even lived there for three years.

I: You did? Tell me about that.

Paula: It was fun. I went after I broke up with a boyfriend. I was eighteen and my aunt was visiting at the time and just on a whim I said, "I'll go with you. I need to kind of get away for a while. I'll go and I'll stay for three months or a semester, so I can come back and deal with school." I just ended up staying. Soon after I got there, just through connections and I knew somebody that worked at a school and I started going to school for interior design and since I was an American I started working also, giving English classes. Teaching English and I was great. I was having a great time and my parents supported everything that I did. It was a nice experience.

I: did that experience change your outlook on anything when you came back?

Paula: What a shady image Americans have in Latin American countries, I guess. And it was a good time of growth and everyone should live somewhere else for a while. Just to experience another culture and get more in tune with... I loved traveling on different vacations to other cities and just really getting to know my parents' culture. (Colombia, 30 years old)

She was able to cope with a difficult emotional situation thanks to the social capital and emotional support that having an extended family in Colombia, and having maintained such transnational family relationships, afforded her. Had she not maintained such connections, she would not have had the opportunity to start anew in a different environment to cope with the situation. It afforded her a time to be on her own, without parental supervision, but in the holding, loving, and caring environment of her family within familiar surroundings which she didn't have in New York City.

VISITING RELATIVES – (RE)ESTABLISHING CONNECTION, CREATING NEW RELATIONSHIPS

The reason for visiting relatives varied depending on who initiated the trips, yet the underlying motive was mainly to meet and acquaint young children with their parents' relatives in their home country. We should not disregard or underestimate the psychological and social need to be in relation with others and to find others who help us feel like we belong and are important. As Josselson argues "relatedness is central – to physical health, to longevity, to meaningful social life, and to the growth and development of the self. (1992, p. 3)". Migration may be viewed as causing the separation of families. For a long time psychologists have worked under the assumption that immigrants did not maintain psychological or social ties with those family members left behind in their home country. These data suggest that immigrants seek to continue relationships with family members in their home country especially if they don't have other family member in their country of residence. Therefore family home visits served to satisfy immigrants' and their children's need for relatedness and to reestablish the continuity of their life project.

> Secure attachment in adulthood, then, is not likely to be demonstrated so much in behavior (although many adult relations have clear attachment rituals, such as birthday celebrations or regular phone calls) as in an inner sense of a peopled world. The securely attached adult feels in proximity to an important other (or others), whether or not that person is geographically close. (Josselson, 1992, p. 51)

Through these visits, immigrants and their children reconnect their 'present' lives with their 'past' lives. The point is to establish a continuity of cultural, social, and psychological connection to their parents' past in the home country, so the children may understand who their parents are today and why their parents act as they do. In the following excerpt, relatedness and tending to the relationship with his mother emerged as an important dimension of John's experience of his first trip to the Dominican Republic. By the time John went to visit his mom, he was 18 years-old:

I: Last time we spoke to you, you had never been to the Dominican Republic before, and now you said you visited once. How did that go? Tell me a little more about that.

John: Oh man it was terrific because my mother lives there. I haven't seen my mother for ten years.

I: She hasn't been able to visit here?

John: I used to talk to her all the time on the phone, and I went by surprise over there. I didn't tell her –

I: Oh, you didn't tell her?

John: I didn't tell her. She almost had a heart attack. Ten years without seeing me? I was a little boy when I came here. And now –

I: -- And suddenly you're there.

John: Yeah. Just like that. Like wow. She started cryin' and stuff like that… (Dominican, 22 years old)

For at least 10 years, John had to maintain and nurture his relationship to his mother through phone calls. His mother lived in the Dominican Republic with his younger brother who had been sent back to the Dominican Republic for misbehaving in school. At first, John didn't express any desire to go to the Dominican Republic. Once he finally decided to go and meet his mother, he wanted to be back to visit her immediately. It was at that point that he started sending money to his mother in the Dominican Republic. He had not been able to go for a second trip because he didn't have enough money to pay for it. A desire to see his mother again drove him to travel, and a desire to maintain and nurture that connection compelled him to help his mom financially. He also has two half-sisters and a stepmother who raised him in New York. It is not hard to see that his encounter with his mother was an emotional one since she was beside herself with happiness to the point of crying. Being able to reconnect to that part of his life must have been a special feeling, so much so that he wants to go back.

The parents of these Dominican and Colombian respondents wanted their children to meet their grandparents, their parents' siblings, and the people who were close to their parents while growing up. The parents' motive and hope is for the children to develop some relationship with those who are important emotionally, psychologically, and socially to their parents. For many immigrant parents, it is important to show their children that in their country, they enjoy a more valued social role and are appreciated by their families and friends regardless of their material reality as immigrants in the United States. Dominican respondents were more likely to have most of their extended families living in the United States. In contrast, Colombian respondents seemed to have fewer family members living in New York and were more likely to remember their visits as children as something enjoyable, and to be excited about the prospect of meeting distant family members in their parents' home country. Andres' description of his experiences going to Colombia as a child exemplify the excited tone common among Colombian respondents:

I: You have been there seven times?

Andres: Yeah.

I: Tell me about that. How long did you stay? Why did you go? What was it like?

Andres: Summer vacations always. I went there the first time when I was five years old basically to see where I was from. That was the reason my parents sent me. Visited my father's side of the family and my mother's side of the family. Loved it. I remember arrivals and meeting all these people that hear so much about you and yet you don't know who they are. You get to know them and you're like, "Oh yeah, you're so and so's cousin." Just different atmosphere. And

> culture and stuff like that. It's awesome. Also how you become a celebrity. "Oh yeah, he's a t.v. American." So you gain notoriety and stuff like that. But I haven't been there in seven years since 91, almost eight now so I'm planning to go there for the millennium and hopefully my mom can join me. She hasn't been there in eighteen years, since I was born. (Colombian, 18 years old)

As Josselson explains "many of the most intense emotions arise during the formation, maintenance, disruption, and renewal of attachment relationships. The unchallenged maintenance of a bond is experienced as a source of security and the renewal of a bond as a source of joy" (1992, p. 45). For Andres, the whole experience was "awesome." He equated the feelings he experienced with how you would feel if one were to be treated as a "celebrity". In an ideal situation, celebrities are often surrounded by people who admire them and show them love; they enjoy many privileges and are well-known wherever they go. So remembering his trips to Colombia brings up memories of feeling loved, cared for, attended to and important to a large number of people even though he had not met them before. It represents an instance of being loved simply for being one's parents' child and therefore the object of unconditional love. Such experiences can contribute to feeling more embedded and attached to one's parents' culture thereby cementing ethnic identities or identification with an ethnic/cultural/social group.

Mauricio's account provides another example of the excitement and happiness that visiting and meeting extended family members produced for some respondents. Even though the reason for his last visit was the death of an aunt, it provided the opportunity for his extended family to gather in one place. Deaths and funerals become some of those attachment rituals that denote a behavioral commitment to honor close relationships.

I: So could you tell me about the last trip – where did you stay mostly and what did you do?

Mauricio: The last trip, I went to – it was in February, not this year but before, when my aunt, you know, passed away. It was great – it was unfortunate we were there – the reason we were there, but it was great, for the first time, the whole entire family got together. That was wonderful. Because some from Barranquilla, some from Medellin, we just – us from New York. We got together.

I: How many people?

Mauricio: It was, in my cousins alone, a bunch of cousins, there must have been like at least fifteen, twenty cousins alone. And I met all my cousins there. But we never were in the same room together. And it was just like – amazing. I said, 'Wow.' And the last time, I'd seen them, we were, you know, younger. I'd see some people when I was young and I see them now today, it was great. It was a sad reason why we were there, but I guess we were so Happy to be together, that that, you know, sadness, kind of like went away, dissipated. It was almost like – we were just so happy to be with each other. We talked, and history, we talked about whatever. The economy, politics, travels, you know to different places. It was more like a gathering. It was wonderful that I got to see everybody at the same time. (Colombian, 30 years old)

It is expected that family members, even those living abroad, would make all efforts possible to accompany others and to say goodbye to a loved one in the home country. Not being able to travel on such occasions is an enormous source of grief and regret for many immigrants. The psychological importance and the positive effect that transnational ties and relatedness represent for those involved is such, that in Mauricio's words, "it dissipated" the sadness. The happiness described so vividly by Mauricio comes from reconnecting to his family, being able to share, on that occasion, the same geographical space with them. It seems unlikely that he would have been so happy to see these relatives, unless they were already psychologically important to him.

If the children initiated the trip, they most likely had visited the home country with their parents in the past and have already developed relationships with relatives there. When past experiences were remembered or associated with positive experiences, the children were likely to return or, at least, to desire to return as adolescents or young adults to reconnect with those relatives. However if their past experiences were remembered or associated with difficult or negative experiences, they were more likely to visit other cities or places of the home country of reference and avoid having to visit their relatives.

I: I'm going to ask you about your relationship to the Dominican Republic. Have you been back? Lots of times. Twenty times?

Jorge: Something like that, yeah.

I: Tell me about when you go – what you do – what's it like for you?

Jorge: I haven't – my relation with the Dominican Republic is pretty much two chapters. The first one was as a kid, going with my parents like every year, usually in the summer and visiting various relatives and staying with them- going out on drives into the countryside with my father and with other relatives. Go to the beach, sort of thing so it's very much a family-oriented kind of cultural immersion thing. The second chapter was back when I was in college, for the second time, finally got myself together and went to NYU and actually went on Spring Breaks with friends. And the majority of my family's clustered in the southern part of the country, so consequently I took my vacations in the north and – ... So, we would go and we would, bounce around to the various bars and we would go to the beach and that was Chapter Two of the Dominican Republic which was very much the giggling foreigners as opposed to cultural members, and that hasn't even happened since 1991

I: So you haven't been since then?

Jorge: No... Finances. Demands on time. Alternate vacations. It was much more a college thing and when college ended, you know, there were other things to do. I would like to go back. It was so much fun. (Dominican, 32 years old)

There were differences in how Colombians and Dominicans experienced their visits as children. Material and social-economic status of the respondents' families in the home country influenced how the children of immigrants experienced their visits to relatives as young children. According to both, the interview and phone survey data, Dominicans were less likely to want to visit their families in their trips as young adults than Colombians. This difference responds to a socio-economic structural difference between immigrant families with a rural vs. urban background in their home countries. According to the in-depth interviews, more than half of the parents (60%)[17] of Dominican respondents interviewed in person had migrated to the United States from rural areas of the Dominican Republic while almost 90% of parents of Colombian respondents interviewed migrated from urban areas in Colombia. This doesn't necessarily represent the distribution of place of origin among contemporary migrants from Colombia and the Dominican Republic from the 1990s to date. The particular

---

[17] This number was computed by adding the number of parents of both cohorts of interviewees that migrated from rural or urban backgrounds, both mother and father and obtaining the respective percentages. Data on rural vs. urban background of parents is not available for all respondents, only for those interviewed in person.

composition of this group of respondents' families with rural vs. urban origins in their home country echoes the particular socio-economic circumstances at a particular historical moment of their migration, as well as, the particular political relationship between the Dominican Republic and Colombia's relationship to the United States. Having a history of political occupation, geographical proximity, and close connection with the United States, it was easier for rural Dominicans to migrate to the United States. On the other hand, until recently it has been more difficult and complicated for Colombians to obtain visas to travel to the United States. Undocumented migration from Colombia has been relatively small given the geographical distance. Colombian immigrants have tended to come from urban areas and have had to demonstrate economic means in order to obtain a travel or student visa. It therefore makes it extremely difficult for a person with a rural background to migrate from Colombia to the United States.

This rural vs. urban difference determined to a great extent the experiences of the respondents in the Dominican Republic and Colombia, especially as children. For these urban Dominican youth accustomed to living in New York City, going to visit family that lived in rural areas was extremely uncomfortable. The rural areas of the Dominican Republic were likely to lack amenities that they had grown accustomed to in urban life like running water, dependable electricity, and indoor plumbing. Dominican respondents, who remembered their visits as intolerable experiences and full of hardships, usually visited family members who lived in rural areas. Their uncomfortable experiences were reflected in their depiction of such visits.

I: So tell me about your last trip there, how I mean, it was two years that you were there-Robert: I didn't really like it?

I: What don't you like.

Robert: I remember the roads were dirt, they weren't even like cement like they are now, uh… holes, there were lights ??? a river I remember, overflowing and there was water, it was just,??? most of the stuff you do in the back of the house the back yard or whatever. A long time ago, a

> country kind of living I guess. (Dominican, 30 years old)

Like Robert, many Dominicans didn't remember their experiences of visiting relatives as young children in a very positive light. When they were old enough to go on their own, Dominicans were more likely to prefer to visit other parts of the country or simply vacation without worrying about social obligations to see their rural relatives. On the other hand, Colombians were more likely to express having enjoyed the experience of meeting their extended family in the home country of their parents. In addition to the love and attention they received from their families in the home country, their visits did not represent a cultural shock of the magnitude experienced by the Dominican respondents. Although they may have experienced some hardships, at least they enjoyed the benefits of urban life such as electricity, running water, cars, stores, street life, and other amenities. Colombians were mainly going to urban areas in another country with roughly equivalent living conditions to those in the United States.

SENDING MONEY – MAINTAINING CONNECTIONS, ATTACHMENTS, AND NURTURING RELATIONSHIPS

One aspect of transnational ties that has received enormous attention is the fact that a large number of immigrants send money back to their home countries (Kasinitz et al., 2008) and continue to do so for extended periods of time even if they make very little money in the United States. Such monetary exchanges are often called "remittances." Although there are many kinds of remittances, such as cultural (i.e. music) and emotional (i.e. letters, calls) among others, monetary remittances have become a topic of importance among many migration scholars. Most research on the topic has focused on the use and potential for economic development that remittances represent for home countries (Kasinitz et al., 2008) and the role remittances plays in transnational parenting (Hondagneu-Sotelo & Avila, 1997; Salazar Parreñas, 2005). Whether the children of immigrants follow their parents' example by sending money to their country of origin is one of the questions posed by Levitt & Waters (2002). Others have discussed how contributing monetarily to their families in their home countries can become a burden and may even be detrimental to their own social mobility in their country of residence (Kasinitz et al., 2008). Smith (2002) highlighted that remittances could represent a source of pride for immigrants who occupy lower social positions in their host country, especially for men, by virtually transforming them into heroes back home for their investments in their home town's infrastructure projects.

An important fact that remains absent from most research about remittances is that immigrants don't just send money to anyone; immigrants send money to their families and, on certain occasions, they may send money to friends. Immigrants, regardless of their ethnic/racial/national group, send money to people who are emotionally close to them and members of their primary or extended family unit. A limited number of researchers (Aguilar, 2009; Drotbohm, 2009) are drawing attention to the need to view remittances as behavioral practices aimed at renegotiating and sustaining relationships with family and communities in the home country. Sending money for philanthropic purposes or to help with community projects is usually done only after the needs of family members have been covered. According to Kasinitz et.al. (2008), immigrant parents send money mostly to children and aging parents living in their home country and, occasionally, to siblings in charge of taking care of aging parents or their children. Once the family members they supported transnationally joined them in the United States or died in their home countries, the financial remittances ceased along with the need for them. Therefore it is not surprising to hear answers such as:

> Fernando: I have no one to send over there. To be honest with you, I don't even know if I have any, well, I do have family left over there but not any family that I stay in touch with, you know? (Dominican, 25 years old)

Exile, political persecution, and trauma affect immigrants' desire or ability to send remittances. For example, in the larger ISGMNY study, Jewish Russian and Chinese immigrants were the least likely to send remittances or have transnational ties to their home countries. This apparent paradigm can be understood by politically and socially contextualizing Chinese and Jewish Russian migration. Most Chinese immigrants in the United States are political or economic refugees who have severed their ties to China. Chinese immigrants usually have managed to bring over most, if not all, of their close family members. The children of Chinese immigrants explained that their parents had never spoken to them about China and that their parents didn't want them to have any ties to China. This was similar for Jewish Russian families who suffered religious persecution in Russia. They left with most of their family members and usually didn't have any more family members living in Russia. Jewish Russian immigrants didn't want their children to visit Russia and never really talked to them about Russia as an idyllic home country to long for. Instead Jewish Russian immigrants longed for Israel as their home country and their children were encouraged to make pilgrimage trips to Israel and not Russia. According to Kasinitz et.al. (2008), Russian Jews and Chinese respondents were the least likely to have ties to their parents' home country while Dominicans (20%) and Colombians (19%) were among the most likely to have ties to their parents' home country.

Connecting and relating to non-migrant family members and friends of their immigrant parents, living in the home country, represents an integral part of the "holding environment… that allows [respondents] to maintain 'continuity of being' enabling the emergence and expression of [their] inner potential" (Winicott, 1975, 1979 as cited Pessach-Ramati & Josselson, 2007, p. 172), and the development of a healthy and resilient self. There are 8 dimensions in Josselson's (1992, 2003) model of relationships: holding, attachment, passion, eye-to-eye validation, identification and idealization, mutuality, embeddedness, and caring/tending for others. These dimensions are all part of developing an individual's identity through their relationship with others. Holding can be describe as the "the experience of being held, contained, supported, and anchored by others"; it can be experienced as external or internalized others without the promise of a continued relationship. As respondents met relatives and other individuals in their trips to their home countries, they seemed to experience being held by these 'familiar-strangers'. Once participants' relationships with specific family members, they have met in their trips, begin to cement through mutual exchange of letters, phone calls, gifts, etc, participants begin to develop to those particular individuals and to experience a level of mutuality, "the creation of a connection that is the product of two" (Pessach-Ramati & Josselson, 2007, p. 169). The following excerpt from Andrea's interview relates just how important and dear these relationships with her family members in Colombia were and continued to be:

I: Has it changed a lot since the last – since you started visiting?

Andrea: Has it changed?

I: Yeah. Do you have a recollection from when you were nine?

Andrea: See I was so naïve, I was still growing up. I- and I had conceptions of a great place to be. And I still see that now. And theirs is a lot of Family and family members in Colombia, and you're just the center of attention. And they're always open to listen and they're so much more, that – I love that. I'm addicted to that. I want that all the time. And I miss it now. You know, I don't know what else to say. I love seeing my grandparents. I love having them, I wish I could have them here, I wish I could see them more often.

I: Do you stay with your grandparents when you're there?

Andrea: I stay with – no I stay at somebody else's house every time I go. I try to stay at somebody else's house – a different house. (Colombian, 27 years old)

Attachments differ from holding because they require the existence of another that provides anchoring and can be expected to respond to ones' needs. "This is the realm of emotional exchange across space, of validation and empathy, of finding ourselves reflected in others and anchoring ourselves in our effects on them. In discovering that others respond to us, we affirm that we ourselves are really here. (Josselson, 1992, p. 92)" In the following excerpt, it is apparent that José has through time developed personal attachments to a number of relatives in the Dominican Republic. He mentions two older uncles of his mom, as well as, an uncle and an aunt who once visited him in the United States, and had since returned to the Dominican Republic. These two older uncles made an impression on José even though he "wouldn't hang out with" them as he would with his friends. Yet, he held them in high regard because he learned from them "the true meaning of living your life to the fullest" and expressed the determination to help keep the remaining older uncle alive.

I: You told us your parents send money to people in the D.R. right? (Yes) As you get older, do you think you will start to send money to someone over there?

José: Probably to my own parents, if they're down there. Because I have, let's see, like I have two uncles over there. They are like the cornerstone of the family. You know, on my mother's side, and one of them died, so I mean, [...] It, you know, I was sad, but at the same time I wasn't that sad, because that was the man, he knew the true meaning of living your life to the fullest. That man did. Oh man. That dude- and when I (emphasis) was there, he was an old man, in comparison with to like if I were gonna hang out, I wouldn't hang out with him, [...], he was the man. [...] But, I got the other uncle over there, like I said, he's the cornerstone and we got to try to keep him as much alive as we can. So, - as long as we're here. (Dominican, 31 years old)

Relationships are maintained through a mutual exchange of emotional, material, or social goods which express to others that we care; that we are with them across borders, space, and time. It is not surprising that some respondents pursued and nurtured their attachments to family members and others in the home country of their parents. Their immigrant parents continued to fulfill their family, social, and moral obligations and expectations to their parents and siblings long after they had migrated and had established families in the United States (Aguilar, 2009; Drotbohm, 2009). Research on household formation and social networks views these behaviors as fulfilling obligations that help maintain the social place of the immigrant in their family or social network. Such research also considers these family obligations an added burden on immigrants' depleted psychological and material resources. The psychological and social benefits received or enjoyed by the immigrant as he/she satisfies the needs of his/her parents or children, are to some extent relegated to the side. For this reason, exploring the dimension of tending and caring in relationships with others is extremely useful and helps us rescue some of the agency and richness of psychological experience involved in helping others across transnational borders. Josselson argues:

> The human need to tend, to offer care, reflects our need to feel needed by others... We choose to offer ourselves in the service of others... We may put aside some of our own needs and demands in the interest of others. In return, we experience joy, which is the emotional accompaniment of the fulfillment of caring... When we care we feel fully in relation to an Other. (1992, p. 162)

The respondents and their immigrant parents 'send money' to their home country as well as, clothes, letters, gifts, etc., in order to care for those individuals who are important to them and who are in need as an expression of love, care, and solidarity. In discussing the concept of caring, Josselson (1992) asserts that in tending to others, one offers not only material but emotional and psychological resources as well. It is in the act of sharing what we have or don't have that we realize the best qualities inside of us and derive pleasure and joy in the process. Therefore, even if it may be difficult and burdensome for some immigrants to send money home, it is necessary to contemplate the idea that it is an exchange among people who have a mutual relationship that provides them emotional and psychological benefits even if these are not easily apparent. Mauricio's family doesn't just send money, sometimes they send small appliances or gifts that they feel are needed by his father's family in Colombia. He also highlights that there is more meaning behind this act; the need to express that, despite the physical distance, they care about those that remained behind.

I: You mentioned that your parents sent money back?

Mauricio: Right.

I: Can you tell me a little bit more about that?

Mauricio: They still do that. To especially... my dad... well, my dad more because my mom, the majority of her immediate family migrated here to the U.S. but my dad he has to send something to his mom. Not that they need the money or anything but just to say, "Hey ma, here's some money. Buy yourself a t.v. or buy yourself a gift or what have you." They still help out.

I: Are you sending any money back to anybody?

Mauricio: I have actually. Just people I meet and I see their condition and you know what, I just share the wealth a little bit. I do the same. (Colombian, 30 years old)

Respondents who eventually joined their immigrant parents in sending money to their relatives in the home country did so after having established personal relations and attachments with particular family members with whom they connected on their visits. This represented an opportunity to realize how privileged they were to be living in the United States and to have the material resources and opportunities they did. In sharing such resources, respondents are connecting to others at a deep emotional level and, to some extent, are cementing relationships that carry the expectation of reciprocity, albeit not material. For many, just knowing that there are other members of the family who value their contributions and express admiration for all their achievements in the United States serves to build a stronger sense of self and identity, to feel supported and loved. Knowing that there are many family members who would potentially be there to help them in a time of need goes a long way to allow them to freely contemplate possible futures and be excited about them. In the following passage,

José tells us that he sent money to his aunt and uncle because they were in need. He trusted that "everybody in the family would chip in" when a family member is in need, including him. It gave him a sort of assurance that if he needed help his entire family will be there for him as well.

I: Have you ever sent money yourself?

José: Yeah, yeah. Actually, to that uncle. That is still alive.

[…]

I: To that uncle. To anyone else.

José: To my aunt back there, I send money to her, 'cause she's kind of a little – well, the situation is she was here and her and her husband get the checks, the Social Security checks from here, they send them over there, but it was something – a problem […] But in that period, I was sending them some money, you know, just – like everybody in the family would chip in, you know, to send them some money. (Dominican, 31 years old)

The quantitative data supported the finding that both groups of respondents, Dominican and Colombian children of immigrants, had similar experiences and reasons to send money and did so at almost the same rate. Table 11 summarizes how often respondents and their parents sent money to their home country in a year. At least 30% of Colombian and 34% of Dominican respondents have at some point sent money themselves or gave money to their parents to help family in their respective home countries. The consistency among the percentages with which parents and respondents from both groups declared that they were sending money underlines a high degree of commonality of experiences with regards to behaviors that help maintain transnational relationships for parents and their children as well.

Table 11. Respondents and Parents Who Sent Remittances to their Home Countries

How often send money to home country	Colombians		Dominicans	
	Respondent	Parents	Respondent	Parents
Never	69.9 %	27.3 %	65.9 %	28.7 %
Once or twice a year	13.3 %	18.2 %	14.2 %	14.7 %
Several times a year	6.6 %	17.0 %	8.4 %	17.9 %
Once a month	7.2 %	18.8 %	8.9 %	19.5 %
2-3 times a month	3.0 %	6.7 %	2.6 %	5.5 %
Every week	-	2.4 %	-	2.6 %

The percentage of respondents who declared sending money 'several times a year' or more was 16.8% for Colombians and 21.9% for Dominicans. These percentages are remarkably close to the percentage of respondents who traveled more than 10 times to the home country of their parents; 14% for Colombians and 21% for Dominicans (see table 7, previous section). This suggests that the more respondents traveled to the home country of their parents, the more likely they were to 'send money more than several times a year.' This supports the qualitative finding that the decision of respondents to send money to their home country emerges from forming stronger transnational relationships and attachments that they deemed important and in need of nurturing and caring

LANGUAGE USE – ENABLING CONNECTION AND MEMBERSHIP

Language is a "central element" of ethnic identity (Deaux, 2000, 2006; Rumbaut, 2002). As children developed psychologically and socially, they acquire the language necessary to connect and communicate with their caregivers, parents, family, and other human beings who have an important role in their lives. "The strongest tie to traditional practices and folklore- medical beliefs, songs, jokes, benedictions, curses, and the like – is through the language in which they developed" (Pearson, 2008, p. 7). Knowledge of one or multiple languages is tied to specific socio-historical contexts in which children develop. It is through everyday use of language in context that children of immigrants encounter and learn about differing worldviews. Zentella emphasizes that "[l]anguage is the vehicle via which a group's ways of "being" and "doing" are learned, while children also learn to use the linguistic codes of their communities in culturally specific ways in order to be communicatively competent, not just grammatically proficient" (2005, p. 15).

Research on language acquisition has demonstrated that children develop their relationship with specific languages in part guided by a desire and need to connect to people in their immediate environment. From an early age, children will try to respond to adults in the language that those adults speak and made the necessary effort to understand them (Pearson, 2008). Different languages are associated with diverse cultural systems that may affect a person's emotional expressions, other-person descriptions, and values (Hong et al., 2000) "The kind of relationship one develops with an acquired language is deeply influenced by the kind of bond one had with one's mother or father tongue – and, by extension with all intimacies and intimate sensations of early life" (E. Hoffman, 2003, p. 51). Research has demonstrated that "speaking with family members in the language of origin can facilitate a sense of interdependence and attachment that also characterized identity, just as the inability to communicate with one's parents in that language can weaken the links." (Deaux, 2006, p. 113)

According to Pérez (1996, cited by Deaux, 2006), middle school children were more likely to speak their parent's native language if their grandparents were living with them. Grandparents are more likely to speak in the native language to children simply because they are less likely to have learned the language spoken outside of the house, especially if they are older. For parents, it is important that the children learned the language of their home country mainly so that they may communicate with their grandparents and extended family. They usually want their children to have a sense of closeness and connection to both of their families. Hong & Chiu (2001) demonstrate the importance that communication and language has for the transmission and maintenance of cultural theories among members of a cultural community. In addition, Robins & Aksoy (2001) point out that the language skills of Turkish-Cypriot children immigrants in Britain allow them to enjoy a cultural mobility and to build cultural and social competencies that native monolingual British children have not experienced.

Language was the most important predictor of visits and of sending money to the home country among these Dominican and Colombian youth. Other researchers have documented positive correlations between language fluency and remittances in the past (Deaux, 2006). Table 12 indicates that both Colombian and Dominican participants grew up in Spanish-speaking households. The majority of Dominican (67.3%) and Colombian (69.9%) respondents reported speaking Spanish while growing up. Yet when they were asked what language they prefer to speak now, about half of Colombian (50.9%) and Dominican (48.8%) respondents prefered English. It is safe to assume that Dominican and Colombian respondents who were born in the United States or arrived before the age of 8 were most likely to say that they prefer to speak English and that respondents who arrived in the United States after age 12 were more likely to prefer to speak in Spanish. However, the fact that a number of Dominican and Colombian respondents, who prefer to speak English, spoke Spanish while growing up indicates that they probably needed to speak Spanish to some family members who did not speak English or were not willing to speak in English in the home. A recent national study of Latino youth by the Pew Hispanic Center described similar findings among Latino youth in general. At least 79% of second-generation Latinos were fluent in Spanish, and close to the 89% of first-generation Latino youth were fluent in Spanish (Pew Hispanic Center, 2009). However, in their national study, the gap in Spanish reading and writing skills between second generation Latino youth (68%) and first-generation Latino youth (90%) was larger. The Pew Hispanic Center (2009) also reported that preference for English dominance only (36%) was less popular than bilingual (41%) and Spanish (23%) language dominance among Latino youth.

Correlational analysis of the ISGMNY data revealed a significant relationship between 'visits to home country' and the summary variable 'language use' for Colombian respondents ($r=.259$, $p<.01$) and for Dominican respondents ($r=.210$, $p<.01$). Thus, it appears that the more respondents visited their parents' home countries, the more likely they were to use their parents' native language, in this case Spanish. There was also a positive correlation between the variables 'how often respondent sends money' and the summary variable 'language use' for both Colombians ($r=.232$, $p<.01$) and Dominicans ($r=.139$, $p<.01$). The more respondents travel to their home country, the stronger their attachments to their families in the home country and the more they use their parents' native language, Spanish. This finding is further validated by the fact that a similar correlation between fluency in the language of the home country and frequency of remittances was reported by Rumbaut (2002). Even though Dominicans don't seem to have as many family members living in the Dominican Republic, they would still need to use Spanish to communicate with people in Dominican Republic during their trips. Such findings contribute to underscore the importance of speaking the language of the home country in maintaining and facilitating the continuation of family and transnational ties for the children of immigrants.

Table 12. Respondents' Language Use

Language use	Colombians		Dominicans	
	English	Spanish	English	Spanish
Language spoken at home while growing up	1.2 %	98.8 %	1.5 %	97.5 %
Language participant used most while growing up	26.4 %	69.9 %	27.0 %	67.3 %
Language participant prefers to speak now	44.2 %	50.9 %	47.6 %	48.8 %

GETTING MARRIED – HAVING CHILDREN: CREATING A LINK BETWEEN PAST, PRESENT, AND FUTURE – HERE AND THERE

The transnational behaviors and attachments maintained by this group of young adults from Dominican and Colombian backgrounds changed across their life course as their societal roles changed and became more complex. At different points in their life cycle, their ethnic/racial/trans/national identity surfaced as an important part of their self-definition, while at other times it took backstage to other life circumstances and/or processes. Levitt (2002) argues that there is a relationship between particular life cycle stages and the intensity of transnational activity among second generation youth. She pointed out that transnational ties "ebb and flow at different stages, varying with the demands of work, school, and family".

A growing number of researchers recognize the importance of considering developmental stages and changes in group membership over time such as Amiot, de la Sablonnière, Terry and Smith (2007), Deaux (2006), Ethier & Deaux (1994), and Phinney (2002), among others. Significant others are important in this process of development throughout the life cycle since social interactions with others and bridging processes help young participants connect new cultural and social meanings to their pre-existent knowledge. Phinney (2002) and Deaux (2006) remind us that it is important to keep in mind while studying acculturation or adaptation of immigrants to their new surroundings, that differences are not necessarily due to such processes and could be the result of changes in personal development. Peggy Levitt (2002) and Robert Smith (2002) documented differences in the type of transnational ties and practices at different life stages. The in-depth interview schedule provided an important advantage making possible a longitudinal reading of the respondents' lives. The interview protocol organized questions in a chronological order from childhood to present adulthood. Retrospective questioning has been used before in the absence of longitudinal studies (Phinney, 2002). Therefore, it was possible to compare the responses of respondents' at different points in their life cycles.

Among these Dominican and Colombian children of immigrants, there was a pattern similar to that of second generation West Indians described previously by Vickerman (2002), where "as children, they had frequently accompanied their parents on visits to the West Indies, but as they grew older they visited less often and almost not at all after they entered college, with its demanding schedule. After college, however, the frequency of contact picked up again, although not necessarily at the same level as when they were young." (p.361). Childhood, adolescence, and young adulthood emerged as periods of transition where important life changes regulated the attention and energy given to (or available for) issues of ethnic/national/racial identity. As described earlier in this chapter, childhood and adolescence involvement in transnational practices was mainly determined and controlled by their parents' own transnational practices and social, political, and economic means. However, as the respondents moved into young adulthood and became more independent, the nature of their interpersonal relationships such as dating, getting married, and having children and the responsibilities associated with them, became an important variable affecting the extent and frequency of their transnational practices. In his ethnography of young Mexican children of immigrants, Robert Smith (2002) found that, "[a]s the second generation moves into adolescence, participation in transnational life becomes incredibly important for many of them, but the demands of young adult life, beginning in their mid-twenties, lessen their ability to participate. In particular, they lose their freedom to travel as they get responsible jobs, have children, and move into their own apartments with their own rents to pay." (p.162)

Table 13. External Context and Social Activities related to Life Cycle Stages

Life stage	Social context	Social Activity
Child	Primary school	Playing/learning to interact with others
Adolescent	Junior /High school	Belonging to a group of friends, dating
Young adults	College/ First Jobs	Expanding horizons, Dating
Adults	Work Marriage	Establishing independence from their parents Becoming a professional Having Children

For adolescents and young adults, dating constituted a contact zone where differing views about race and ethnicity between respondents and their parents were worked out, both among Dominicans and Colombians. Most respondents reported having dated people from many ethnic backgrounds in their youth. Who respondents dated had more to do with who was part of their social circle and where they lived, than a personal choice to search and date people from a specific racial or ethnic background. Yet, by the time they made the decision to get married or find life partners, respondents who partnered with members of other ethnic/racial groups (other than Latino/Hispanic or Latin American backgrounds) were in the minority (about 30%). Quantitative analysis of the ethnic/racial background of respondents' spouses demonstrates that respondents in this study married mostly within their ethnic/racial group (Hispanic/Latino and other Latino groups), even if it was not their same national group. An earlier study by the Pew Hispanic Center obtained similar results of interracial marriage (32%) among Latino second-generation, although it increased by the third generation (57%) (Suro & Passel, 2003).

Table 14. Ethnic/Racial Background of Respondents' Parents and their Spouses[18]

	Colombians			Dominicans		
Race	Mother	Father	Spouse	Mother	Father	Spouse
White	24.6 %	25.7 %	24.5 %	14.8 %	15.5 %	22.2 %
Black, African American	1.8 %	3.6 %	7.5 %	10.2 %	11.7 %	12.7 %
Asian	-	-	-	1.1 %	-	-
Native American	1.8 %	1.2 %	-	1.0 %	1.6 %	-
Spanish	4.8 %	3.6 %	1.9 %	4.3 %	4.1 %	3.8 %
Hispanic	40.1 %	38.3 %	45.3 %	30.8 %	30.8 %	29.7 %
Latino	4.8 %	4.2 %	3.8 %	2.8 %	3.1 %	1.3 %
Colombian	16.2 %	14.4 %	1.9 %	-	-	-
Dominican	-	-	3.8 %	22.6 %	20.1 %	11.4 %
Puerto Rican	-	-	3.8 %	-	-	3.8
Some other race	3.6 %	4.2 %	5.7 %	5.8 %	6.4 %	6.3

[18] The columns do not add to 100% due to missing data.

Whether the respondents chose to marry Colombians, Dominicans, or other Latinos consciously or unconsciously, cannot be determined from these data. However it remains an interesting finding, that although most respondents expressed openness to date people from different ethnic/racial backgrounds, their marriage patterns did not coincide with such attitudes. According to the survey self-reported data, more than half of Colombian respondents (66.2%) and Dominican respondents (56.3%) married partners from the same national origin or another Latino group (See table 14). I suggest that such marital choices are influenced by thoughts about 'progeny' and 'legacy' that arise as respondents contemplate the idea of getting married and having children. They may in fact begin to worry about what legacy they will pass on to their children and may discover more in common with other Latinos than with Whites, African Americans, Asian Americans or other ethnic/racial groups when it comes to childrearing beliefs and practices.

Dominican and Colombian respondents, who lived in the Dominican Republic and Colombia for extended periods of time, were more likely to marry or date recent immigrants from their national group than to marry other U.S.-born Latinos or co-nationals. Respondents who married or considered marrying and having children with individuals from a different ethnic/racial group emphasized the importance of having a partner who valued their culture (national and panethnic) highly and was willing to share and learn more about it. This may provide a sense of reassurance that their culture will be transmitted to their children as well. One such example can be seen in Rogelio's rationale for why it was alright that his sister married an African American man:

I: Did they say you should or shouldn't marry a person of Dominican background?

Rogelio: They said it would be great if I married a Dominican woman but again, it has to do with if they are smart. There are even smart people who are stupid. But eventually I believe even the smart can be stupid. No. I would be nice. But someone who has understanding of the culture. Not someone who is ignorant and can't speak a

> lick of Spanish. That doesn't understand Spanish. Like let's say, in my sister's case, where she married this African American guy. He doesn't speak Spanish that well, but he understands like there's no tomorrow. He understands totally because he has always grown up with Spanish people around him. And he knows Spanish words and he hangs out. He loves Dominican beer. Something like that where they are not ignorant and they won't stop themselves from learning. That they know enough but they want to learn more. (Dominican, 29 years old)

When respondents became parents, being able to transmit cultural and historical background knowledge to their children became important. Ensuring the continuation of family traditions and cultural customs represented an effort to rescue their parents' past and reconnect respondents' present experiences with their family's historical memory. It also allowed Dominican and Colombian participants to envision their lives and their children's lives projected into the future creating a sense of continuity across time (past, present, future) and space (geographical boundaries). As Josselson eloquently asserts "[b]y interpreting our lives in the same terms as those who have come before us and passing on these stories to the next generation, we ensure a continuity of our existence that outlasts ourselves (1992, p. 185)." It is by looking into our parents' own upbringing and understanding where they are coming from, what has shaped their experiences, and their ways of being that we can truly evaluate and understand our place in the story of our families and socio-historical context. This is precisely the reason why Claudia enjoyed her visit to her parents' home country:

I: -- How was that experience for you?

Claudia: Great. I loved it.

I: You liked it?

Claudia: Loved (emphasis) it.

I: What did you like the most about the D.R.?

Claudia: The (word) it's quiet. Your whole family's there. You get to see where your ancestors grew up, you know, just get a feel of how your family was raised. Even the ones that aren't alive now, but it's just a nice place to be. You go to the countryside and you get to relax. (Dominican, 25 years old)

"Our embeddedness within a culture provides us fables and myths by which to evaluate our lives and our relationships and thereby determine if they are 'coming out right' (Josselson, 1992, p. 185)." By maintaining and pursuing transnational ties, the children of immigrants have an opportunity to enrich their collective memories (Bikmen, 2007; Deaux, 2006) with the stories and histories of their extended families in their home country. They were also able to attach real life details such as smells, images, and feelings to the tales and stories told by their parents and often grandparents. Many Dominican and Colombian respondents discussed being able to see the place where their parents grew up, being able to attach faces to names they have heard so many times. These activities were invaluable for them in order to understand, even in a minuscule manner, the dimensions of their parents' decision to move to another country in the hopes of ensuring a brighter future for their children.

Through the continuation of transnational ties, immigrant parents achieved some measure of acknowledgment of their loss and dilemma inscribing it in the collective memory of their family and group. Their pain and history are no longer only personal stories, but a shared reality of displacement, resiliency, and hope. As Newman reminds us:

> [R]emembering –forcing individual memories of pain and suffering into the public domain where they may be heard, and their burden shared – is a prerequisite for genuine reconciliation... Therefore, it is essential to create both social and political spaces in which death, destruction and personal

> losses can be recognized, and their traumatic effects acknowledged. (2003, p. 46)

Therefore transnational ties create a contact zone between geographical and time boundaries where such acknowledgement can be co-constructed by parents, their children, and their families in the home and host countries.

On the other hand, these transnational ties also allowed Dominican and Colombian respondents an opportunity to fill in the blanks, to understand where those taken-for-granted traditions, rituals, and beliefs came from, claim the collective memories for themselves and find their place in it. It was an opportunity to discover that they are not alone in their struggle and that they had something valuable to offer future generations. Robins & Aksoy (2001) discussed similar findings among their Turkish-Cypriot participants who were children of immigrants. The Turkish-Cypriot participants did not discuss their cultural or ethnic identity as political attachments to national community, but rather talked about being able to transmit values and cultural traditions, ways of 'being and doing' to their children. Paula narrates how she came to terms with her own story, her parents', her husband's and how she was passing that on to her child.

I: When you were growing history, traditions, stuff like that?

Paula: Yeah, it just would be... I was very inquisitive so they always volunteered any sort of information about that, their childhood stories, holidays and why they celebrated. Granted I may have fallen asleep on them a few times. But yeah, they volunteered plenty of information.

I: Obviously you made the effort to learn on your own?

Paula: Yes.

I: If you have children, will you teach them about Colombia?

Paula: Absolutely. I had already planned that. And teach them about everything about their background. Like I said, my fiancée, he is Greek background and Puerto Rican background. I myself wanted to learn about it so that I can… he doesn't know anything about it so I wanted to learn as much as possible so that I could have something valid to pass on.

I: About his side also?

Paula: Of course. Just the way I taught him about mine. And taught him by taking him there and by hanging around my family.

I: You took him to Colombia?

Paula: Yes.

I: Why do you think that's important to you? To be able to pass that sort of information along?

Paula: It's an identity thing. It kind of establishes me being who you are and what you are and where you come from. It's different elements that make up what you are, what you look like. (Colombian, 30 years old)

Most Colombian and Dominican respondents affirmed that they wanted to take their children to their parents' home country even if they themselves had never been there. Whether that would happen in the end depends as much on their motivation as on their socio-economic means and the demands of their jobs among others. Besides learning about their parents' and their grandparents' history and families, respondents often highlighted that it was important for them to show their children there were other ways of being and living beyond the United States. Some Dominican and Colombian respondents spoke about how traveling and maintaining transnational contacts elicited a new appreciation for the many opportunities that living in the United

States afforded them. Others spoke about how seeing and understanding other of ways of living and being exposed the fact that dominant U.S. culture and ideologies were not the only value systems available to structure their lives by, and that alternative modes and views about life existed and were possible. Andrea exemplified the desire to offer their children alternative views of the world beyond the United States.

I: So when you have children, will you want them to go to Colombia?

Andrea: Yes. (I: Why?) Why?

I: You want them to get acquainted with the culture?

Andrea: Totally. I want them to know where they came from. I want them to know where their grandparents came from. I want them to know this is how people lived, and you've got luxuries, and I want them to know that there is more to life than being in the United States. (Colombian, 27 years old)

Sandra, another respondent, echoed Andrea's response:

I: Do you think that will be important for your children?

Sandra: I hope so, yeah. I hope to instill that in her too.

I: Puerto Rican history too?

Sandra: Yeah. It will be a little hard with her. I'm bombard her from two sides. (laughter)

I: Why do you think that will be important for her?

Sandra: Because I think it's important. I know it's also important for her to know that she is an American, because she was born here in North America, but I also think it's important for her because she's going to speak Spanish and because she's going to be involved in that culture, for her to know more about her background. Our background, actually.

I: So you plan for her to be bilingual?

Sandra: Oh yes. She already is. (Colombian, 28 years old)

Even though cross tabulation analysis demonstrate the majority of respondents did not have children at the moment (see table 15), it is important to highlight that even childless respondents envisioned immersing their future children in transnational ties and initiating family visits to the home country to acquaint their children with it and to introduce them to their extended families there. Most respondents wished to continue their transnational relationship to their parents' home country and extend that experience to their children. Whether respondents were able to realize their wishes or not is uncertain.

Table 15. Percentage of Respondents with Children

Number of Children	Colombians	Dominicans
0	76.5	58.8
1	15.7	23.7
2	6.0	10.4
3 or more	1.8	7.1

Maintaining a balance between cultures and countries as they raise their children was an important concern for respondents, especially for those who had partners from different ethnic/racial backgrounds. They emphasized a desire to establish a balance where neither culture or country would be more important than another. This preoccupation stemmed from their understanding of being a product of the coming together of two cultures and identities, their parents' and the United States' mainstream culture they grew up in. As discussed in the previous chapter, respondents did not want to privilege any one culture and expressed that both were equally part of their experience. Ideally they would want their children to feel the same way and to appreciate their cultures in a similar manner. The yearning for achieving a balance between cultures, countries and worlds for their children is evident in Rogelio's and Deyanira's answers:

> I: Being Dominican and children.
>
> Rogelio: Yes, I mean, I want to have a child who's more -I wouldn't want them to be more Dominican than German or more American than German, just a piece of each - know about each thing. That's what I would say is the most important thing -to know about it. More than anything. (Dominican, 29 years old)

Deyanira added:

> I: How do you plan to raise your daughter?
>
> Deyanira: I would like to think that I have created a balance between the two worlds. I do think it is important for her to learn the language. To learn about the culture, speak the language, eat the food, share the traditions, the holidays and all that. My family and I are very close so I think that she will have that instilled in her. (Dominican, 30 years old)

Rogelio and Deyanira sought a constant process of achieving balance between the different cultural, linguistic, and social fields they and their children inhabit, rather than searching for "unity" and "simplicity". As Dorfman beautifully puts it, they are not looking for "the victory of one tongue over the other one but rather a cohabitation, [their] two languages [and cultures] reaching a truce in order to help the body they were lodged in to survive (2003, p. 33)." As children of immigrants, they were constantly striving to achieve a "new consciousness" forged in the midst of their transnational experiences that embraces ambiguity and change.

SUMMARY

The findings in this chapter demonstrate that having close family members in their parents' home country is a good predictor of strong ethnic identity and transnational involvement. Transnational practices and involvement were anchored in family relationships, new and old, that developed beyond transnational borders. Transnational ties were also a tool immigrant parents used to ensure continuity in their lives by maintaining communication with their families and, in the process, cementing roots for future transnational relationships of their children. Most respondents had gone to their parents' home country as children and many returned subsequently to visit those family members with whom they had established relationships with. Almost fifty percent of respondents had visited their parents' home country 1-3 times and about 30% had done so 4-9 times. Among some immigrant families, sending children to their home country was a child-rearing practice that helped them cope with undesirable and less than optimal social and structural conditions such as lack of access to good neighborhoods and schools.

Visits and sending remittances to the home country are commonly used to measure the level of transnational involvement of immigrants and their children. However, in their efforts to understand what drives and sustains these practices, researchers have overlooked the fact they are behaviors with the purpose of establishing, nurturing, and sustaining interpersonal relationships. Such behaviors are bound to continue as long as those interpersonal relationships exist, hold meaning and value for respondents and while social, economic, and political contexts permit them to flourish. By sharing resources (psychological, social and economic) respondents connected to others at a deep emotional level which provided satisfaction, joy, and pride. The importance of social networks for resiliency and psychological well-being has been well-documented. In addition, this chapter highlights the interconnectedness between language use and the desire to connect with specific others. Language use (as a measure of preference and actual use) and transnational behaviors (visits and remittances) were highly correlated. Respondents who reported greater usage of Spanish were more likely to travel to their parents' home country more frequently and send money to relatives there.

Life cycle and life stages were found to be intimately tied to the types of respondents' transnational practices and their frequency. This was not a linear relationship. On the contrary, transnational ties and practices were shaped by the social activities, demands and expectations particular to specific life stages. Transnational practices and how they were subjectively experienced differed as people move through life as children, adolescents, young adults, and, later, as new parents. Getting married and having children were two life stages in which ethnic, national, cultural, and racial identities gained saliency as respondents contemplate what kinds of families they wanted to form and what values and cultural norms they wanted to transmit to future generations. So far, these findings have highlighted how similar the psychological experience of managing multiple identities, cultures and norms, and maintaining transnational relationships are among both, Colombian and Dominican respondents. However, the chapter that follows uncovers the ways in which the experiences of Dominican and Colombian children of immigrants differ as they encounter social, economic, and political structures.

CHAPTER 5

Encountering Social Structures

Bronfenbrenner's ecological development model (Bronfenbrenner & P. A. Morris, 1998) places the child at the center within concentric and overlapping social spheres of family, school, friends, and work. The child's development is continuous and simultaneously being shaped by her/his social interactions and her/his immediate economic, social, political and physical surroundings, changing as she/he grows up. In this chapter, I move beyond discussing the respondents' relationships with their families across borders and their psychological and social implications to exploring the interconnections and multiple intersections of local and trans- local, national, and trans-national social structures and institutions such as race, gender, nationality, ethnicity, social class that shape the social reality experienced by these Colombian and Dominican respondents.

Most participants expressed feeling at peace and satisfied with where they were in life. However, some respondents had more social and institutional capital and opportunities to achieve higher levels of education and improve their future quality of life than others. In this sense, the respondents may be said to travel two different life trajectories. Rather than highlighting how these two groups differed in their levels of achievement, I will focus on social processes and structures that control their access to educational, civic, and economic opportunities. Their narratives illustrate how differing experiences with respect to social class, gender, and race intersect to place these children of Dominican and Colombian immigrants in different places within the socio-economic and racial hierarchies of New York City.

Even though they might come to a social interaction or situation with the same set of psychological experiences of ethnic/national/racial identity and knowledge from their families, the outcome of that interaction depends on how they are judged by others in terms of race, gender, and social class among other variables as a combination of economic and cultural capital (according to Bourdieu's (1984) definition). Despite having similar social and psychological experiences growing up as children of immigrants in New York City among their family and friends, Colombian participants had access to better schools, more opportunities to attend college, and entertained a wider number of possible futures than Dominican respondents. Ten years later, "[s]tudents who begin with the greatest economic disadvantages [still] receive the least enriching educations and end up with fewer, less valuable, and historically deflating diplomas" (Fine, 1991, p. 26).

Taking advantage of the chronological design of the phone survey and the in-depth interviews, I have organized this chapter by focusing on specific moments of transition in the respondent's lives. Transition points are especially important because they open or close opportunities and possible futures. Lareau & Weininger referred to these moments as 'key transition points at which individuals commit to one or another of multiple paths" (2007, p. 1). The decisions made at these key transition points are sometimes made by parents and, other times, by respondents themselves. Using transition points such as, choosing a neighborhood to live in, deciding whether to graduate from high school and go on to college or not, dating and choosing a marriage partner allow me to explore how the intersectionality (Cole, 2009; Mahalingam et al., 2008) across social constructs of race, gender, ethnicity, national origin, and social class among others, are embodied in participants' lives and contribute to their decision making process. Exploring the intersectionality of social constructs recognizes that no social group is homogeneous and that respondents' locations within these social structures makes visible the power relations inherent in such structures, i.e. race, sex, phenotype, social class, cultural capital, etc. (Mahalingam et al., 2008) By concentrating on these transition moments we can consider both the agency of respondents and their parents in making these decisions while illuminating how social and structural constraints limit their possible choices.

UNEQUAL ACCESS: REPRODUCING SOCIAL INEQUALITIES

According to the quantitative and qualitative data, Dominican and Colombian respondents differed on personal income, educational attainment, parent's educational attainment and phenotype (skin-color) which place them differently in the socio-economic and racial hierarchy of the United States. In general, the patterns that emerged indicate that Dominican children of immigrants had a harder time accessing quality schools and the education necessary to aspire to college; left high school before graduation in greater numbers; were more likely to get pregnant in high school; had fewer opportunities to find good-paying jobs; and were more likely to report experiencing discrimination than Colombian respondents.

Reviewing the survey data reveals interesting comparisons of socio-economic status among young Colombian and Dominican respondents after controlling for their national origins. Participants were asked what their current personal gross income was for the year 1998 (see table 16). The percentage of Colombian and Dominican respondents that would be considered earning below poverty levels ($12,000 or less) was virtually equal for both groups at 44% for Colombians and 43.6% for Dominicans. Since this was a sample of young adults, many of them were not fully employed or had not entered the workforce at the moment. However, household median income for Colombians was consistently higher compared to Dominican households in New York City in 1990, 2000, and-2010 (Bergad, 2009, 2011). According to the 2010 U.S. Census, the median household income in New York City for foreign born Colombians was $58,050 and $70,100 for domestic born Colombians compared to $40,200 for foreign born Dominicans and $41,800 for domestic born Dominicans after adjusting for inflation (Bergad, 2011). At least 24% of Dominican and 14% of Colombian households earned less than $20,000 while 21% of Dominican and 38% of Colombian households earned $75,000 or more (Bergad, 2011). These data suggests that the children of Colombian immigrants are doing better economically and have more financial resources than those of Dominican background. This may also help explain the slightly higher number of visits to the home country reported by Colombian respondents (see table 7). However in New York City, Latinos/as in general remained economically disadvantaged with the lowest median household income of $45,300 in 2010 and the lowest increase between 2000 and 2010 compared to Blacks, Whites, and Asians (Bergad, 2011). Many Colombian and Dominican respondents replied that lack of economic resources was a major factor in determining whether or not, and how often, they visited their parent's home country.

Samson (2000) argues that those who have "lower educational capital and less economic resources are particularly likely to end up in ethnically defined niches on the labor market, while better skilled immigrants are much less dependent on such niches and immigrants with some economic capital may choose between ethnic or mainstream business opportunities" (cited by Wimmer, 2007, p. 22). In other words, the educational attainment differences among Colombian and Dominican respondents described above help explain differences in income since having some college education provides access to better-paying jobs. The fact that the percentages of respondents who had a college degree or above was almost the same may help explain the small difference between Colombian and Dominican respondents earning above $40,000.

Table 16. Respondent's Personal Gross Income in 1998

Personal Gross Income	Colombians	Dominicans
Less than $12,000	44.4 %	43.6 %
$12,000 – 19,000	14.6 %	18.7 %
$20,000 - 29,000	10.4 %	16.0 %
$30,000 - 39,000	20.8 %	12.7 %
$40,000 and above	9.8 %	9.0 %

The pattern of educational attainment among Colombian and Dominican respondents indicates Dominican respondents achieved lower levels of educational attainment (see table 17). It is important to highlight that the greatest variance is concentrated at the level of having 'less than high school' and at the mid-range level of 'some college or vocational school.' Dominican respondents were twice as likely to not have graduated high school compared with Colombians. It is troublesome that the educational system of a global city, like New York City, would produce a cohort of young adults where 17.6% percent report having less than a high school education. However, the more striking difference between the two groups was that more than half of Colombian respondents (61.7%) were enrolled in college or had some college experience compared to less than half of Dominican respondents (46.8%). However, Colombians and Dominicans achieved equally at the higher levels of educational attainment by graduating from a 4-year college or pursuing graduate education. Despite enrolling in college at greater levels, Colombians were as likely as Dominicans to have a 4-year college degree and to have some graduate education. Among the general Latino/Hispanic population of New York City, 25 years of age and older, Dominicans had lower high school and college completion rates, 60% and 13% compared to Colombians with 78% and 24% respectively in 2010 (Bergad, 2011)

Table 17. Respondent's Level of Education

Level of Education	Colombians	Dominicans
Less than High School	8.4 %	17.6 %
Graduated High School or GED	13.2 %	19.6 %
Some College or Vocational School	61.7 %	46.8 %
4-year College	14.4 %	12.5 %
Some Graduate School	2.4 %	3.6 %

In her work with second generation Italian young adults in Germany, Kirsten (2007) concluded that ethnic differences in achievement disappeared once educational and social class origins were taking into account. If current income levels of respondents are connected to their educational attainment levels, it is appropriate to inquire about the variables and life circumstances that influenced respondents' academic decisions to stay in school and eventually apply to college. To answer these questions, I explored the quantitative data for differences among respondents that related to their personal experiences with schools. I then turn to the qualitative interviews to understand the processes and meaning making behind the decisions made by respondents.

CHOOSING A NEIGHBORHOOD

Quality of Schools

The most important variables in facilitating high school graduation and college enrollment were quality of schools attended by respondents, their immigrant parents' cultural capital, and transnational social network which may be viewed as transnational social class. As (Weininger & Lareau, 2007) emphasize, despite the fact that cultural capital is acquired in the home and the school via exposure to a given set of cultural practices – and therefore has a social origin –, it is liable to be perceived as inborn 'talent' and its holder as 'gifted' as a result of the fact that it is embodied in particular individuals. Moreover, because the school system transforms "inherited" cultural capital into "scholastic" cultural capital the latter is predisposed to appear as an individual "achievement" (2007, p. 2).

According to the survey data, Colombian respondents were more likely to have attended some higher performing schools in New York City than Dominican respondents. At least 24.3% of Colombian respondents attended a high-performing school compared to only 6.6% of Dominican respondents. On the other hand, Dominican respondents (29.2%) were more likely than Colombian respondents (3.9%) to have attended a low performing school (see table 20). Given the system of funds allocation used by New York City, quality of schools is closely tied to neighborhood real estate values and the income of neighborhood residents (Fine, 1991; E. Lee & Burkam, 2002; Li, 2010; C. Suárez-Orozco & M. M. Suárez-Orozco, 2001). According to the 2008 American Community Survey, Colombians in New York City were more likely to live in housing units they owed (34%) than Dominicans (18.1%) which might suggest higher access to better funded schools for Colombians (U.S. Census Bureau, American Community Survey, 2009a). In her ethnography about students who decided to leave or stay in high school, Michelle Fine pointed out how "low-income students disproportionately attend dropout-prone schools."(1991, p. 23) For that reason, the likelihood of having access to quality schools is intimately tied to the neighborhood where a child's family lives. With some exemptions, most children in New York City are enrolled in zoned schools determined by their home address.

Table 18. Quality of High Schools (according to quartiles) Attended by Respondents

Quality of school (Quartiles)	Colombians	Dominicans
Highest Performing	24.3 %	6.6 %
Above Average	20.4 %	15.6 %
Average	23.3 %	19.8 %
Below Average	28.2 %	28.8 %
Lowest Performing	3.9 %	29.2 %

Table 19. Quality of Schools Respondents Attended by Borough

Quality of School (Quartiles)	Bronx	Brooklyn	Manhattan	Queens	NJ Metro
Highest Performing	2.4 %	19.0 %	14.3 %	59.5 %	-
Above Average	8.2 %	36.1 %	11.5 %	44.3 %	-
Average	9.3 %	26.7 %	10.7 %	53.3 %	-
Below Average	11.7 %	5.8 %	23.3 %	59.2 %	-
Lowest Performing	32.9 %	17.7 %	40.5 %	7.6 %	1.3 %

The distribution of quality of schools in each of the five New York City boroughs is not equal. Therefore, it is not surprising to find that some neighborhoods and boroughs have a higher share of low performing schools while others have a greater share of high performing schools (see table 19). In this case, high performing schools (59.5%) and above average schools (44.3%) were overly represented in Queens while the lowest performing schools were highly concentrated in the Bronx (32.9%) and Manhattan (40.5%). Respondents were affected by their parents' decision to live in a specific neighborhood. Ironically, for many immigrant parents choosing a neighborhood to live is not much of a choice at all. Many immigrants are forced to live in neighborhoods where rents are cheap and close to possible jobs. Since ethnic enclaves and ethnic social networks are usually the primary source of jobs and information for new immigrants (Kasinitz et al., 2008), opportunities for the children of immigrants are restricted to the neighborhood resources and conditions available where their ethnic enclaves have flourished.

Parents' Cultural Capital

Residential segregation and structural racism channel and determine what inmigrant communities would be accepted or not in particular neighborhoods. Dominicans with lower incomes and darker skin-tones seemed to find themselves living side by side with Puerto Ricans and African-Americans in neighborhoods characterized by socio-economic disinvestment while other light skinned Latin American immigrants have made their way into more working and middle class neighborhoods (Kasinitz et al., 2008). A number of researchers have pointed out that "[a]lthough differences in language and customs diminish over generations, phenotypical (racial) differences do not. Visibility, or identifiability, is clearly a factor in discrimination, as well as in the maintenance of ethnic identity." (Phinney, 2002, p. 76)

At the time the survey was conducted, Jackson Heights and East Elmhurst, middle class neighborhoods in Queens were, and still are, home to the largest Colombian community in New York City (Bergad, 2011). Dominicans have settled in large numbers in Washington Heights in Manhattan which was home to the largest concentration of Dominicans in the city followed by the South and Western part of the Bronx and the Greenpoint area of Brooklyn (Aparicio, 2006; Grasmuck & Pessar, 1991; Kasinitz et al., 2008). However, as of 2011, the Bronx has become the borough with the largest share of Dominican residents (Bergad, 2009, 2011). Therefore, Dominican respondents were more likely to find themselves attending a poorer performing school than Colombian respondents simply because of their residential patterns. As table 3 shows, the majority of Colombian respondents (72.9%) lived in Queens while Dominicans were distributed about the city with the largest concentrations in Manhattan (28.5%), Brooklyn (22.4%) and the Bronx (17.6%). In general, the schools Colombians attended were much better than the schools Dominican respondents had access to.

Kasinitz and colleagues (2008) pointed out Dominicans with more socio-economic resources actually chose to live in the Latin American neighborhoods of Queens. If we consider rent prices a proxy of neighborhood quality, it can be said that Colombian respondents lived in better neighborhoods than Dominican respondents. In fact, Dominicans median gross rent payments ($924) were less than the median gross rent paid ($1,114) by Colombians (U.S. Census Bureau, American Community Survey, 2009a). They also observed that "although [Queens] neighborhoods are run down by suburban standards, they actually afford access to decent schools and have less crime than poor inner city neighborhoods" (Kasinitz et al., 2008, p. 30). Most respondents had spent most of their school years living in the same neighborhood and a few had moved a number of times.

Understanding social class as the combination of economic and cultural capital allows us to examine the effects of immigrants' and their children's social class as they integrate into their adopted country of residence, in this case the United States and, more precisely, New York City. Professional immigrants encounter difficulties in utilizing their skills and credentials as new immigrants in the United States. Latin American immigrants in the United States, as all non-English speaking immigrants, have the added difficulty of encountering a different language they must master in order to substantiate their education and credentials. Some educated immigrants may find it difficult to substantiate their education and learn a new language, and must turn to less-skilled jobs with relatively low wages. These factors could lead to the mistaken conclusion that migration evens out economic inequalities among immigrants by putting everyone in the same socio-economic position regardless of their pre-migration social class and socio-economic status.

Initially, the quantitative data suggested that, despite having similar family income levels in New York City while growing up, Colombian and Dominican respondents' families differed in their cultural capital and how they made use of it. Both Dominican and Colombian immigrant parents with higher cultural capital in the form of higher educational attainment levels were able to recapture some social mobility and access to more resources to ensure opportunities for their children to succeed than immigrant parents who had lower levels of education, despite great sacrifices and hopes. One important way in which they deployed their transnational cultural capital relates to how they navigated the residential landscape and the educational system in New York City. They effectively tapped into a reality denounced by Bourdieu where,

> Modern systems of schooling are far more adept at validating and augmenting cultural capital inherited from the family than are at instilling it in children who enter the institution with few or none of the requisite dispositions and skills... the educational systems of modern societies tend to channel individuals class destinations that largely (but not wholly) mirror their class origins. (Weininger & Lareau, 2007, p. 2)

An analysis of variables that influenced educational attainment among children of immigrants in the original study, (Kasinitz et.al 2008) demonstrated that parental level of education was the single strongest predictor after controlling for ethnic group, age, gender, parents home composition, number of siblings and times they have moved from one neighborhood to another between ages 6-18. Other researchers have documented a strong relationship between the educational level of immigrant parents and their children's educational attainment levels (van Ours & Veenman, 2001; Rothon, Heath, & Lessard-Phillips, 2009) even as they move to college (Lareau & Weininger, 2008). Van Ours & Veenman (2001) found that even though children of immigrants from Turkey, Morocco, Surinam, and Dutch Antilles in the Netherlands had higher levels of education than their parents, lower levels of parental education had an adverse effect on the likelihood of their children being enrolled in a curriculum track geared towards university attendance.

Unfortunately, Dominican respondents were in a more disadvantaged position than their Colombian counterparts simply because fewer Dominican parents were in a position to capitalize on their transnational cultural capital. Almost half of the Dominican immigrant parents were reported to have less than a high school education compared to Colombian immigrant parents (see table 20). The percentage of Dominicans (40%) and Colombians (22%) above the age of 25 who did not graduate from high school according to the 2010 census were quite similar to the rates of high school non-completion rates of respondents' parents (Bergad, 2011). Bergad (2009) suggests that the low level of high school completion among Dominicans were linked to large share of foreign born (89%) among the population 25 years of age and older. According to the phone survey, the parents of Colombian respondents in general graduated from high school in greater numbers (36% of mothers, 35.9% of fathers) than the parents of Dominican respondents (21.2% of mothers, 27.4% of fathers). Another point worth mentioning is that Dominican immigrant mothers had relatively lower educational levels compared to their partners than did Colombian immigrant mothers.

Table 20. Level of Education of Respondents' Parents

Level of Education	Colombians		Dominicans	
	Mother	Father	Mother	Father
Less than High School	30.0 %	27.5 %	51.3 %	44.9 %
Graduated High School or GED	36.0 %	35.9 %	25.2 %	27.4 %
Some college or vocational school	17.3 %	16.8 %	17.7 %	14.0 %
Graduate College (BA)	10.7 %	13.7 %	5.2 %	10.6 %
More than BA	6.0 %	6.1 %	0.6 %	3.1 %

The fact that the parents of Dominican respondents have lower levels of high school graduation than the parents of Colombian respondents may be linked to a number of social, political, and economic differences between Colombia and the Dominican Republic. My findings suggest that Dominican respondents were not doing as well as Colombian respondents because Dominican immigrant parents were more likely to have migrated from rural areas or small towns in the Dominican Republic than Colombian immigrant parents. Wimmer (2007) proposes that un-skilled immigrants are likely to find it hard to leave ethnic enclaves given that they are less likely to find jobs outside ethnic labor market niches, in fact limiting their chances of affording to live in neighborhoods with better school districts.

In addition, having a rural background would be associated with lower cultural capital available to navigate life in New York City and its school system. Not only are these immigrants adjusting to life in a different country, but they would also be adjusting to urban life in general. As indicated previously, United States' visa requirements and procedures for Colombian citizens made it almost impossible for rural migrants to enter the United States unless they crossed the border undocumented. Less restrictive visa and immigration policies towards the Dominican Republic, especially before the 1990s, made it possible for rural workers and migrants to enter and settle in the United States. Therefore, one largely understudied variable affecting children of immigrants' achievement is whether their parents come from urban or rural backgrounds.

The effect of social class before migration lingered as transnational cultural capital among immigrant parents and communities. As Scahill remarks, "[c]lass habitus is, of course, a collective phenomena reflecting group adaptations and adjustments to historical necessity and struggles won and lost" (1993, p. n.p.). Although immigrant parents have high expectations for their children, these usually involve achieving a higher level of education than their parents' and some degree of social mobility. However, these expectations are relative to parents' cultural capital: if a parent did not finish high school, graduating from high school is already an achievement beyond their own; while a parent who graduated from college would probably expect no less than a college education for her/his children. Parents who come from rural areas may underestimate the need of having a college degree to secure descent jobs. Beyond that, they simply would not have the skills and knowledge necessary to navigate an intricate system that reproduces social class inequalities instead of challenging them (Li, 2010). "The Dominicans and South Americans had more limited information. Parents were often not aware of the specialized high schools or did not realize that the quality of early schooling might make a big difference for their children's future" (Kasinitz et al., 2008, p. 153).

Despite disadvantaged and difficult circumstances, parents with more transnational cultural capital used a number of strategies to offset their lack of economic resources and ensure their children had access to descent schools. At least in one case, a Colombian respondent explained how his parents decided to live in a public housing project in Queens, so they could afford to send him to Catholic school from first grade through high school. Colombian parents and some Dominican parents actually sacrificed space and luxuries in order to be able to live in a good neighborhood with better schools. It was not strange for Colombian families to have parents sleeping in the living room because they could only afford a smaller size apartment rather than move to a "poor" or "bad" neighborhood often times associated with racial and residential segregation patterns. Racism and discrimination on the part of Colombian parents were directed towards African-Americans and Latino groups who were stereotyped as 'poor' and 'uneducated', such as Puerto Ricans, Mexicans, and Dominicans. Many Colombian parents associated neighborhoods with a high concentration of individuals of African ancestry with higher levels of violence and poverty which they actively avoided. In the following excerpt, Lina described how it was more important for her parents to live in a "good" neighborhood than have a bigger apartment.

I: Oh gosh, wow. So, you stayed there, until you were, until you moved to this apartment now?

Lina: We lived there until 1987, and then they bought the apartment that I live in now, which was a little bit better but it was also small, because it was only a one-bedroom apartment.

I: Oh, gosh.

Lina: Yeah. Like, we always lived in small areas, because they didn't want to live in a bad neighborhood, where they can afford to live in a bigger apartment or a house or whatever.

I: Right, exactly.

Lina: So, they just always felt that they would compromise space for a good neighborhood.

I: Wow. So, where did you sleep? Did you sleep like in the living room?

Lina: Well, fortunately, they always gave me the bedroom. So, I had the bedroom when we were in the one-bedroom, and then they would sleep in the living room.

I: Right. Wow. Gosh.

Lina: But it was very uncomfortable. Because normally you know, you want to have your friends over. And it's like your visit would always be in the bedroom. (Colombian, 34 years old)

TAKING ONE'S PLACE IN SOCIETY - GRADUATING FROM HIGH SCHOOL OR NOT? COLLEGE?

Deciding to stay in high school or to leave is an important decision that children of immigrants make every day. In doing so, adolescents and young adults are exercising their limited agency and freedom in the midst of social and economically adverse conditions. Unfortunately, the fact remains that those who are most critical of the system, challenge it – however counterproductive it may be –, and are more keen to unequal school and labor market arrangements in their lives, abandoning the system and in a way, further limiting their situations. Socio-economically disadvantaged students are adept at reading a school culture that does not hold high expectations for them (Daiute & Fine, 2003; Fallis & Opotow, 2003) and often times search for meaning and satisfaction in other spheres such as the job market and the family where they may feel fully valued. Making it to their high school graduation or not, is intrinsically tied to the intersection of social class, race, gender, and sexuality. Cutting class and pregnancies were precursors to leaving high school and not pursuing college educations which were particularly salient among this group of respondents. Colombian respondents were more likely to obtain a high school degree and move on to a college education. Colombian respondents had the advantage of attending much better schools than did Dominican respondents. Dominican respondents made it to college in fewer numbers and were more likely to leave high school to find jobs and to become teen mothers. Sadly, the reality for these young Colombian and Dominican respondents was not different than that described by Michelle Fine almost two decades ago:

> Older children and only children, children of Puerto Rican [and Dominican] parents, children raised by grandmothers, and children who were poor were fine candidates for dropping out of high school. Inversely, younger children, those not from the United States [with fewer siblings and more educated parents]... and those with fathers residing at home (a synonym for *additional income*) were more likely to graduate. Public high schools may 'work' relatively well for the children of [educated immigrants] and for the younger children of America's poor. Today, however, urban poverty means that the oldest child in a family will unlikely make it to twelfth grade. (Fine, 1991, p. 133)

School (Dis)Engagement – Schools Failing Poor Children

Cutting class to hang out with friends is a behavior that is usually associated with truancy and school absenteeism. A number of researchers have connected truancy and cutting class with increased high school dropout rates and risk for substance abuse and school violence (for a review of relevant studies see Puzzanchera, 2000). A disturbingly high number of these studies classify 'cutting class' as a behavioral indicator of violent and criminal potential and its "treatment" usually revolves around school punitive policies (Fine, 1991; Nishino et al., 2009; Puzzanchera, 2000), rather than considering strategies to engage and motivate disengaged students through extra-curricular activities, creative pedagogies, culturally and socially relevant curriculum (Fallis & Opotow, 2003). Boredom, lack of inspiring teachers and curriculum are the most common reasons listed by students for 'cutting class' and 'playing hooky'(Webster & E. Ayala, 2006), including Colombian and Dominican respondents in this study.

Jessica, a Dominican girl, described why she cut class and what her mom's reaction was. Her story reveals the criminal justice approach that many inner-city high schools have taken to deal with students' absences and school disengagement. There were serious consequences as her mother pointed out. Jessica was scared. However, she was not scared into going back to school. Rather the 'truancy policies' were successful in getting Jessica off of the streets and into her home but not back to school.

I: So you told us that—we'll go to high school now—you said you went to Samuel Gumpers?

Jessica: Yeah, 7th Boulevard. It looked *like a jail* on the outside. It was surrounded by *factories, a funeral* home, some stores down the block.

[…]

I: So that's what you did in junior high school when you cut?

Jessica: Yeah, if we weren't there we were at each other's houses, watching TV.

I: So why did you cut in junior high school?

Jessica: Because it was boring. I would wake up, you know, we'd be on the bus and we just wouldn't feel like going. We'd get off the bus near Yankee Stadium, go to the handball courts, then get back on the train. That was when the *truant patrol* wasn't as strong as it is now, I mean, I got caught in the ninth grade by the *truant patrol*, and I didn't play hooky after that. If I was, I didn't leave my house.

I: How did your mother feel about that?

Jessica: When I got home—… And I got home, I start crying, I don't know why, I guess to make it seem like I felt bad when I was really made that I got caught, and my mother, she finished all my sentences for me. I said, "Mommy," she said, "you cut," I said, "yeah," she said, "you got caught by the *truant patrol*," I said "yeah." She said she didn't punish me because the scare was enough, which is true. I didn't go to any other school after that; if I played hooky I just stayed at home or went to somebody's house in my neighborhood, I didn't leave my block.

[...]

I: But how about after that? Did you play hooky again?

Jessica: Oh yeah, I don't know if you'd call it playing hooky, I just didn't go. I woke up in the morning, I was ready—I was always the last one to leave my house—and I just wouldn't go. (Dominican, 21 years old, emphasis added)

Most Colombian respondents said that they did not really cut class because they couldn't or did not really think of it. Colombian respondents were fortunate to attend better and best performing schools where they were likely to find learning environments much more engaging than in the poorly performing schools attended by Dominican respondents. Students attending Catholic schools found it harder to get away from school in general. Whether Catholic schools were more engaging or simply stricter is difficult to determine. In Anibal's case (below), even though he cut class, he was not able to leave the building and found himself in detention most of the time. It's interesting that he seemed to have developed a trusting relationship with the person in charge of his detention which perhaps he lacked from his teachers.

I: Did you sometimes cut class?

Anibal: Naw. Cut class in the sense that my mother didn't know, no. Because if I did that, Catholic school they'll call up your parent right away. "Why isn't he here." And I already had enough detention so I had at one point three indefinite detention and another 65 to serve after they told me that those three indefinites went away. So I had detention... I was a lifer in detention. Forget about it. I stayed in detention. I don't know if you was in detention much but you know when you're in detention so often that you get to know

> the person who is holding detention, that they just ask you run errands for them because they know you ain't going nowhere and they know you got to come back. The next day or whatever. So that was me. They used to send me on errands after school. "Here go do this. Take this down to the athletic office." "Alright." Everybody looking at me like, "Damn, why you not in detention?" "I'm here for life. I've been here too long. I put in my time." (Dominican, 28 years old)

Anibal's experiences (above) contrast sharply with those of Jacqueline (below). Most of all, Jacqueline's sense of agency and purpose permeates the text. She was extremely skilled and determined to find the right place for herself. What is lacking in her narrative are her parents and their role in the whole process. One definitely gets the feeling that she was not lost in the background at school and that she felt it was a demanding program with high expectations for her, "making it to the Westinghouse Competition", all important factors in avoiding teenage pregnancy and leaving school (Plotnick, 1992 cited by Kasinitz et al., 2008).

I: In fourth grade you were in Honors? How did you feel about that?

Jacqueline: I liked it. I liked it.

I: What happened in high school?

Jacqueline: I was still in Honors in high school, but what happened was they don't really have - when I applied to high schools, I didn't know where to go so I applied to a school in Forest Hills. I don't know if you know the schools there. But I didn't get in because it was a computer lottery. So I didn't get in there, so I decided to take the test for Special Ed schools, Stuyvesant, Brooklyn Tech, and I took it and I passed it. When I went to see

> Stuyvesant, I felt very out of place. Everyone I saw taking the test was Asian. Every One. And I mean coming from the junior high school where it was Hispanic. I mean, it shouldn't have been an issue but it was. I was looking around, I was -I'm not gonna fit in here. It was my first time - I mean, everything I had done up until then was in Queens, taking the train all the way to Manhattan, downtown, was like a new thing. So I decided not to go there. So I applied to another school, to Van Buren which is in Queens Village, just by chance, and the reason I applied and went there was because they offered me what they call a scholar's institute which is a new program they were piloting. That was the first year that they did it. They took like about sixty or eighty kids and they made a whole new program called New Curriculum. We didn't have lunch period. They put us - *they were training us for the Westinghouse Competition.* It was all AP classes, Regents, so it was very hard. I really didn't enjoy it because we were there until 9th period. Class after class. (Colombian, 27 years old, emphasis added)

Embodying consequences – Learning to Love and Care

Even though both, young girls and boys, were equally affected by poor teacher expectations and lack of engaging and relevant curricula, the consequences of cutting class were radically different for both. While boys found themselves labeled as 'truants' and 'behavioral problems', girls likely found themselves experimenting with relationships and bearing their consequences, immersed in life all too soon. Again poor, older children, with absent fathers were most likely to get pregnant before finishing high school. McLanahan's (2001) analysis of the connection between single-parenthood and teenage pregnancy adds a gendered perspective on achieving high school graduation or not (cited by Kasinitz et al., 2008, p. 102). Regardless of race, ethnic group, gender and family characteristics, "having a child" was the largest predictor of non-graduation from high school among respondents. Only 58.8% of Dominican respondents did not have children at the time of the survey compared to 75.6% of Colombians (see table 15 and Kasinitz et al., 2008).

Poverty and poor neighborhood safety increased the potential for teenage pregnancies among Dominican young women. Dominican respondents, like Dharma (a teenage mother of 2), did not hang out in the street when they cut class, because their parents "warned" them of the dangers of being in the street. Instead, when Dominican young women cut class, they either stayed in their own houses or hung out in a friend's house in order to stay away from the streets. Being alone in a house with their boyfriends did not help reduce the risk of unwanted or unplanned pregnancies. Teenagers are eager to experiment and feel loved and valued, making sexual experimentation part of teenage life.

I: So when you got left back in the ninth grade that happened because you were cutting classes and it was absences?

Dharma: No, it was more cutting class.

[…]

I: What way were you raised? In the Dominican way?

Dharma: Yeah, I was raised in the Dominican way.

I: You were kept at home, you didn't hang out in the streets?

Dharma: Oh exactly. Now it's different. Now teenage years change. You just want to hang out with your friends. I never did that. That's why I probably ended up with kids but…

I: Explain that to me. Because the stereotype is "oh, it's the girls hanging out in the street that end up with kids." But you're saying, "I never hung out in the street."

Dharma: I never had anything to do. So… cause it's more like if you're hanging out in the street and you get pregnant, you'll probably end up having an abortion cause they like… my sister, she'll know what taking care of babies is like, so she'll be like, "I like the street so I'm not dealing with that." She knows. So, if you have the experience, you'll be better off.

I: Which experience?

Dharma: Like I never had a baby experience. I never saw one of my friend raise a baby or it just `happened. See, now my sister is going through this. She takes care of my kids when I go to school sometimes at night. And she'll be like, "Ah huh, I'm not having babies now because I like to party." See, if you like to party you can't have babies because who's going to take care of them? (Dominican, 18 years old)

Lack of experience and knowledge about sexual education, pregnancy, and parenthood places teenagers at a disadvantage. As the oldest child, Dharma felt she did not have the advantage of seeing someone deal with having a child as a teenager. She seemed to think that if she had known how hard it would be and how many things she would have to give up, she would have done things differently. Respondents who became pregnant as teenagers were more likely to have a second child within the following two years further hampering their chances of continuing their education. Dharma herself had her first child at sixteen and a second child at eighteen. Among female respondents, those who were teenage mothers were also more likely to still be in a relationship with their high school boyfriend, now a husband or partner, than those who had children after high school.

I: How did having a child affect your life?

Yadira: Depressing.

I: Why? Or how?

Yadira: How? Because it wasn't planned, and--I don't regret having him, I enjoy my kids--but it wasn't something that I wanted, both of them. They're there because of my mom, so that sometimes brings me down, because I probably would have been somewhere else, somewhere further in life, and right now I'm pretty stuck. (Dominican, 24 years old)

Among the interviewees, Colombian women more often discussed having parents who were strict and had more rules about dating and school. Their parents did not allow them to bring their boyfriends into their rooms. Usually, their boyfriends were expected to meet the parents and wait in the living room. Colombian young women expressed having fewer opportunities to cut class and when they did, their parents had knowledge of it. The following excerpt illustrates how Colombian parents exerted control over their daughters' behavior.

I: And you don't have any kids, right. Let me ask you, do you think Colombian or Hispanic families in general have a different way - the ones here in the United States have a different way of raising kids than other Americans?

Stephanie: Yes. (I: - what are the differences?) It goes back to why I moved out of my parents' house. Very strict. Very strict. I was the only one who was twenty two years old and had a curfew among anyone that I knew. Very very strict. I have to be very proper at all times, you know, if some poor guy had the unfortunate event - have to go meet me at my house, he'd have to come in, go into the living room, couldn't go anywhere near my room, couldn't go anywhere in there and had to sit in the living room and wait while my father and my brother, sometimes, when my brother got older, both of them watching and staring at him, and my mother served him soda or whatever, watching Oh! There's no doubt. It's like growing apples in the banana fields. It really is. The method of raising is very different.

[...]

I: Did you ever cut class?

Stephanie: No, I never had the guts to cut class. I think on occasion, maybe one or two times in my entire school career, not counting college, in my entire school career I think I cut maybe like half a class. I showed up like half an hour late when the class was half done, and said 'I got caught up in this,' that was my way of cutting class. I was petrified they'd call my parents. (Colombian, 32 years old)

Even if the women graduated from high school without getting pregnant, postponing pregnancy was the best way to increase their chances of completing college. In fact, how far young female respondents took their education was intimately tied to whether they had children or not. Having children at any age represents a drain on economic and emotional resources making it extremely hard, if not impossible, for young adults to manage college as well as raising a family. This did not mean that respondents who had children of their own abandoned aspirations to further their education but it did mean those aspirations had to be postponed indefinitely. Many hoped that once their children were older, they would be able to return to school. Claudia and Sharina were well aware of the implications that pregnancies had for their own and their friends' educational aspirations.

I: Have you been enrolled since you graduated from BMCC or thought about going back to school?

Claudia: Oh yeah, I'm definitely going back but I'm waiting for my fiancé to finish his Masters.

I: He's gonna finish his Masters and then you'll go back. What is he getting it in?

Claudia: Same program.

[…]

I: You got the degree and everything?

Claudia: Yep. It took me a long time, 'cause I got pregnant with my son, so I had to stop and then go back part- time. (Dominican, 25 years old)

And Sharina's response:

I: What order are most of your friends doing?

Sharina: It varies because my friends that are currently in college with me, it's the same thing. Either you go to school full time, work part time or some of them don't work at all and they are just continuing their education. They are not likely to get married. One of them did get married and had a baby and she is still going to college. A lot of my girlfriends from high school came out pregnant so their whole steps are way different. First they had the baby. They are still not married. But now they are working and going to school. Working first and then trying to go to school part time. (Dominican, 18 years old)

MARRIAGE AS RITE OF INCORPORATION – PARENTS AND CHILDREN NEGOTIATING (TRANS)NATIONAL SOCIAL, RACIAL AND CLASS HIERARCHIES

Although the concept of 'rites of passage' (Van Gennep, 1977) has mainly remained within anthropological realms, it seems to be useful in theorizing what might be occurring at the intersection of race, class, ethnicity/race when immigrant parents and their children are considering the prospective marriage scenarios for their children. In his theorizing, Van Gennep (1977) insisted that transition periods in individuals' development do not occur in a vacuum. Development transitions in the life course of a person are intrinsically interconnected to significant others and family members. These transition periods, such as childhood, adolescence, adulthood, marriage, having children, passing away, are events that are bound to involve others and in the process will reinforce or re-evaluate a persons' worldview and the social place they hold within that particular social group. (Stewart & Healy, 1989)

Marriage would be considered a rite of incorporation where at least one individual leaves physically (or symbolically), her/his family/social group and enters into the partner's family/social group. Research on immigrants racial prejudices and stereotypes have mostly focused on how they affect individuals' intergroup and cross-racial contact, (S. C. Miller, Olson, & Fazio, 2004), as well as, to what extent are adolescent cross-cultural and cross-racial relationships affected by their parents' racial attitudes (Edmonds & Killen, 2009; Edmonds, 2006). However, studies that investigate how marriage decisions are affected by parents' racial attitudes, especially attitudes of immigrant parents, are almost nonexistent. A search of PsycInfo database yielded only two references (1 journal article & 1 dissertation) out of the first 100 hits, that looked at parental racial attitudes and their effects on their children's cross-racial relationships, focusing on contact and intimacy (Edmonds & Killen, 2009; Edmonds, 2006).

An important finding in this study is that immigrant parents, regardless of national origin, do hold racial prejudices that extend to their own national/ethnic/racial group. Despite the hegemonic discourse of *mestizaje* that circulates in Latin America, and among Latin American and Latinos/as in the United States, there is a racial hierarchy deeply enmeshed with social class to the point of masquerading as mere social class differences. Recent research has theorized that Latin American ideologies of race categories fall within a "racial continuum", in contrast to the "one-drop rule" used in the United States to assign racial categories (Roth, 2004). Respondents and their parents, both Colombian and Dominican, were aware that racial dynamics in the United States differed from those in their home countries. These Dominican and Colombian young adults were quick to assert that their experiences in the United States did not fit the White nor Black/African American categories. Respondents racialized the Hispanic/Latino/Spanish category by emphasizing cultural differences in norms, values and especially child rearing practices and not necessarily skin color. Consistent with census data, Dominican respondents were more likely to identify as black and considered themselves dark-skinned than Colombian respondents.

Given the history of racism and negative stereotypes about Haitians in the Dominican Republic, skin color functioned as a heuristic cue (S. C. Miller et al., 2004) for socio-economic status among immigrant parents regardless of their own race. This suggests that even black Dominican parents have internalized the belief that dark skin color implies social and economic disadvantages. It is possible that Dominican immigrants may have appropriated racial discrimination discourses to a greater extent than Colombian immigrants. Racism against Haitians has historically been legitimatized by the Dominican government and, in the past, the state has instigated racial violence at the Haitian-Dominican border. In contrast, Colombian immigrants historically have not experienced in Colombia the level of racial violence and overt discrimination exercised by Dominicans towards Haitians in the Dominican Republic. Racial attitudes among Colombians have largely been theorized as economic and cultural capital differences which still allow skin color to function as a heuristic cue of socio-economic status.

Both Colombian and Dominican respondents disagreed with their parents' racial attitudes and did not feel that it affected their own decisions about who they dated or befriended. Cross-racial dating, although not common, was not an issue for them but more the result of physical proximity and residential segregation patterns. For example, Dominicans were more likely to have dated African-Americans or Puerto Ricans, and Colombians were more likely to have dated other Latinos including Puerto Ricans or Whites. Both Colombian and Dominican respondents reported that their parents had made it known to them that dating African-Americans was not acceptable and highly discouraged respondents from dating or marrying someone darker than themselves. In this young woman's story, the abuse described seemed to have been attributed to having violated racial and cultural boundaries.

I: Did your parents think it was important to marry someone who spoke Spanish?

Yadira: Yeah.

I: Why do you think that was important to them?

Yadira: Because they saw what I was going through with the different race.

I: Who did you date?

Yadira: My son's father is African-American, and I had a difficult...

I: __________

Yadira: _______They had their reasons. I was abused.

I: Physically?

Yadira: Yes.

I: So they basically didn't like him because he was abusive, not because he was African-American?

Yadira: Well, I shouldn't say that it was racism, but they spoke on it, like, "it's not good to mix your race with... their culture, they have their own manners, their own," you know, but I didn't see it like that back then. (Dominican, 24 years old)

As Jacqueline explains (below), her parents had concrete ideas about who was not 'marriage material'. This young woman identified Puerto Ricans, Dominicans, and Mexicans as the 'taboo' race/ethnic groups to stay away from in her parents' perspective. Among Latin American immigrants in New York City, these Latino groups are perceived to be doing the worst in socio-economic status (actually they are), therefore there is a desire to differentiate oneself from them. She also highlights the importance of context and residential patterns. For Jacqueline, it would be taboo to date Puerto Ricans or Dominicans who are most visibly at the bottom of the socio-economic ladder among Latinos in New York City. On the other hand, for her cousin what would be problematic is to date Mexicans who are at the bottom of the Latino racial/ethnic hierarchy in Texas.

I: Did your parents ever express expectations about the type of person you should marry or whether you should marry?

Jacqueline: Yeah, Hispanic. I'm sure your mom did too. (Laugh)

I: General Hispanic or Colombian or -

Jacqueline: They never specified but I think, I always think Colombian would be great. Actually they did, they did. They never said 'Colombian' but they did say not this, not that.

I: Can you tell me about the 'not this, not that.'

Jacqueline: Yeah. Not Puerto Rican, not Dominican, that was about it 'cause that's usually what you see around here. I'm sure they told my cousin in Texas, not Mexicans.

I: Did they ever talk about skin color?

Jacqueline: Yeah. They really preferred the lighter shades.

I: Lighter shades meaning Colombian?

Jacqueline: In general.

I: Was it important that the person spoke Spanish?

Jacqueline: Yeah. They preferred it, just because it was easier for them to communicate. (Colombian, 27 years old)

Gender played an important role in the negotiation of marriage and race. Fathers were more likely to have stronger opinions about the race of possible husbands than did respondents' mothers. This was so even when the father himself was dark-skinned and had married a white Dominican woman. It seemed that previous difficult experiences of rejection and negative reactions towards their own cross-racial marriage, did not dissuade immigrant parents from following the cultural script about race. As might be expected, patriarchal family dynamics were focused on exerting control over the daughters' dating patterns, rather than the son's. All over the world, women are still viewed as guardians of culture and family honor (Pettigrew, 2006). This held true for both Colombian and Dominican female respondents. From this perspective, cross-racial/cultural friendship need not pose a threat to the family social position and stability, yet dating and to that extent considering cross-racial/cultural marriage, would represent a family threat. This young Colombian woman believed that her parents would tolerate racially diverse friendships, but not for a serious relationship.

Lina: They can be a little prejudiced.

I: Ok. But was it- Do you know if it was- Could you explain that a little more? Like, what would they say?

Lina: I guess they wouldn't be too happy if I ever brought home a black guy. [laughter]

I: [laughter] Ok. How about friends, could you have black friends, would they still be…

Lina: Yeah, they were ok.

I: But they're worried if you got into a-

Lina: A relationship, yeah.

I: Ok. A serious relationship.

Lina: Yeah. (Colombian, 34 years old)

Young adult men received different reactions from their parents. Apparently, parents were not as worried about their sons marrying black Latino women although they repeatedly preferred 'lighter' skin tones. However, their girlfriends' parents did not allow their daughters to consider Dominican young men as potential partners. As Anibal relates, race was not the only factor against them. Dominican men were perceived to be more patriarchal and 'machista' than other Latino men. This was mentioned both by Dominican women and men in the study.

I: Was being Dominican ever an issue in the relationship?

Anibal: Well initially, because like I said, the stereotypes for Dominican men being womanizers or ???, you know how they say that. Usually when I meet a girl and they're like, "Oh, you're Dominican. Got to watch out for you." I'm like, "No, no, I'm not like that." I have to show them I'm different. So basically it does come up in the beginning. "Oh oh, I've got to watch out for you." And I'm like, "No, no, it's not like that."

I: How about with their parents?

Anibal: Well, I spoke to that before. Yeah, definitely, at times it was an issue. And at times the girl would stop calling me. Not that we weren't cool anymore but it's just she couldn't have that relationship. Not boyfriend/girlfriend. Friends alright, fine. But boyfriend/girlfriend is totally different.

I: Did it only happen with Puerto Ricans?

Anibal: No. White parents too. With white parents, what it was a lot of... not a lot but at times it was just a matter of just not knowing about me. And that plus the fact that I'm a man and that's their daughter so that confused them a little but it really wasn't too bad but it did happen. It's just that I didn't pay any mind to it. I just let it roll off my back. (Dominican, 28 years old)

Rosa's description of her parents' views on race and marriage (below) support findings highlighting the role of education and cultural capital in rationalizing racial prejudices and to the extent that more educated parents might able to consider other variables such as personality, level of education, socio-economic status, and avoid making decisions based solely on race categories. Miller and colleagues (2004) documented differences in the way less educated White and non-White parents rationalized their racial attitudes about whether their daughters might marry a White or a non-White partner. More educated parents were more likely to entertain other variables in making their assessments. Rosa's mother, as well as her father, migrated to the U.S. from a rural area in the Dominican Republic. Her father did not have high school education and so lower levels of education might explain their strong reactions towards considering potential dark-skinned partners for their daughter. In Rosa's context, the only options available seemed to be White, Latino or African-American men. Asian men are not mentioned as an option.

I: Did your parents express any expectations about the type of person you should marry or whether you should marry at all?

Rosa: My mother, she said if I was going to marry, marry somebody my own race, my own ethnicity rather or marry somebody white.

I: That's pretty different. (laughter) How did she explain number one and number two?

Rosa: Because she didn't want number three.

I: Which was?

Rosa: African American. That's the three choices because you can marry an African American, you can marry a Latino or you can marry a white. She says white or Latin is fine but just don't bring anybody black home.

I; And the reason being?

Rosa: My mother is racist.

I: Is she light skinned?

Rosa: No. She's a little bit lighter than me.

I: Like my complexion?

Rosa: Yes.

I: And your dad is dark skinned?

Rosa: Yeah.

I: And she says "Don't marry a dark-skinned man?"

Rosa: And so does my father.

I: Did your parents have strong opinions about whether you should date people who spoke Spanish? Was that a big issue? When you said white, I suppose it didn't matter.

Rosa: It didn't matter as long as you were light.

I: How do you feel about that?

Rosa: Well, back then and still now I believe that you should date anybody that you choose to date, based on personality and nothing else. I don't think the color of your skin really matters. The ethnicity. Of course there's differences but... (Dominican, 19 years old)

As I indicated previously, at least in one case the Colombian respondent's parents decided to live in public housing in Queens. The particular public housing was racially segregated with mostly African-American tenants. Mauricio's parents lived there to be able to send him to Catholic school from primary school through high school. This strategy yielded positive results since Mauricio had finished his bachelor's degree from a well-known university at the time of the interview. On the other hand, it created a conflicting situation. Most of Mauricio's friends and girlfriends while growing up were African-Americans. He was surrounded by African-Americans at home even if when at school it was mostly a white student body. His parents were not too happy to see him dating African-American girls and it might be assumed that their hope was that upon having a college education he would have access to a non-Black dating pool.

I: Did your mother or father ever express any expectations about the kind of person you should marry?

Mauricio: Yeah, they did actually.

I: What did they say?

Mauricio: Well, someone like me. Not Colombian or something like that but someone with an education. Someone career-minded. My dad wanted us, being that we grew up in a black neighborhood, always dating black girls and it's funny one day my younger brother come upstairs and said, "Hey, I have a girlfriend. She's black." My dad had a fit. "Why is everyone you bring up here black? Why is that?" "Well, dad, it's where we live." So he was, "Oh yeah, good point."

I: Was he upset?

Mauricio: I guess he would like to see some interest in our culture and our people or what have you. But if that wasn't available to us... If he did, I'm sure he would have done it in a humorous way but I don't think he made it a stern point like only date your kind.

I: So your parents never talked to you about you have to date a certain type of girl? Skin color?

Mauricio: No. But they did say they would like us to but it wasn't… (Colombian, 30 years old)

As an example of how racial attitudes are mediated by educational level, Sharina's grandmother, a well-educated woman, focused more on the need to find an educated husband with drive and potential for social mobility. In contrast her mother tried to sabotage any desire Sharina might had to consider a dark-skinned husband by joking about what their children would look like. This strategy was used by parents in an effort to create an image of how undesirable a cross-racial union would be. Although language and customs may change over generations, skin color remains visible (Phinney, 2002) potentially exposing future generations to discrimination and racism. It stirs fears of race mixture as undesirable and taboo. It is a hard argument to respond to since it uses guilt to dissuade young people from steering too far from the path of cultural and racial purity.

I: Did your parents ever say anything good or bad about other people based on skin tone, hair texture, facial or body characteristics?

Sharina: Yes.

I: Like what?

Sharina: Like my mother would be, "Please don't marry a guy with nappy hair because your kids are going to come out with happy hair." Or my biological father is very… he was like a white boy. Very light skinned. I mean whiter than white. He would be, "?????" And he would always tell me, "You better not marry no dark skinned dude." And I would be, "But I'm colored. I'm not white. What are you trying to tell me?" He would be, "No, you are not colored. You're just right. But don't get married with anyone dark." Comments like that.

I: Darker than you?

Sharina: Yeah. They would say, "?????" I'm like "Oh, that's great. That's so racist."

I: How do you feel about people in your ethnic group with lighter or darker skin than you?

Sharina: It doesn't really affect me. Only when I know they are Spanish, I really know that you're Spanish and you make believe that you are white. Or you make believe you are black and you be, "No, I'm not Spanish." That really offends me. Okay, obviously you think being white or black is better than being Spanish. What is up with that? I don't know. My mother was very well off in Dominican Republic so to me it's not like I came from ancestors that were bums in the street, begging for money. And that's why I'm, "I'm not Dominican. Blah, blah, blah." That's about it.

I: Did your parents, grandparents or other relatives ever discuss *mejorando la raza*?

Sharina Yes.

[...]

Sharina: My grandmother really didn't discuss it by color or who you married. She discussed it more about education, because my grandfather and her were educated and they were just smart enough to have a business. And build off their business. But she would always say, "In America you can't do that cause all the top people that have businesses are educated."

I: So it was more by education than economic status?

Sharina: Yeah, everyone else in the family would be, "You need to marry somebody with blue eyes, green eyes...." Or something. Whatever they believed was beautiful. Because I have a cousin that thinks that we need to marry black. I'm talking about super black, if the lights go off... she believes that is what beauty is. So whatever they would believe beauty is, that's what they would prefer. But my grandmother was more get an education. And she always told me, "Don't get married now. Do not get married too young. Don't listen to these people. They don't know what they are talking about to get married young." (Dominican, 18 years old)

On the other hand, some of the difficulties and questions raised by considering cross-racial/cultural marriages are all too real for young adults and their families. Marrying someone implies creating a future together and making decisions about what they want for their future children. Negotiating parenting styles and expectations is hard enough among two individuals from the same socio-economic and ethnic backgrounds, let alone reconciling different cultural ideologies about childrearing practices. And then, there is the issue of enabling communication and connection. Deciding what language children will be spoken to at home becomes an important decision. It will in part determine to what extent grandparents will be able to communicate with their grandchildren or not. Immigrant parents of children raised in the United States may already feel alienated from true intimacy with their children by virtue of language differences and experiences they may not be able to relate to, such as dealing with racism while growing up (Tummala-Narra, 2009). Respondents' parents may fear the prospect of not being able to communicate and connect deeply with their grandchildren, if their own children do not raise them within what's culturally familiar to their immigrant parents. Immigrant parents fear the uncertainty of a future they cannot control or predict.

I: Did your parents every say anything good or bad about other people based on skintone –

Andrea: Yes. My parents are racists.

I: Like what did they say?

Andrea: My father has a saying, whenever he sees somebody of African American decent that they should fill up the holes in the streets with them. That's pretty racist.

I: From what you said so far, I think you don't agree with that, basically.

Andrea: No.

I: Did your parents, grandparents or other relatives ever discuss '*Mejorando la Raza*?"

Andrea: Yes.

I: So that was something that you, even if you marry a Colombian it shouldn't be like a dark Colombian.

Andrea: Ironically enough, my mother has two sisters and they -the three of them married white men with blue eyes and blond hair. So, it's been an issue in the family, the way they expect you to go for - They Know Better Than That To Come Near Me when it comes to that, but that's not gonna be an issue.

I: Would you say that maybe when you were younger, that affected you at all, your attitude when you dated people?

Andrea: My very first boyfriend was from the Dominican Republic, and he had nappy hair and dark skin and my mom crushed me because of that. And she used to make fun of me, and she used to tell me, "I'm gonna see you with two kids, fighting with their hair to get ponytails out of them." She used to be cruel. Yeah, they were totally against it. (Colombian, 27 years old)

The need to connect through shared experiences is also present for respondents, regardless of social group. The standards of what needs to be shared in order to establish an intimate relationship varies depending on each respondent's own lived experiences. For some, language is paramount, for others it is not; for most, bicultural backgrounds are important, for others they are not. Research among adolescents documented that even if immigrant adolescents believed in cross-racial/culture and had many cross-racial/cultural friends, those relationships were not intimate relationships. Intimate relationships continued to be primarily with members of their same racial/cultural background (Edmonds & Killen, 2009). Shared experiences and the need to feel truly valued and reflected by the other seem to determine whom we really trust and make ourselves vulnerable to.

I: Did they say you should or shouldn't marry a person of Dominican background?

Anibal: No, they would love that. They'd be like, "Yeah. She's Dominican? Yeah? Marry that one." But it's not like they said only marry a Dominican.

	It's not like they said that. It's just that, that's what they would prefer, of course. That's their own culture.
I:	Do your parents think you should date or marry someone who spoke Spanish?
Anibal:	Yeah.
I:	Is that important to them?
Anibal:	Yeah, pretty important. I guess they don't want.... basically it's all like I stated before, it's just a matter of you're more comfortable with things you already know. So of course, you'd like... if someone is going to come into your family, you'd like them to be as familiar with you as possible. Have similar things in common, as much things in common as possible.
I:	What about race? Did your parents have strong opinions about that?
Anibal:	Yeah, they did. I guess they try to hold them back a little bit but it still came out towards me to try to show me whatever. It still came out a little bit. Of course, like I said they are old fashioned so of course, anyone darker they are like.....tend to shy away from. Even though we have dark people in my family. My family as it is ranges in all shades. So it's funny but yeah. (Dominican, 28 years old)

SUMMARY

This chapter explored the multiple intersections of Dominican and Colombian children of immigrants and social structures in their local, national and transnational contexts. It documented how gender, race, and social class intersected and placed Dominicans and Colombians in different life trajectories by shaping the educational, socio-economic, and political resources available to them. Despite sharing the social and psychological experience of growing up as children of immigrants, Colombians' access much better schools allowed them to entertain and pursue a wider number of possible selves and opportunities than Dominican respondents. Having attended much better schools due to residential choices, Colombian respondents were more likely to live in working and middle-class neighborhoods, graduate from high school, move on to and graduate from college, ensuring a certain level of social mobility. On the other hand, Dominican respondents lived in poorer neighborhoods, as a result of racial segregation and lower income levels, and were more likely to attend some of the lowest performing schools in the city, become alienated from school and leave or become teenage parents in effect limiting their opportunities to attend and graduate from college.

However parents' cultural capital in the form of educational attainment and social class pre-migration were instrumental in ensuring access to better opportunities for their children, like moving to neighborhoods with better schools or sending them to Catholic schools. The majority of this cohort of immigrant parents from Colombia migrated from urban areas and had higher levels of educational attainment as a result. In general, they came from higher social class backgrounds than the immigrant parents from the Dominican Republic. Dominican respondents and their parents' access to social mobility and educational opportunities were further constrained by having darker skin color than Colombians. Dominican respondents and their families were more likely to experience residential segregation and discrimination due to their darker hues. They also reported encountering racism and discrimination within their own ethnic/national origin communities and sometimes within their families. Racial discrimination was most salient in the realm of romantic relationships and marriage. Parents did not want their children to date or marry individuals darker than them. Although respondents did not agree with their parents' racial attitudes, the majority of respondents married other co-ethnics/nationals or other Latinos. They looked for partners with whom they had shared experiences of being raised within Latino/Latin American culture having immigrant parents or social proximity. Again, being able to maintain connection and cohesion within the family unit was crucial and so it was important that their partners could communicate with their parents and be willing to embrace their culture. Finally the following chapter provides some conclusions and discusses implications of the findings for practice and theory.

CHAPTER 6

Conclusions and Discussion

> … we are concerned with possibility, with opening windows on alternative realities,
> with moving through doorways into spaces some of us have never seen before…
> we are interested in breakthroughs and new beginnings,
> in the kind of wide-awakeness that allows for wonder and unease and questioning and the pursuit of what is not yet.
> (Greene, 2001, p. 44)

> Thus the writer embraces story and memory as an act of restitution to all those stories and memory expelled from official history, a dangerous and fertile *embrace* that releases repressed or forgotten human energies.
> (Mignolo, 2000, p. 25 emphasis added)

In an effort to present some concluding remarks, I want to take you to the spaces and theories that inspired and helped frame my analysis and writing of this book. In order to ponder the conclusions and implications that can be derived from this study, I feel the need to engage with you in closing the *escenario* (stage) as Cuban ethnologist and writer, Fernando Ortíz, would call it (Davies, 2000). Understanding what was behind the expressions "in-betweenness", "here and there, and nowhere", was at the heart of taking on the challenge to explore what it meant psychologically to live in those "in-between" and "here and there, and nowhere" spaces. In the beginning, it seemed to me that respondents and even scholars were at a loss for words or concepts that could capture the essence of that psychological space "in-between". My own thinking about it changed dramatically when I encountered Holloway's thesis about identity and the world of "doing":

> If the world is looked at from the point of view of doing, it is clearly impossible to say 'the world is,' or 'things are,' or 'I am'. From the perspective of doing, it is clear that everything is in movement. The world is and is not, things are and are and are not, I am and I am not. The contradiction that is inherent in these statements presents no problems if we think in terms of doing: in doing I go beyond myself, the world moves beyond itself, and so on. The change in me that is implied in my doing means that I am and I am not. But once the doing is broken, once the doing is subordinated to the done, movement is halted and the statement that I am and I am not seems incoherent. Once doing is ruptured, it is no longer doing and contradiction that prevail. Identity rules, contradiction is flattened. The world is, that's the way things are: if we say 'the world is and is not; that's the way things are and are not,' these now seem meaningless, illogical statements. (Holloway, 2002, p.57)

Then, conceptualizing identity in a way that does not reduce it to "power-over" and re-instates participants' experiences into a taxonomy of identity meant adopting the language of "doing" to make explicit that things, feelings, experiences, perceptions, and stories occurred in specific times and spaces which are constantly changing. It emphasized the fluidity and dynamism inherent in any process of identification or identity negotiation among individuals and groups. This socio-psychological approach emerges as an important psychological contribution to the migration literature.

Looking at phenomena as "doing" liberated me from the need to flatten statements such as, "Because I'm neither Gringa nor Latina, because I am not any one thing," and take them for what they were; moments of resistance to adhere to an identity discourse that subordinates and pathologizes difference and Otherness. I began to see in these statements as a bold desire to subvert the categories imposed by society and hold on to the wholeness of their experiences regardless of outside forces. I understood that "It is when the flow of doing is fractured that power-to is transformed into its opposite, power-over" (Holloway, 2002, p. 28). It took me back to a meeting in Queens, NY at a community church about 8 years ago led by a representative of the United States Census Bureau. The goal of the meeting, or so I thought, was to introduce a pilot questionnaire to the community for the purpose of testing the race and ethnicity question of the American Community Survey in Queens, which had been selected as the most ethnically and linguistically diverse borough of the country. Beyond the fact that the meeting was a mere informational lecture and the presenters were obviously not serious about receiving feedback or engaging the community, I was struck by some of the statements made by one of the census representatives, a Latina women herself, which went like this:

> "Nosotros los Hispanos no sabemos como definirnos, eso de escoger más de una opción es ignorante. Tenemos que aprender a escoger una sola opción y decidirnos de una vez por todas que somos." (We Hispanics don't know how to define ourselves; choosing more than one option is ignorant. We need to learn to chose only one option and decide once and for all what we are. – my translation)

I could not believe she was calling people ignorant for choosing 'White' and writing in 'Latino' or 'Colombian', or choosing 'Black' and writing in 'Dominican', or choosing 'Some other race' and writing in Cuban, etc. Those "ignorant Hispanics" who refused to choose one option were making her life difficult. She felt the need to control their 'power-to' identify as they wished, and turned it into 'power-over' their categorization. "It is not that everything stands still, but everything is locked into a perpetual continuity, everything is repeated, everything moves forward on track" (Holloway, 2002, p. 57) in order to maintain the status quo.

Since the beginning, this project has been about transgressing limits, be it genre, disciplines, histories, national borders, gender, race, class. It has been for me a way to rescue "hidden scripts" (Scott, 1992) of resistance, forgotten stories of connection (Galeano, 1992), about honoring the resiliency of family and relationships of solidarity, and "decolonizing knowledge" (L. T. Smith, 1999) by restoring from the periphery of intellectual canons the work of Latin American intellectuals. In many ways, it could be considered in the tradition of contributing to a

> "Trans"-modernity, in contrast [to post-modernity that] demands a whole new interpretation of modernity in order to include moments that were never incorporated into the European vision… The emergence of other cultures, until now depreciated and unvalued, from beyond the horizon of European modernity is not a miracle arising from nothingness, but the return by these cultures to their status as actors in the history of the world-system. (Dussel, 2002, p.223)

Particularly, the goal of this research was to understand how children of immigrants from Colombian and Dominican backgrounds negotiated social identities within transnational social fields; whether and why they maintained transnational ties; and how they interacted and were affected by social structures and institutions in their lives. The following pages highlight the main findings and make some statements about how they advance our psychological knowledge about re-negotiating multiple identities, living within transnational social fields, sustaining and initiating transnational ties, dealing with social stratification and institutionalization and considering a new framework of "transculturation" for studying encounters between new cultures, ethnicities, and social groups especially for migration research.

SUMMARY OF FINDINGS

Identity Negotiation within Transnational Social Fields

Despite their differences in national origin, social class, historical backgrounds, and educational experiences, Dominican and Colombian respondents shared similar socio-psychological experiences of identity negotiation as children of immigrants. Growing up in New York City with immigrant parents marked a common experiential component for both groups which potentially parallels the experiences of children of immigrants from other national groups, especially from Latin America. As children of immigrants, Colombian and Dominican respondents navigated two or more cultural, ethnic/national origin *habitus*

(Bourdieu, 1984, 2008), defined as a set of dispositions and practices that shape one's behavior and are based on past experience. In other words, *habitus* can be understood as the whole of norms, practices, expectations and beliefs that are passed through socialization within a specific social group in the course of everyday activities. Bourdieu (2008) uses the term *cleft-habitus* to refer to a situation in which a person lives among several habitus at once, such that it is "the product of a 'conciliation of contraries' which then inclines one to the 'conciliation of contraries"(2008, p. 103). In the case of children of immigrants, the different cultures or *habitus* they had to conciliate were the national origin culture of their immigrant parents and the mainstream culture of New York City where respondents grew up. Respondents' ethnic/national/cultural origin identities were anchored in cultural traditions appropriated and reproduced in the diaspora by their immigrant families. The family served as a cultural/national origin referent for the social group, and acted as a 'remooring' (Deaux & Ethier, 1998; Ethier & Deaux, 1994) context for respondents' identity negotiation. Respondents' immigrant families functioned as a remooring context that extended beyond national borders to encompass transnational family members as well.

Colombian and Dominican respondents dealt with their multiple cultural realities by comparing and contrasting situations, cultural norms, and ways of doing things and made decisions based on what they deemed most appropriate for the particular (time and space) situation. Respondents agreed and disagreed with specific aspects of each culture, while holding and respecting both. For example, they did not like their parents' racial attitudes and racism, but deeply valued their parents' family values. On the other, they valued civil liberties and diversity in United States mainstream culture but disliked the idea of family defined as just immediate family members (i.e. parents and children). Colombian and Dominican children of immigrant managed their social identities through the mechanism of social comparison and audience assessment which provides support for a social identity performance framework. Complexity was not a source of psychological stress for these youth. On the contrary, they felt fortunate and proud of being able to draw from multiple cultural frameworks which may contribute to their overall optimism about life and resiliency despite limited circumstances.

Transnational relationships and practices

Do children of immigrants maintain transnational ties? The answer is yes; most of them do to varying degrees, at different times in their lives and for different reasons. Why do they do it? It represents the continuation of their families' life projects. How long would they continue to do it? As long as they have family members and close family friends living in their home countries. Of course, there were other reasons (social, political, and economical) that motivated Dominican and Colombian children of immigrants and their descendents to establish or maintain transnational ties to their parents' home country. However, one way or another, these motivations involved family or were facilitated by family members who lived in their parents' home country, Colombia and the Dominican Republic in this case. Transnational ties were (re)negotiated between parents and children, the former made possible their initiation and maintenance while the latter decided whether to continue them or not and to what extent. Josselson's (1992, 2003) multidimensional model of relatedness and Bronfenbrenner's ecological model of human and child development (Bronfenbrenner & P. A. Morris, 1998, 2006) were especially useful in understanding the importance of maintaining relationships with family and friends in the parents' home country for children of immigrants' personal and social identities.

For respondents and their immigrant parents, relatedness in the form of family and close family friends was found to contribute to "physical health, to longevity, to meaningful social life, and to the growth and development of the self (Josselson, 1992, p. 3)." For parents, it was important to establish a connection between their children and their grandparents (and other family members) who continued to live in Colombia or the Dominican Republic. Researchers have documented lower levels of depression among children who have good relationships with their grandparents (Ruiz & Silverstein, 2007). From the perspective of respondents, having additional family members who expressed love and concern for them was enjoyable and appreciated. It created a 'holding' environment and social 'embeddedness' (Deaux, 2006; Josselson, 1992, 2003) within which they could continue to develop a healthy and strong sense of identity as part of that cultural/ethnic/national origin group. A lot of attention has been given to remittances sent by immigrants to their home country and to whether the children of immigrants would follow this behavior, overlooking the social and psychological reasons behind it. My findings demonstrate that remittances contributed to the relatedness dimension of 'caring/tending for others'. Relationships formed through communication and travel were maintained and nurtured through behaviors that denoted reciprocity and mutual solidarity. They represented not only the fulfillment of family obligations but an opportunity to deepen valued relationships and to express gratitude and care for others. Remittances and communication were the result of establishing personal relationships with specific individuals who held an esteemed position in the respondents' hierarchy of relationships. Respondents did not engage in transnational remittances or continue communication with casual acquaintances. Remittances were the result of deep connection and personal investment in particularly important relationships.

In this relational context, language was more than a simple ethnic or cultural marker. Speaking Spanish represented a vehicle for potential deep emotional connection, especially with those persons who did not speak English. The findings suggest that respondents who were highly invested in maintaining intergenerational and transnational relationships were more likely to speak Spanish and attached more importance to speaking Spanish as part of their cultural identity. The importance of transnational ties and their relationship to ethnic/cultural/national origin identity was strongest at particular points in the respondents' life cycle involving particular interpersonal relationships. According to Bronfenbrenner's ecological development model, a child develops through a series of increasingly complex interactions with other persons, events, objects, or environments. As respondents grew up, their understanding and self-identity development took different expressions. Ethnic identity did not really enter respondents' minds until they encountered children and members (teachers and administrators) of other ethnic/cultural/national origin groups at school. As young adults, college became the stage of identity negotiation especially informed by learning historical and socio-political facts about their own group and interacting with others. As Wimmer asserts "[e]thnic groups therefore do not grow naturally from the social cohesion between individuals that share culture and origin, but result from acts of social distancing and closure vis-à-vis member of *other* categories" (2007, p. 14).

Marriage and having children represent two transitional points when ethnic,/cultural/national origin identities assumed added importance. Choosing a person to share their life with and who could potentially be the father or mother of their future children, involved considering the role of culture and cultural/ethnic practices in respondents' lives. Even respondents who valued inter-group contact and inter-group dating in high school and college had a difficult time envisioning marriage and having children with members of a racial/ethnic/cultural group whom they viewed as markedly different from theirs. Edmond and Killen's (2009) findings reflect similar patterns of inter-racial contact decreasing with age and level of intimacy. Most respondents felt it was very important that their possible wife or husband be able to speak Spanish so they could communicate with their immigrant parents. They also wanted to take their children to visit their parents' home country at some point. These findings imply a paradigm change in the way social psychologists look at inter-group relations to understand "[t]he *motivation* of resistance as not simply an avoidance of insight or a fear of change, but as a dialectic between preservation and change – a basic need to preserve the continuity of self-experience in the process of growth by minimizing the threat of potential traumatization" (Bromberg, 1998, p. 206)

Access Denied, Transnational Social Class and Race Relations among Latino/as

Despite having similar social and psychological experiences of growing up as children of immigrants in New York City among family and friends, Dominican and Colombian respondents had different experiences with social institutions and structures resulting in unequal access to opportunities such as finishing high school, going on to college, and fulfilling their psychological, social, and economic needs and desires. The level of education of their parents and family socio-economic status proved to be the strongest predictor of respondents' educational achievement, second to having a child. Particular migration histories of the Dominican Republic and Colombia directly shaped the composition of Dominican and Colombian immigrant communities and the social and cultural capital available within each community in New York City. Another important factor that mediated the educational achievement of respondents was the quality of the schools they attended. Colombians respondents were fortunate to attend much better performing schools in general than did Dominican respondents as a by product of the neighborhoods where they lived. In the end, Colombian respondents achieved higher educational levels which was directly tied to having parents who were better educated, came from urban backgrounds, and had, on average, higher socio-economic status prior to migration that were transformed into cultural capital in their present place of residence. On the other hand, the Dominican immigrant families, from a comparable year of migration cohort, had a different socio-economic profile with lower levels of education, higher likelihood of rural backgrounds and lower socio-economic status to build on. These findings do not negate that within groups, the Dominican and Colombian community in New York City today have representation in all levels of the City's socio-economic hierarchy.

Two transition points (Weininger & Lareau, 2007) were particularly instrumental in shaping respondents' access to opportunities for educational success: (1) choosing a neighborhood which determined the quality of schools available to respondents and the level of poverty and social disorganization in their environment, and (2) deciding to stay or leave high school as a consequence of (dis)engagement in school, 'cutting class' behavior, and teenage pregnancies. Focusing on these moments highlights the consequences of decisions made by parents and children within limit-situations. These transition points were examples of immigrant parents making the best use they could of their social and cultural capital, as they chose among neighborhoods they could afford. At the same time, for some children staying in alienating, poorly funded and overcrowded schools was not necessarily the most enticing option. Staying off the streets in questionable neighborhoods combined with lack of knowledge about safe sexual practices placed young girls in a difficult position and increased their chances of becoming teenage mothers.

Getting married, a third transitional point was an opportunity to (re)negotiate transnational social, racial, and class hierarchies. Deciding who to marry, often overlooked in social psychological research, was a pivotal moment where race, class, and gender mattered for in-group and out-group marriages. Choosing a partner represented a moment of inter-personal and inter-generational dialogue and negotiation. The role of parents' opinions and cultural theories in their children's choice of marriage partners has been under-theorized, especially as it refers to racial attitudes. Marriage constituted a 'contact zone' where the racial attitudes of parents, based on their experiences in the home-country as well as in New York City, encountered the racial beliefs and attitudes of their children, which were based on their experiences growing up in New York City. Understanding marriage as a rite of incorporation, in which a third person is brought into the family group was important. Doing so brought forth anxieties about the well-being of future generations and the continuation of personal stories, historical memories, and cultures. Marriage became a site where race, class, and gender guided decisions that question the limits of contact theories about inter-racial/ethnic relations. Not surprisingly, it was darker skinned Dominicans who suffered the brunt of in-group and out-group discrimination and racism.

NEPANTLA AS A SAFE SPACE FOR "TRANS"IDENTITIES – THE CONTACT ZONE WITHIN

Both Colombian and Dominican respondents grew up navigating two or more ethnic/national origin cultures. Different metaphors have been used to describe what that psychological space looks like such as, hybrid, hyphenated, cross-border and bicultural identities to name a few. Most of these terms build on an assumption that the psychological experience of living in-between worlds is equivalent to experiencing the self as divided. A hyphenated identity uses a hyphen to signify the co-existence of two separate worlds, one ethnic and the other national i.e. Mexican-American or Dominican-American. Cross-border identity has usually been used to discuss identity issues where adjacent geographical borders are crossed such as the Mexico-USA border and identity issues among Mexican-Americans. Bicultural identity assumes a comparative approach between different cultures or cultural frameworks but overlooks the existence of other combinations besides adversarial or contradictory claims. Hybridity as a post-colonial term has been used to talk about the feeling of in-betweenness. However, I find the negative connotations associated with the word hybrid troubling, especially within Latin American history. A hybrid connotes 'inferiority', 'damaged', 'impure', and in many spheres is associated with the term 'mongrel'. However in my reading of Colombian and Dominican respondents' stories, their self experience is anything *but* divided. Despite feeling like they had different selves as situations, contexts and audiences changed, they did not describe feeling divided or compartmentalized psychologically. Both Colombian and Dominican respondents described feeling like different selves were enacted or took different positions, yet they still felt as parts of one encompassing self. They refused to define themselves with any one term alone, and describe a sense of self that was dynamic, creative, and in constant flux. They resisted dichotomies and categorization, but were willing to appropriate labels if the situation demanded it.

I struggled with finding a language to express these experiences of feeling in-between; of feeling never fully American, never fully Dominican, but somewhere in between; sometimes more American, sometimes more Colombian,[19] never any one thing. For me, it was important to capture and understand the process of negotiating identity within different spheres of social life that could travel across psychological domains. Disappointed with her metaphor of crossing borders, Gloria Anzaldúa used the concept of *Nepantla* that goes beyond her theories of borderlands by recapturing un-theorized social, psychological, and spiritual spaces inhabited by those who live in-between worlds. Characterized as a way of seeing and reading the world, her concept of *Nepantla* travels across contexts and issues i.e. gender, race, ethnicity, class, sexuality. According to Anzaldúa, Nepantla "is a stage that women and men, and whoever is willing to change into a new person and further grow and develop, go through. The concept is articulated as a process" (1999, p. 237). Therefore as I have said before,

> And I now called it *Nepantla*, which is a Nahuatl word for the space between two bodies of water, the space between worlds. It is a limited space, a space where you are not this or that but where you are changing. You haven't got into the new identity yet and you haven't left the old identity behind either

---

[19] Colombian-American as a term has not really been introduced to migration literature and has not yet really been appropriated among immigrants or North American mainstream.

> – you are in a kind of transition. And that is what *Nepantla* stands for. (Anzaldúa, 1999, p. 237)

The key being that it is a space connecting two or more points, cultures, perspectives as a bridge would. For most 'cultural straddlers' or 'hyphenated individuals", the bridge becomes the space where they spent most of their time, feeling like they have not really arrived at any one destination, always in transit. Why then appropriate a Nahuatl word to name this psychological space? As a tool, a symbol of the capacity to de-colonize knowledges, to go beyond western academic traditions, and enunciate the voices of those Non-European views that through globalization are intersecting and questioning European and North American modes of theorizing. Recognizing that "[t]he vision of cosmic harmony is threatened when the languages capable of expressing opposites held in balance (*multitude-person*) are forcibly replaced by the European languages that can only express these concepts in the awkward approximation of hyphenated pairs…"(Fischlin & Nandorfy, 2002, p. 383), I use a Latin American indigenous metaphor that refuses to be reduced to opposites, instead embracing complex relationships and the wholeness of human experience echoed in these respondents' interviews.

As a psychological space of in-betweenness, *Nepantla* travels well to several psychological domains such as gender, race, ethnic identity, national identity, cultural identity, etc. Persons who defied identity classifications and categorizations based on stable, mutually exclusive and unchanging categories such as, female-male, immigrant-non-immigrant, white-black, hetero-homo, that obscure diversity and the continuum of experience, share the experience of feeling in-between worlds. Individuals who cross boundaries and resist indexing can be said to develop identities that move beyond established categories and transgress 'acceptable' ways of being embodying "*trans*-identities" (i.e. trans-ethnic, trans-national, trans-racial, trans-gender, trans-cultural). Hybrid identities, bi-cultural identities, cross-border identities and hyphenated identities could be considered all instances of "trans-identities" with different particularities. Researchers and psychologists have begun to recognize 'trans-identities' in some social domains such as trans-gender theorizing, 'trans-ethnic' identity and more recently 'trans-racial' families and adoptions. Trans-national identity as such has received less attention within North American psychology.

Children of immigrants, in this study, did not discuss a 'transnational' identity as such, if national identity is tied to claims of citizenship in a nation-state. Despite identifying with national origin groups and maintaining transnational ties across geographical borders, respondents did not talk about a national identity as citizens of their parents' home country. They felt part of the same national origin/cultural background but did not feel the need to participate in the political life of their parents' home country, with very few exceptions. Their national identity and citizenship were tied to the United States as a nation-state. For example, most respondents would not entertain joining the military forces of the Dominican Republic or Colombia because it was not their country; they considered New York City (United States) their home. There could be differences between Colombian and Dominican respondents who were born in the United States compared to those born outside the United States given the strong association between country of birth and national identity in western societies. Future research should explore the complex relationship between the definitions and content of racial, ethnic and national-origin identities among second generation immigrants. If national-origin could be equated with classification as an ethnicity among children of immigrants, then trans-ethnic might be an adequate term. Yet if an ethnic identity has been racialized, as in the case of Hispanic/Latino/a, would one call it a trans-racial identity?

DE-COLONIZING THE TERMS OF ENCOUNTER – TRANSFORMING THE '*CHOQUE*' INTO AN '*ABRAZO*'

Individuals living in *Nepantla* and enacting trans-identities are adept at embracing complexity and dealing with ambiguity. Psychological research has begun to explore the capacity of dealing with complexity and ambiguity by studying concepts like social identity complexity, which has been associated with positive personal and interpersonal outcomes, including more positive inter-group out-group perceptions and attitudes (Schmid, et.al. (2009). Ehrensaft and Tousignant (2006) suggested that managing contradictions in a conciliatory way rather than a battleground with winners and losers, may help individuals construct narratives that are more resilient in the face of war and social conflict. Research among a group of high school African American and Latino students concluded that students who maneuvered "best the social boundaries between their ethnic peer cultures and their school environment were the cultural straddlers – students who demonstrated multiple cultural competences and deployed varied cultural tools and resources to strike a more effective balance among the various cultural spheres in which they participated" (Carter, 2006, p. 322). Bromberg has gone as far as defining psychological health as:

> [T]he ability to stand in spaces without losing any of them- … 'Standing in spaces' is a shorthand way of describing a person's relative capacity for making room at any given moment for subjective reality that is not readily containable by the self he or she experiences as "me" at that moment. It is what distinguishes creative imagination from both fantasy and concreteness, and distinguishes playfulness from facetiousness. (Bromberg, 1998, p. 142)

Theories of double-consciousness (DuBois, 1903; Upegui-Hérnandez, 2009), cross-border and *meztiza* consciousness (Anzaldúa, 1999, 2002; J. Ayala, 2005) have emphasized the difficult emotional work and potential stress associated with living between worlds. However, Dominican and Colombian respondents did not linger or make much of the possible contradictions or incongruencies between their worlds. Their interview answers suggested that maneuvering cultural/ethnic differences did not represent a big stressor in their lives This doesn't mean that dealing with reconciling different *habitus* in one's life is a simple matter. An analysis of power relations is necessary for understanding what are situations that would arouse psychological stress and which are not. When we are dealing with groups who have been subordinated and oppressed, psychological stress is likely to be present in people's daily struggles, such as the double-consciousness of African-Americans described by DuBois at the turn of the century and in the case of *mestiza* consciousness where Mexican and Indigenous heritage may be treated as inferior and devalued. However, the Dominican and Colombian young respondents in this study grew up in New York City. Part of their "American" identity, as experienced in New York City, meant tolerance and validation of differences, at least in the public discourse. Whether or not it was present in people's daily life is another issue. For these Latina/o young adults being an "American citizen" was intimately tied to being different, being 'ethnic' and being proud of what made you different, yet being able to appreciate and embrace others in their differences. One might say, they were truly the generation of multiculturalism and diversity. Whether young Latinas/os from other parts of the country would respond in the same way remains a question. Outside New York City, Dominican and Colombian respondents reported experiencing discrimination and racism. Therefore an analysis of power relations remains necessary when dealing with issues of in-group/out-group relations and immigration experiences across the United States.

What we can take away from these young Dominican and Colombian youth is their willingness to literally *abrazar* (embrace) uncertainty, complexity, and ambiguity as a positive force. These young adults subverted the 'terms of encounter' in a way that opened up spaces to truly recognize and validate *others* in their difference. Those of us that have grown up in – apparently – homogeneous contexts are potentially subject to seeing change as "… a cultural crisis of the first order that cannot help but generate profound anxiety because, by definition, it threatens 'the basic assumptions which have been identified with the existence of the culture, and which the individual, as a participant in the culture, has identified with his own existence. (May, 1977 cited by Gordon, 2003, p. 239)" Children of immigrants on the other hand, seemed ready to acknowledge that their lives were full of ambiguity and contradictions. Yet they felt empowered by the possibility to choose among their options. Rather than being puzzled and lost in the midst of options, they felt privileged and grateful. Kasinitz and colleagues (2008) alluded to it pointing out that "… the interaction of structure and culture opens up choices, particularly for the second generation. The fact that they have choices, and that they are often conscious of the fact that they have choices, is perhaps more than anything the distinct advantage of the second generation" (p. 86).

Why is this important? Because these Colombian and Dominican youth understood that "[i]gnorance and contemplation go hand in hand in this opening gesture, a speech act of profound importance for how it establishes an alternative structure of encounter, one that requires both a recognition of one's ignorance of difference as well as the need to contemplate difference in a meaningful way" (Fischlin & Nandorfy, 2002, p. 75). Their lives and interpretations are a reminder that,

> Precisely because most accounts are more or less true to the perspectives they adopt, the way out of this discontinuity seldom lies with a blanket rejection of one perspective over another, a simple “right” or “wrong”. Instead, the most constructive and creative response is to search for a larger horizon, a new way of thinking that is broad enough in scope to do justice to both accounts… A shared horizon, on the other hand, is more inclusive than neither text alone and often connects them on the level of implications, not explicit claims. (R. E. Miller & Spellmeyer, 2008, p. xx)

It is this embodied understanding of complexity of life and the arbitrariness of categories that engenders possibilities for social change. A life experience of not fully fitting in particular boxes sharpens their perspective-taking skills and nurtures possibilities to question not only cultural systems, but other kinds of social, economic, political and institutional arrangements that to most might appeared unchangeable and self-evident. They assumed the challenge of diverse, apparently conflicting cultural and ideological frameworks willing to find points of connection and conciliation, rather than safely remain within socially accepted ways of being.

DE-COLONIZING “TRANS”CULTURATION – A LATIN AMERICAN ‘ETHICS OF RADICAL INTERCONNECTEDNESS’

Let’s hold ’marriage’ as a metaphor for what Galeano (Fischlin & Nandorfy, 2002) might call an *abrazo* between cultures. In order to avoid a *choque* (clash) between cultures in a marriage, each partner must be able to trust their partner, to be vulnerable to their partner’s gaze, be willing to commit to a common agenda and to reach compromises on the most difficult issues. It is a moment where two cultures meet in order to make an*other* part of their group based on love, reciprocity, respect, and solidarity. The ethics of encounter assumed by theories of assimilation and acculturation of immigrants into their host countries are devoid of ‘reciprocity’, ‘mutual recognition’, ‘solidarity’ and ‘trust’. At their outset, theories of assimilation and acculturation are framed by a discourse of distrust, fear, meritocracy and unwillingness to self-examination. Anglo-

American and European ethics of encounter have been based on a desire to 'civilize' the 'uncivilized', to impart the metropoli's knowledge on the uncivilized Others who are "devoid" of it, without contemplating the possibility of learning anything from those Others. Most research on migration has sought to understand how the immigrant assumes or adapts to their host culture, leaving an analysis of the role of 'host' unquestioned. Mary Louise Pratt's (1991) conceptualization of 'contact zones' as a place where cultures and groups meet is a very helpful concept that allows us to look at all parties involved as part of the dialogical relationship of contact. However, it belies its own story of appropriation and neo-colonization.

In an effort to anchor these concluding remarks on an intellectual tradition that would connect my North American academically trained self with my Latin American intellectual self, I uncovered a long forgotten and colonized theory of "transculturation" postulated by Cuban ethnologist and writer Fernando Ortíz in 1940 (for a detailed discussion see Davies, 2000). Having embraced Pratt's concept of 'contact zones' as a wonderfully rich space for discussing immigration, I was not prepared for the disappointment of my findings. I was taken aback by the fact that once again North American and European intellectual traditions had pushed Latin American knowledges to the periphery. Despite using the term 'transculturation' in the title of her book, Pratt barely dedicates a footnote to acknowledging Ortíz as the Latin American colleague who coined the term six decades earlier. Would she have done the same if it had been a term authored by Foucault? Fernando Ortíz did not merit mention in her index, yet his concept was paraded in her title. However, transculturation as a theory has a parallel intellectual life within Latin American philosophy and literary criticism that is probably unknown to most North American academics. The ironies and points of connection with the invisibility of immigrants and children of immigrants' transnational lives are many.

By the 1940s, Latin American intellectuals had begun to express inconformity with the mostly anthropological Anglo-American terminology used to address encounters among cultures and movements of people across geographical borders by denouncing the moral imperialism behind them. Fernando Ortíz presented in his book *Contrapunteo cubano del tabaco y del azucar* (1940, for a discussion see Davies, 2000; Hirabayashi, 2002) a critique of the term "acculturation" mainly used in the United States to refer to what at the time was known in Britain as "cultural contact". However, Ortíz's criticism of western anthropological traditions and the usefulness of Ortíz's theory of 'transculturation' as a more appropriate term were introduced to North America and Europe by anthropologist Bronislaw Malinowski, who at the time wrote in its preface: "It is an ethnocentric word with a moral connotation. The immigrant has to "acculturate" himself; so do the natives, pagan, heather, barbarian or savage, who enjoy the benefits of being under the sway of our great Western culture" (Malinowski, 1940 cited by Davies, 2000). Fernando Ortíz understood that the Latin American experience of contact among cultures was different from Spain's and the United States'. He acknowledged that Cuba was different from Spain because it had a 'vibrant' Black culture and its mulatto culture differentiated it from the United States. He concluded that 'acculturation' could not explain the Cuban case since Black and African culture had permeated much of Cuban culture and co-existed with indigenous and Spaniard traditions as a result of *mestizaje* (race mixing) which is considered unique to the Latin American colonial experience. Fernando Ortíz conceived of 'transculturation' as:

> [A] process in which something is always given in return for what one receives, a system of give and take… a process from which a new reality emerges, transformed and complex, a reality that is not a mechanical agglomeration of traits, or even a mosaic, but a new phenomenon, original and independent… an exchange between two cultures, both of them active, both contributing their share. (Malinowski, 1940 cited by Davies, 2000)

According to Davies (2000), the basis for Ortíz's criticism of 'acculturation' was the lack of discussion of power, control, coercion, and inequality by its proponents. He was also deeply bothered by the assumption that the process of acculturation was unilateral and unilinear, and omitted the situation when one culture is considered inferior to others. In the process of transculturation, disadvantaged groups chose to appropriate certain aspects of the dominant cultures for particular reasons, at the same time that the dominant culture adopted cultural practices that stemmed from the subjugated groups even if it wanted to deny it. In the end, *all* groups *were changed* in the process even if only some were able to self-reflect on it. Transculturation, as used by Ortíz, demanded an analysis of power and emphasized that

> … subordinated groups are anything but inert when determining relations with dominant and metropolitan cultures. Even in situations of extraordinary unequal power… subordinated groups are highly *selective* and *inventive* in absorbing materials from the metropolis, and they develop many ways of maintaining cultural integrity. When the process of selection and invention are fractured into the picture, what once appeared as a simplistic dynamic of incorporation is better characterized as a dynamic of *trans*culturation. (Hirabayashi, 2002, p. x)

The concept itself has reappeared in the work of cultural anthropologists like Asian American Lane Ryo Hirabayashi (2002) by highlighting its consideration of power relations, dialogical/dialectical process, dynamism, and mutual interdependence. I suggest that *transculturation* could be a fruitful theoretical notion for framing the experiences of immigrants and their children. Feminist psychologist, Lillian Comas-Diaz (1987) used the concept in an article about Puerto Rican women who maintained what would be considered "transnational ties" between Puerto Rico and the United States mainland, although technically they are not considered immigrants by many given the fact that Puerto Rico is a U.S. territory. She found particularly useful the concept because it allowed her to discuss the colonial relationship of Puerto Rico vis-à-vis the United States and how women's gender roles changed in the midst of this cultural exchange.

Transculturation acknowledges respondents' agency in making decisions about how to conciliate and combine their cultures in the midst of unequal cultural and material power relations. Recognizing that cultural change is a mutual and dialectical process in which we are, and have always been, mutually-implicated (losing/letting go and appropriating new cultural practices) might in the end help us have a less fearful attitude in approaching cultural change. We might be able to better invest our time in finding ways to connect our bridges in an *abrazo* instead of a *choque,* or both, and may come to understand that:

> A bridge… is not just about one set of people crossing to the other side; it's about those on the other side crossing to this side… It's about honoring people's otherness in ways that allow us to be changed by *embracing* that otherness rather than punishing others for having a different view, belief system, skin color, or spiritual practice. (Anzaldúa, 2002, p. 4)

ON BRIDGING PSYCHOLOGICAL QUESTIONS – THROUGH SECONDARY ANALYSIS OF SOCIOLOGICAL QUALITATIVE DATA

Throughout the analysis and writing process, I have strived to create a narrative that might be *(trans)*disciplinary and *(trans)*methodological, in which different types of data reinforce each other, inspire new questions, or provide unexpected answers. In a way, going to other fields of knowledge has allowed me to find connections (trans-connections) to other researchers (sociologists, anthropologists, literary writers) who have thought about the same issues albeit in different ways. This theoretical and methodological journey has been about crossing borders and going beyond the categories, topics and methods used within our social psychological discipline where the transnational life of immigrants and their children has not been a priority. In many ways, our psychological field remains subject to what Glick-Schiller and Wimmer outlined as "methodological nationalism" that manifest itself in three different forms:

> 1) ignoring or disregarding the fundamental importance of nationalism for modern societies;… 2) naturalization, *i.e.,* taking for granted that the boundaries of the nation-state delimit and define the unit of analysis; 3) territorial limitation which confines the study of social processes to the political and geographic boundaries of a particular nation-state. (2003, p. 577)

This oversight is at the heart of my decision to go beyond psychological literature to understand the complexity in the experiences of children of immigrants' negotiation of identities and transnational interpersonal relationships. The intellectual work itself became a trans-migration project of sorts which inevitably brought me back to my initial relationships with psychology. Despite maneuvering in other fields with some ease, although at times I felt as a stranger within psychological circles and theories, I remain a psychologist who moves between places. Outside of psychology, I advocate for the psychological experience of immigrants and their children and within psychology, I advocate for exploring concepts such as transnational social fields and national identities.

One of the lessons of crossing disciplinary borders was that in the process one learns about commonalities as well as differences between the disciplines. I feel as though I understand more profoundly what makes me a psychologist and not a sociologist, than I did before writing this book. One must become a good translator, versed in different disciplinary jargons becoming bilingual, multilingual, and 'trans'lingual in the process. At first it was not easy; there were a lot of moments of confusion, of feeling like I was better prepared to write a sociological or anthropological book than a psychological one. It was a process of continuous immersion, travel, and translation. But in the end, much like immigrants with multiple 'trans-'identities, I feel that I can talk to different audiences and in different contexts, which makes my work stronger. Knowing just how much knowledge and understanding I have gained in the process, the most difficult decisions were always about what to leave out.

One of the major difficulties in this process was to understand how psychologists think differently, compared to sociologists, when it comes to creating survey measures and instruments. As I pondered over the phone survey for questions that would speak to my social psychological concerns, I was excited with the vast amount of contextual data on class, race, neighborhood, school, and work experiences but was dismayed at the small number of questions that touched on psychological issues such as perception of discrimination and racism. Most of the socially contextual questions were categorical and nominal, and did not lend themselves to the exploration of variation within groups. Finally, the most psychologically promising survey questions were not useful as a result of extremely low sample sizes, which suggested that phone surveyors did not press for answers to these questions as they did for others. Fortunately the qualitative interviews provided fertile ground for psychological cross-fertilization. The in-depth interview protocols permitted participants to speak freely and make associations about subjects they were not directly asked about. The qualitative data lent itself to a wider range of possible psychological explorations than did the quantitative data. However, the quantitative data was extremely useful in contextualizing findings and analyzing how gender, race, ethnicity, and social class affected respondents' transnational experiences.

Beyond disciplinary concerns, there were many challenges associated with conducting a secondary analysis of qualitative and quantitative data. One of the biggest challenges was coming to terms with not being able to ask the questions that I would have wanted. Having access to both the survey and qualitative interviews was extremely important for gathering psychological insights from the primary data. The order of the chapters itself represents a sort of road map of themes that appeared in the qualitative and quantitative data. Issues of identity negotiation and psychological experiences of respondents were mostly assessed from the in-depth interviews, while data about respondents' experiences of gender, class, and race were visible both in the survey and the interviews. Social class was not directly discussed in the interviews, but there were a number of questions related to it in the survey. The chapter about transnational ties and relationships represents a mixture of both types of data. An interesting finding was that although in the phone survey there were few answers to questions about prejudice, experiences and perception of racism and discrimination (very small sample size); there was material in the interviews that suggested respondents did have experiences with racism and discrimination. More interestingly, they described instances of racism or discrimination even if they did not classify them as such. In many instances, experiences of discrimination were rationalized or explained away as something else, even as they described their occurrence within their homes, families and community spaces.

Another challenge qualitative secondary analysis presented was the inability to experience the relationship between the researcher and the participants. This happened in a number of ways. First of all, not having collected the data eliminated the possibility of developing an interpersonal relationship with the interviewee that usually provides so much psychological insight for qualitative researchers. One may obtain an approximate glimpse of the data collection by reading interviewer notes (Goodwin & O'Connor, 2006). Even though I did not use the interviewer notes, I was able to discern different interviewer styles from reading the interview transcripts. My own secondary analysis procedure was a little different from the primary research. I read all interviews in their entirity before I began to code and highlight themes. In the original research, the coding procedure involved having a coder divide and create initial themes. Subsequently, different coders coded the parts of the interviews that had been identified as speaking to the larger codes. Theme coders did not necessarily have knowledge of the context of the interview itself. However my findings validate many of the claims and conclusions made in the primary research and its publications. Therefore, my project speaks in many ways to the validity of qualitative research, the possibility of assessing the reliability of qualitative findings, and the value of qualitative secondary analysis.

Although some researchers would argue that analyzing interview transcripts without listening to the tape-recorded interviews hinders the quality of interpretations, I feel that I achieved a relative closeness to the interviews. One of the reasons why I chose to subsample Dominican and Colombian respondents from the larger sample was my intimate cultural and historical knowledge of these communities. Such knowledge allowed me to reflect on how respondents' interviews resonated with my own cultural knowledge and experiences with these groups. In other words, it was important for me to be able to see real persons lifted out of the transcript and to be able to imagine myself as a virtual observer of the interview, as if I had been there. I feel that this would have been much harder to do if I had selected to analyze transcripts of Chinese or Russian Jewish participants. In some ways, being a cultural insider helped reduce the distance between me and the interviewee/respondent. Personally knowing the interviewers who were matched with each interviewee helped me fill in information about the possible relational context of the interview. Interviewers were matched with interviewees by gender, ethnicity, and national origin whenever possible which arguably increased the level of rapport. This was not the case with the survey phone questionnaires, which obtained remarkably different answers to their race and ethnicity questions.

An ethical challenge that emerged in doing the secondary qualitative analysis was the issue of confidentiality and consent. Most qualitative data are not collected with the intention of being available for secondary analysis. The process of designing consent forms should consider whether the researcher is likely to make the data available for secondary analysis of variables and research questions other than those described in the consent form given to participants in the course of the primary study. In many ways, my research questions were in-line with the research questions asked in the primary study, but in other occasions this may be different. In this case, the database was collected with the explicit intention of making it available for qualitative secondary analysis.

Throughout this book I have referred to participants in the study as respondents in order to make clear my relationship to them and avoid misconstruing the extent of my knowledge. I have changed the names of all participants and used names of personal friends and people I know (from the same particular national group) as way to make respondents real to me and make myself accountable to them in the writing. I did not write anything that I would not say about my friends. On the other hand, the stories in this book reflect my friends and family's transnational stories as well.

This project was not without limitations and shortcomings. There are a number of things that could be improved in future studies. For example, in an effort to highlight the parallel experiences of children of immigrants, I did not differentiate between foreign-born and U.S.-born respondents, so called '2nd generation' and '1.75 or 1.5 generation' in the analysis. I grouped them together to highlight how their social and psychological experiences were defined by being children of immigrants primarily raised in New York City. However, there might be differences in the labels they use to identify themselves. U.S.-born Dominican and Colombian respondents might be more likely to identify using a pan-ethnic label such as Hispanic or Latino than foreign-born Dominican and Colombian respondents. There may be differences among U.S. born and foreign-born Dominican and Colombian respondents in how likely they are to prefer to speak English vs. Spanish and to intermarry which might have been obscured in my analysis.

The original study was initiated in 1999 and the sample was drawn among young children of immigrants then. As a result, Dominican and Colombian respondents' parents had mostly migrated before the 1990's. This is an important factor shaping the large numbers of parents' with documented status and citizenship rates reported by respondents. Many likely undocumented Dominican and Colombian immigrant parents would have had the opportunity to regularize their immigrant status through the 1986 amnesty legislation. Therefore, findings with regards to immigrant status are not representative of the experiences of Dominican and Colombian children of immigrants and their parents today. Findings related to parents' level of education are problematic as well. They are based on the respondents' report of parents' education and the qualitative interviews revealed that many respondents were not really aware of their parents' education. For that reason, I decided to make a comparison of rural vs. urban backgrounds as a proxy for cultural capital closely related to level of education and social class.

Another limitation is related to an interviewer effect that shaped the length and depth of interview data. Some interviewers were more engaging and prompted longer responses eliciting follow-up information that approximated to the quality of depth we have come to expect in psychological semi-structured interviews. However other interviewers were less engaging and followed a more close-ended structured interview approach that yielded fewer descriptions and shorter concise answers with limited follow-up. This more close-ended interview style reduced the opportunity for themes not outlined on the interview protocol to surface. This effect was coupled with an interviewer's gender effect among Colombian respondents producing more elaborate and in-depth transcripts from female respondents compared to male respondents' transcripts. Despite this and other limitations outlined above, this book makes clear contributions to psychological theory as well as to migration literature and opens possible areas for psychological research that would further help us understand how children of immigrants manage complexity and negotiate identities and lives within transnational social fields.

WHAT LIES AHEAD: FINAL THOUGHTS

The findings presented in this book offer important contributions to both social psychological and migration literatures about children of immigrants' transnational experiences. It highlights areas that merit further research, and have implications for social and psychological practice. Most importantly, this research has been

> ... concerned with possibility, with opening windows on alternative realities, with moving through doorways into spaces some of us have never seen before... [with] releasing ... from fixed categories and measurable competences... interested in breakthroughs and new beginnings, in the kind of wide-awareness that allows for wonder and unease and questioning and the pursuit of what is not yet. (Greene, 2001, p. 44)

These findings demonstrate that Dominican and Colombian children of immigrants dealt with their psychological experience of growing up within transnational social fields in similar ways, however their experiences with social structures differed according to where they were placed by others within race, gender, and social class hierarchies. This implies that children of immigrants from other national groups, including other Latino immigrant groups, may negotiate their sense of selves and multiple identities within transnational social fields as did Dominican and Colombian children of immigrants.

However, how children of immigrants from different national groups, other than Colombian and Dominican, are treated socially and what opportunities they have is likely to depend on how they are differently positioned within race, gender, and social class hierarchies by others, especially those that hold positions of privilege within such hierarchies. In other words, the subjective experiences of juggling multiple identities among Chinese and Indian children of immigrants are probably quite similar to the experiences of Latino children of immigrants growing up in New York City. Yet, the social dimensions of their experiences are bound to be shaped by the migration histories of their parents as well as by how they are perceived by other groups in the United States. Above all, the psychological experiences of these Dominican and Colombian children of immigrants challenge the social construction of labels and categories of identity, and make them less likely to respond to stereotypes based on those categories (Shih, Bonam, D. Sanchez, & Peck, 2007). They possessed alternative counter-stories that helped them question the validity of such stereotyping. Future research should explore the process of identity negotiation of children of immigrants from other national groups to establish whether they are comparable or not.

The experiences of Dominican and Colombian respondents demonstrate that managing multiple identities and maintaining transnational ties may serve as a source of resiliency and strength among these youth. It has been suggested that "these youth are better able to maintain a sense of pride and healthy self-esteem... [where] energies are freed up and mobilized for the work of day-to-day coping" (C. Suárez-Orozco & M. M. Suárez-Orozco, 2001). Such emotional strength allowed them to be less fearful of change and difference, be more open to learning from others, and to work together towards social change and a more inclusive society. In the process, they can teach us that "we must be prepared to give up the illusion that cultural and ethnic purity has ever existed, let alone provided a foundation for civil society" (Gilroy as cited by Hutnyk, 2005, p. 83). This implies rethinking assimilation and acculturation models that center on flattening difference and overlook the dialectical nature of cultural encounters. Perhaps more attention should be given to how to embrace change in a more positive way and embrace the arrival of new immigrant groups as an opportunity to revaluate long-held dominant views. Additional research can highlight how immigrants bring social remittances with them to their host countries as well. Perhaps moving away from a language of "host" and "home" countries to a language that focuses on places of settlement or residence, would contribute to viewing immigrants as part of our communities and not as 'intruders'.

A major implication of this study is the importance that family relationships beyond national borders have for the well-being of children of immigrants. This is especially important in the context of increasing anti-immigrant sentiment, evidenced by laws such as Arizona's SB1070, calls for the intensification of detention and deportation of undocumented immigrants, and for closing the Mexico-U.S. border through militarization and wall-construction. Transnational ties and relationships allow both immigrant parents and their children to stay connected with relatives across generations and geographical borders. Such relationships were sources of happiness, deep emotional connection, feelings of pride, self-worth, and self-esteem that contributed immensely to respondents' psychological well-being and sense of hope and motivation. Therefore punitive measures and closing borders can only impede and sever the opportunities that children of immigrants and their parents have for meaningful interaction with their immediate and extended families across borders.

In fact such policies contribute to deny the subjectivity and psychological well-being of children of immigrants and their families:

> Where as power-to is a uniting, a bringing together of my doing with the doing of others, the exercise of power-over is separation. Those who exert power over the doing of others deny the subjectivity of those others, deny their part in the flow of doing, exclude them from history. Power-over breaks the mutual recognition: those over whom power is exercised are not recognised... the doing of the doers is deprived of social validation: we and our doing become invisible. (Holloway, 2002, p. 28)

Further research is needed to establish the negative consequences of social policies that inhibit and restrict the ability of children of immigrants and their parents to stay connected with their families across borders in a deep meaningful way. Relationships forged transnationally were most important when they were cemented by personal face-to-face interaction, even if it was only possible occasionally. Therefore, the ability to move freely between countries is essential to the well-being of children of immigrants and their families.

Researchers should continue to investigate how transnational involvement and relationships contribute to children of immigrants' social and psychological well-being. Marriage and having children was found to be an important context for renegotiating racial hierarchies and revisiting/cementing transnational ties to one's ethnic/national origin culture and parents' home country. Language use was instrumental to enable connections and relationships with family members both in the United States and abroad. A concern for being able to transmit one's cultural heritage and family historical memory factored greatly in these Dominican and Colombian respondents' decisions about whom to marry. Much inter-cultural contact theory restricts itself to the exploration of inter-group contact among friends and encounters among strangers. However, there is little research addressing the reasons why such contact does not yield greater rates of cross-racial or cross-ethnic marriages. Understanding how cross-racial and cross-ethnic marriages deal with cultural, racial, and ethnic differences can shed light about how individuals can intensely engage with each other without fear of change in truly inclusive ways.

Finally, this study demonstrates that social class and racial inequalities are usually obscured by a discourse of ethnic differences in achievement and social mobility. As Freire, Martín Baró, and Galeano have called for, this book:

> ... interrogates the mythification of domininant structures' widely disseminated master narratives. Freire has remarked how people are made passive... "by the oppressors' depositing myths indispensable to the preservation of the status quo". (cited by Fischlin & Nandorfy, 2002, p. 147)

Apparent ethnic and cultural differences disappeared in the face of socio-economic and racial structures designed to produce the appearance of cultural differences. Structural conditions such as quality of neighborhood, quality of schools, owning a home, skin color, and parents' cultural capital were more important predictors of variance in educational achievement among respondents than experiences of juggling multiple cultures and being children of immigrants. Life opportunities available to Dominican and Colombian youth were shaped by how they were socially identified and perceived by others which were manifested in residential segregation patterns and lack of access to good schools for those who could not afford to live in working or middle-class neighborhoods. Migration continued to reify social inequalities by transforming cultural capital acquired pre-migration into a form of transnational social class that gave more highly educated immigrant parents, from urban backgrounds, the upper hand over less educated immigrant parents, from rural backgrounds. Therefore, if we are looking to ensure that children of immigrants have equal opportunities to achieve their goals academically and enter the job market, we must focus on reducing inequalities within social structures.

Although behaviors like dropping out of school and getting pregnant as a teenager can often be perceived as behavioral outcomes of acculturative stress or stressors related to the migration process among children of immigrants, this study suggests that, more importantly, respondents had differential access to quality schools and engaging school environments which were instrumental in respondents' decisions to stay or leave schools. Even though respondents may have experienced daily life stressors related to their status as children of immigrants such as, lack of parental supervision and increased family obligations at home, those were not the reasons respondents referred to when discussing their decisions to leave school or have a child as an adolescent. Dropping out of school and getting pregnant in high school was most likely to occur among respondents who were enrolled in poor performing, over-policed, and overcrowded schools. Cutting class was a pivotal marker of disengagement with schools, perceiving schools and teachers as disinterested in their success and educational futures, and losing trust and giving up on an educational system that did not seem to be there to help them pursue their goals and dreams. The findings presented in this book demonstrate that our public schools are failing precisely the students who need them the most and, at the same time, they are reproducing racial and social inequalities that limit the opportunities of these youth to fulfill their academic, social, political and economic potential. We should understand that what is good for children in general is equally, if not more, important for children of immigrants. As this study suggests, having access to good schools, caring teachers, and a supportive and engaging school environment are essential to ensuring children of immigrants have opportunities to succeed in school and entered the job market on their own terms.

Finally, and not less importantly, this book offers insight into racial practices that occur among Latino groups in New York City. Contrary to what some believe, there is racism and discrimination within the Latino community even in the intimacy of families. It discussed how children of immigrants and their parents negotiated different racial attitudes and beliefs within the domain of romantic relationships and marriage. This is not surprising as marriage denotes formal and integral incorporation and acceptance of others into one's family. It is here where parents' racial attitudes become more salient and are challenged by their children. Additional research is needed to help us understand how *mestizaje* functions as a hegemonic discourse that obscures the continued importance of race among Latino groups and Latin American immigrants. The existence of a large number of classifications and categories depicting different degrees of African descent and levels of whiteness among Latin Americans does not mean that racialization processes and race are not pervasive in Latin America or among Latinos in the U.S. Therefore, doing away with racism and discrimination requires more than coming up with a more detailed and accurate taxonomy of classifications. Rather, it necessitates that we challenge the underlying assumptions behind the entire project of racialization; the need to employ racial explanations to discuss social inequalities; and the need for those who are privileged to maintain their privilege.

This book brings a transnational lens to the psychological study of identity formation and explores how children of immigrants develop identities and make sense of them within transnational social fields. It highlights the interconnectedness and intersectionality between national, ethnic, racial, and transnational social identity processes and the inadequacy of traditional ethnic and racial identity models within psychology. It explores the psychological implications of transnational ties and relationships, as well as, the psychological content of transnational identities formed in the multiplicity of transnational life. It contributes to expand the literature about Colombian, Dominican and other Latino immigrants by exploring the effects of class and race differences within and across national groups as well. Finally, this work emphasizes the importance of viewing the experiences of immigrants and their children as part of a larger life project that rests in the continuity and connection between pasts, presents, and futures, between memories, goals, and hopes that nurture their motivation, resiliency, and humanity.

APPENDIX A

Description of Quantitative Variables

Micro Level

Age:
Participants were asked their age at the moment of answering the survey.

Immigrant Generation:
Participants' age at immigration was assessed by asking: "At what age did you first come to the United States to live?" If the participants arrived in the United States to live before the age of 7 years old or where born in the United States, they would be considered 2nd generation immigrants. If the participant arrived in the United States between the ages of 7 and 12 years, they will then be considered 1.5 generation.

Respondents' Educational Attainment:
The phone survey asked participants about the highest grade of schooling completed they had completed at the moment. Their answers were coded as "Less than High School", "Graduated High School or Completed GED", "Some College or Vocational School", "Collcgc Degree (BA/BS)" and "Graduate Studies (Beyond BA/BS).

Number of Children:

Respondents were asked if they have children and how many.

Language Behavior:

In order to established patterns of language use and preference among respondents, the survey asked several questions. Those questions include: What language spoken at home while growing up?, What language used most while growing up?, What language they prefer to speak now? And how often they watch ethnic programming?

Meso Level

Parent's Country of Origin:

Participants were asked "…your parents are…" Responses were coded as "Colombian" or "Dominican" if at least one of the parents had been born in Colombia or Dominican Republic.

Parents' Educational Attainment Prior to Migration:

The phone survey asked participants about the highest grade of schooling completed by their parents in their home country. This was asked separately for the mother and the father. Their answers were coded as "Less than High School", "Graduated High School or Completed GED", "Some College or Vocational School", "College Degree (BA/BS)" and "Graduate Studies (Beyond BA/BS).

Parents' Relationship Stability:

This was measured by asking whether their parents were still together or not, and/or if their mother/father was dead.

Number of Siblings:

This variable measured the number of siblings the respondents have in order to compare family size of the groups.

Transnational Practices:

This variable measured the extent to which respondents performed transnational behavior or practices. Several questions were asked covering a range of possible behaviors such as, how many times they have visited their parents' home country, whether they ever lived in their parents' home country for more than 6 months (why?), and whether they or their parents send money to their home country.

Macro Level

Social Class in U.S.:

It was operationalized as the participants' household annual income for the calendar year 1998. The respondents were asked their household annual income: "the income of everybody who lives in your current household, including wages, salaries, interest, dividends, and all other incomes." This item was recoded as a nominal variable such that "Below Poverty Line (less than $12,000)", "At Poverty Line ($12,000 - $19,000)", "Working Poor ($20,000 - $29,000)", "Working Class ($30,000 – $39,999)" and "Lower Middle Class (40,000 and above.)"

Home Ownership:

This variable was used to assess whether participants were currently living in a house they owed or whether they were paying rent. This question was important because home ownership have been associated with social mobility and higher socio-economic levels. In addition, the quality of schools has been related to higher levels of home ownership in communities.

Race:

The list of racial categories used in this part of the survey corresponds to that approved and used in the 2000 United States Census. This means that Latino/Hispanics was not available to participants as a racial category. Latinos/Hispanics were expected to choose "White" or "Black". It they didn't chose one of the categories given, the interviewer chose "Some other race" and asked the respondent to specify as a write in. Respondents were also asked about the race of their parents and their spouses or partners as well. They were also asked "What was the primary ethnic or racial background of the people in this household?" At this point they could among the following: "Asian", "Hispanic", "Black- not Hispanic", "White- not Hispanic" or "Something else". If they chose "Hispanic" then they were further asked to chose among: "Dominican", "Colombian", "Ecuadorian", "Peru", "Puerto Rico" or "Something else."

Neighborhood Social Characteristics:

As a way to approximate the quality of social conditions existent in the participants' neighborhood, I used a question from the survey that inquire whether people use drugs in the open in their neighborhood. The assumption behind this choice is that people using drugs openly in the streets represents a proxy for socio-economic problems in the neighborhood and lack of institutional resources.

Quality and type of Schools:

This variable was computed by the ISGMNY study. Participants that had attended high school in New York City were asked the name of the high school they attended. Then the researchers of the ISGMNY study created a high school quality index based on data retrieved from the Division of Assessment and Accountability of the New York City Board of Education for the year 1995. It was assumed that there had not been major performance differences in New York City high schools between the 1980's and 1990's. A number of correlations were performed among the different variables and those that do not contributed significantly to graduated rates were eliminated from the index. The variables remaining were converted into z-scores and divided into 5 quartiles of performance from lowest to highest. The different high schools were also classified as "NYC public high school", "NYC catholic high school", "Public high school outside of NYC" and "Private/catholic high school outside of NYC"

APPENDIX B

Respondents' Educational History and Household Characteristics

Colombian Women

Interviewee	Age	Enrolled in College	Married	Children
Diana	26	Yes (4 yr college)	No	Yes (1)
Andrea	27	Yes (4 yr college)	No	No
Lina	34	Finished (BA)	No	No
Marta	21	No (started, didn't finish)	No	No
Paula	30	Yes (4 yr college)	No	No
Sandra	28	No (started, didn't finish)	Yes (in HS)	Yes (1)
Isabel	23	Yes (2 yr college)	No	No
Yohana	32	Yes (4 yr college)	Yes (in HS)	Yes (2)
Stephanie	32	No (started, didn't finish)	No	No
Jacqueline	27	Finished (BA)	No	No
Carolina	29	No (started, didn't finish)	Yes	Yes (1)

Dominican Women

Interviewee	Age	Enrolled in College	Married	Children
Sharina	18	Finished (BA)	No,HS boyfriend	No (father in PR)
Claudia	25	Finished (AA)	Engaged, HS boyfriend	Yes (1)
María	26	Finished (BA)	No	Yes (1)
Deyanira	30	Finished (BA)	Divorced	Yes (1, in HS)
Jessica	21	Enrolled (4 yr college)	No	No
Yadira	24	No (dropped out of HS)	No	Yes (2, in HS)
Monique	29	No (started, didn't finish)	Engaged	No
Dharma	18	NA (Enrolled in HS)	Yes, HS boyfriend	Yes (2)
Marisol	27	Finished (BA)	Yes	Yes (1)
Rosa	29	Finished (BA)	No	No
Yesenia	18	NA (in HS)	No	No

Colombian Men

Interviewee	Age	Enrolled in College	Married	Children
Marcos	24	No (started, didn't finish)	No	No
Andres	18	Yes (4 year college)	No	No
Mario	23	No (started, didn't finish)	No	No
Federico	26	Finished (AA)	No	No
Carlos	25	Finished (BA)	No	No
Mauricio	30	Finished (BA)	Yes	Yes (1)
Gustavo	24	NAVY – Vocational School	Yes (in HS)	Yes (2)

Dominican Men

Interviewee	Age	Enrolled in College	Married	Children
Anibal	28	No (didn't finish)	No, Separated	Yes (1)
Robert	30	No (dropped HS, GED)	No, w/Partner	Yes (2)
José	31	Finished (BA)	No	No
Jorge	32	Finished (BA)	No, Engaged	No
Aurelio	22	No (dropped HS, GED)	No	No
Fernando	25	No	No	No
George	28	No (2 yr college DR)	Yes	Yes (1)
José Luis	21	Yes (4 yr ollege)	No	No
Danilo	20	Yes (4 yr ollege)	No	No
John	22	No (dropped HS)	No	No
Jeremy	21	Yes (4 yr college)	No	No
Anthony	23	Yes (Graduate School)	No	No
Marco	19	No (dropped HS, GED)	No	No
Rogelio	29	No (started, didn't finish)	Yes	No

References

Aguilar, F. (2009). Labour migration and ties of relatedness: Diasporic houses and investments in memory in a rural Philippine village. *Thesis Eleven*, *98*(1), 88-114. doi:10.1177/0725513609105485

Alba, R. (2005). Bright vs. blurred boundaries: Second-generation assimilation and exclusion in France, Germany, and the United States. *Ethnic and Racial Studies*, *28*(1), 20-49. doi:10.1080/0141987042000280003

Alba, R. (2009). *Blurring the color line: The new chance for a more integrated America* (1st ed.). Cambridge, MA: Harvard University Press.

Alba, R., & Nee, V. (2003). *Remaking the American mainstream: Assimilation and contemporary immigration.* Cambridge, MA: Harvard University Press.

Alba, R., & Silberman, R. (2009). The children of immigrants and host-society educational systems: Mexicans in the United States and North Africans in France. *Teachers College Record*, *111*(6), 1444-1475.

Álvarez, J. (1991). *How the Garcia girls lost their accents*. Chapel Hill, NC: Algonquin Books of Chapel Hill.

Álvarez, J. (2004). *Before we were free*. New York, NY: Dell Laurel Leaf.

Álvarez, J. (2010). *In the time of the butterflies* (Reprint.). Chapel Hill, NC: Algonquin Books of Chapel Hill.

Amiot, C. E., de la Sablonniere, R., Terry, D. J., & Smith, J. R. (2007). Integration of social identities in the self: Toward a cognitive-developmental model. *Personality and Social Psychology Review*,

11(4), 364-388. doi:10.1177/1088868307304091

Anzaldúa, G. (1999). *Borderlands la frontera: The new mestiza* (Second Edition.). San Francisco, CA: Aunt Lute Books.

Anzaldúa, G. (2002). (Un)natural bridges, (un)safe spaces. In G. Anzaldúa & A. Keating (Eds.), *This bridge we call home* (pp. 1-6). New York, NY: Routledge.

Aparicio, A. (2006). *Dominican-Americans and the politics of empowerment*. Gainesville, FL: University Press of Florida.

Arana, M. (2002). *American chica: Two worlds, one childhood*. New York, NY: Delta Trade Paperbacks.

Ayala, J. (2005). *Corporate fogs and mestiza visions: Parallels between student and institution experiences in a faith-based college* (Dissertation). New York, NY: City University of New York. Retrieved from ProQuest. (845782101)

Ayala, J. (2006). Confianza, consejos, and contradictions: Gender and sexuality lessons between Latina adolescent daugthers and mothers. In J. Denner & B. Guzman (Eds.), *Latina girls: Voices of adolescent strength in the U.S.* (Illustrated edition., pp. 29-43). New York, NY: New York University Press.

Bargal, D. (2006). Personal and intellectual influences leading to Lewin's paradigm of action research: Towards the 60th anniversary of Lewin's 'Action research and minority problems' (1946). *Action Research*, *4*(4), 367-388. doi:10.1177/1476750306070101

Basch, L., Glick-Schiller, N., & Szanton-Blanc, C. (1994). Transnational projects: A new perspective. In *Nations unbound: Transnational projects, post-colonial predicaments and deterrritorialized nation-states* (pp. 1-48). Amsterdam: Overseas Publishers Association.

Benet-Martinez, V., Leu, J., Lee, F., & Morris, M. W. (2002). Negotiating biculturalism: Cultural frame switching in biculturals with oppositional versus compatible cultural identities. *Journal of Cross-Cultural Psychology*, *33*, 492-516.

Bergad, L. W. (2009). *The Latino population of New York City, 2008* (Latino Data Project Report No. 32). New York, NY: Center for Latin American, Caribbean and Latino Studies - The CUNY Graduate Center. Retrieved from http://web.gc.cuny.edu/lastudies/latinodataprojectreports/The%20Latino%20Population%20of%20New%20York%20City%202008.pdf

Bergad, L. W. (2011). *The Latino Population of New York City, 1990-2010* (Latino Data Project Report No. 44). New York, NY: Center for Latin American, Caribbean and Latino Studies - The CUNY Graduate Center. Retrieved from http://clacls.gc.cuny.edu/files/2013/10/The-Latino-Population-of-New-York-City-1990-2010.pdf

Bermúdez Torres, A. (2003). *Gender and forced migration: The experiences of Colombian refugees living in London* . Unpublished Dissertation. London: Queen Mary, University of London.

Bermúdez Torres, A. (2005). *Armed conflict, peace processes and forced migrants* (Forced Migration Online Research Guide No. FMO039). Forced Migration Online. Retrieved from http://www.forcedmigration.org/guides/fmo039/

Bermúdez Torres, A. (2006). *Colombian migration to Europe: Political transnationalism in the middle of conflict* (working Paper No. 39). London: Centre on Migration, Policy and Society, University of Oxford.

Berry, J. W. (1997). Immigration, acculturation and adaptation. *Applied Psychology, 46*, 5-68.

Berry, J. W. (2001). A psychology of immigration. *Journal of Social Issues, 57*(3), 615-631.

Bhatia, S. (2002). Acculturation, dialogical voices and the construction of the diasporic self. *Theory & Psychology, 12*(1), 55-77.

Bhatia, S. (2007). *American karma: Race, culture, and identity in the Indian diaspora.* New York, NY: New York University Press.

Bhatia, S., & Ram, A. (2001a). Rethinking 'acculturation' in relation to diasporic cultures and postcolonial identities. *Human Development, 44*, 1-17.

Bhatia, S., & Ram, A. (2001b). Locating the dialogical self in the age of transnational migrations, border crossings and diasporas. *Culture & Psychology, 7*, 297-309.

Bikmen, N. (2007). *History, memory, and identity: Remembering the homeland in Exile* (Unpublished Dissertation). New York, NY: The CUNY Graduate Center.

Bourdieu, P. (1984). *Distinctions. A social critique of the judgment of taste.* Cambridge, MA: Harvard University Press.

Bourdieu, P. (2008). *Sketch for a self-analysis.* (R. Nice, Tran.). Chicago and London: The University of Chicago Press.

Bromberg, P. M. (1998). *Standing in the spaces.* Hillsdale, NJ: The

Analytic Press.
Bronfenbrenner, U., & Morris, P. A. (1998). Bioecological model of human development. In W. Damon & R. M. Lerner (Eds.), *Handbook of child psychology: Theoretical models of human development* (1st ed., pp. 793-825). New York, NY: John Wiley and Sons.
Bronfenbrenner, U., & Morris, P. A. (2006). Bioecological model of human development. In W. Damon & R. M. Lerner (Eds.), *Handbook of child psychology: Theoretical models of human development* (6th ed., pp. 793-825). New York, NY: John Wiley and Sons.
Butterfield, S. (2004). "We're just Black": The racial and ethnic identities of second-generation West Indies in New York. In P. Kasinitz, J. H. Mollenkopf, & M. C. Waters (Eds.), *Becoming New Yorkers: Ethnographies of the new second generation* (pp. 288-312). New York, NY: Russell Sage Foundation.
Carter, P. L. (2006). Straddling boundaries: Identity, culture, and school. *Sociology of Education*, *79*(4), 304.
Charmaz, C. (2000). Grounded theory: Objectivist and constructivist methods. In N. Denzin & Y. Lincoln (Eds.), *Handbook of qualitative research* (Second ed.). London: Sage.
CIA - The world factbook. (2010). Washington, D.C.: Central Intelligence Agency. Retrieved from https://www.cia.gov/library/publications/the-world-factbook/geos/co.html
Clifford, J. (1994). Diasporas. *Cultural Anthropology*, *9*(3), 302-338.
Cole, E. R. (2009). Intersectionality and research in psychology. *American Psychologist*, *64*(3), 170-180.
Colic-Peisker, V., & Walker, I. (2003). Human capital, acculturation and social identity: Bosnian refugees in Australia. *Journal of Community & Applied Social Psychology*, *13*, 337-360.
Collier, M. W., & Gamarra, E. A. (2003). The Colombian diaspora in South Florida: A report of the Colombian Studies Institute. Presented at the XXIV International Congress of Latin American Studies Association, Dallas, TX.
Comas-Diaz, L. (1987). Feminist therapy with mainland Puerto Rican women. *Psychology of Women Quarterly*, *11*(4), 461-474.
Daiute, C., & Fine, M. (2003). Youth perspectives on violence and injustice. *Journal of Social Issues*, *59*(1), 1-14.

Davies, C. (2000). Fernando Ortiz's transculturation: The postcolonial intellectual and the politics of cultural representation. In R. W. Fiddian (Ed.), *Postcolonial perspectives on the cultures of Latin America and Lusophone Africa* (pp. 141-168). Liverpool, UK: Liverpool University Press.

Deaux, K. (2000). Surveying the landscape of immigration: Social psychological perspectives. *Journal of Community & Applied Social Psychology*, *10*, 421-431.

Deaux, K. (2006). *To be an immigrant*. New York:, NY Russell Sage Foundation.

Deaux, K. (2008). To be an American: Immigration, hyphenation, and incorporation. *Journal of Social Issues*, *64*(4), 925-943.

Deaux, K., Bikmen, N., Gilkes, A., Ventuneac, A., Joseph, Y., Payne, Y. A., & Steele, C. M. (2007). Becoming American: Stereotype threat effects in Afro-Caribbean immigrant groups. *Social Psychology Quarterly*, *70*(4), 384-404. doi:10.1177/019027250707000408

Deaux, K., & Ethier, K. (1998). Negotiating social identity. In J. Swim & C. Stangor (Eds.), *Prejudice: The target's perspective* (pp. 301-323). San Diego, CA: Academic Press.

Deaux, K., & Martin, D. (2003). Interpersonal networks and social categories: Specifying levels of context in identity processes. *Social Psychology Quarterly*, *66*, 101-117.

Development aid at a glance 2010: Statistics by region (Development Co-operation Report). (2010). Development Aid at a Glance. France - Washington, DC: Organization for Economic Co-operation and Development. Retrieved from http://www.oecd.org/document/11/0,3343,en_2649_34447_2002187_1_1_1_1,00.html

Dion, K. K. (2006). On the development of identity: Perspectives from immigrant families. In R. Mahalingam (Ed.), *Cultural psychology of immigrants* (pp. 299-314). Mahwah, NJ: Lawrence Erlbaum Associates Publishers.

Dorfman, A. (2003). The wandering bigamist of language. In I. D. Courtivron (Ed.), *Lives in translation: Bilingual writers on identity and creativity* (1st ed., pp. 29-38). New York, NY: Palgrave Macmillan.

Drotbohm, H. (2009). Horizons of long-distance intimacies: Reciprocity, contribution and disjuncture in Cape Verde. *The*

History of the Family, *14*(2), 132-149.

Duany, J. (2005). Dominican migration to Puerto Rico: A transnational perspective. *Centro Journal*, *17*(1), 242-269.

DuBois, W. (1903). *The souls of black folk* (1990th ed.). New York, NY: Vintage Books.

Dussel, E. (2002). World-system and "trans"-modernity. *Nepantla: Views from the South*, *3*(2), 221–244.

Eckstein, S., & Barberia, L. (2002). Grounding immigrant generations in history: Cuban Americans and their transnational ties. *International Migration Review*, *36*(3), 799-837.

Edmonds, C., & Killen, M. (2009). Do adolescents' perceptions of parental racial attitudes relate to their intergroup contact and cross-race relationships? *Group Processes & Intergroup Relations*, *12*(1), 5-21. doi:10.1177/1368430208098773

Edmonds, C. M. (2006). The influence of perceptions of parent racial attitude and intergroup contact on adolescent cross-race relationships. *Dissertation Abstracts International: Section B: The Sciences and Engineering*, *66*(12-B). Retrieved from http://search.ebscohost.com/login.aspx?direct=true&db=psyh&AN=2006-99012-276&site=ehost-live

Ehrensaft, E., & Tousignant, M. (2006). Immigration and resilience. In D. L. Sam & J. W. Berry (Eds.), *The Cambridge handbook of acculturation psychology*, Cambridge handbooks in psychology (1st ed., pp. 469-483). Cambridge, MA: Cambridge University Press.

Escobar, C. (2004). Dual citizenship and political participation: Migrants in the interplay of United States and Colombian politics. *Latino Studies*, *2*, 45-69.

Espín, O. (1997). *Latina realities: Essays on healing, migration, and sexuality*. Boulder, CA: Westview Press.

Espín, O. (2006). Gender, sexuality, language and migration. In R. Mahalingam (Ed.), *Cultural psychology of immigrants* (pp. 241-258). Mahwah, NJ: Lawrence Erlbaum Associates Publishers.

Espiritu, Y. L., & Tran, T. (2002). "ViệtNam, Nước Tôi" (Vietnam, my country): Vietnamese Americans and transnationalism. In P. Levitt & M. C. Waters (Eds.), *The changing face of home the transnational lives of the second generation* (pp. 367-398). New York, NY: Russell Sage Foundation.

Ethier, K., & Deaux, K. (1994). Negotiating social identity when contexts change: maintaining identification and responding to threat. *Journal of Personality and Social Psychology, 67*, 243-251.

Faist, T. (2001). Dual citizenship as overlapping membership. *International Migration and Ethnic Relations, 3*, 1-43.

Fallis, R. K., & Opotow, S. (2003). Are students failing school or are schools failing students? Class cutting in high school. *Journal of Social Issues, 59*(1), 103-119.

Farley, R., & Alba, R. (2002). The new second generation in the United States. *International Migration Review, 36*(3), 669-701.

Fine, M. (1991). *Framing dropouts: Notes on the politics of an urban public high school.* Albany, NY: State University of New York Press.

Fischlin, D., & Nandorfy, M. (2002). *Eduardo Galeano : Through the looking glass.* Montréal and New York: Black Rose Books.

Foner, N. (2001). Transnationalism then and now: New York immigrants today and at the turn of the twentieth century. In H. R. Cordero-Guzmán, R. C. Smith, & R. Grosfoguel (Eds.), *Migration, transnationalization & race in a changing New York* (pp. 58-86). Philadelphia, PA: Temple University Press.

Foner, N. (2002). Second-generation transnationalism, then and now. In P. Levitt & M. C. Waters (Eds.), *The changing face of home the transnational lives of the second generation* (pp. 242-254). New York, NY: Russell Sage Foundation.

Foster, R. J. (1991). Making national cultures in the global ecumene. *Annual Review of Anthropology, 20*, 235-260.

Fouron, G. E. (2003). Haitian immigrants in the United States: The imagining of where 'home' is in their transnational social fields. In B. S. A. Yeoh, M. W. Charney, & C. K. Tong (Eds.), *Approaching transnationalisms: Studies on transnational societies, multicultural contacts.* Massachusetts, MA: Springer.

Fouron, G. E., & Glick-Schiller, N. (2002). The generation of identity: Redefining the second generation within a transnational social field. In P. Levitt & M. C. Waters (Eds.), *The changing face of home the transnational lives of the second generation* (pp. 168-210). New York, NY: Russell Sage Foundation.

Frank, R., Akresh, I. R., & Lu, B. (2010). Latino immigrants and the U.S. racial order: How and where do they fit in? *American Sociological Review, 75*(3).

Fuligni, A. J., & Pedersen, S. (2002). Family obligation and the transition to young adulthood. *Developmental Psychology, 38*(5), 856-868.

Galeano, E. (1992). *The book of embraces*. New York, NY: W. W. Norton & Company.

García-Coll, C., & Marks, A. K. (2009). *Immigrant stories*. Childhood development in cultural context. New York, NY: Oxford University Press US.

Glasser, B., & Strauss, A. L. (1967). *The discovery of grounded theory: Strategies for qualitative research*. New York, NY: Aldine.

Glick-Schiller, N., & Fouron, G. E. (1998). Transnational lives and national identities: The identity politics of Haitian immigrants. In M. P. Smith & L. E. Guarnizo (Eds.), *Transnationalism from below* (pp. 130-159). New Brunswick, NJ: Transaction Publishers.

Glick-Schiller, N., & Fouron, G. E. (1999). Terrains of blood and nation: Haitian transnational social fields. *Ethnic and Racial Studies, 22*(2), 341-366.

Golbert, R. (2001). Transnational orientations from home: Constructions of Israel and transnational space among Ukrainian Jewish youth. *Journal of Ethnic and Migration Studies, 27*(4), 713-731.

Goodwin, J., & O'Connor, H. (2006). Contextualising the research process: Using interviewer notes in the secondary analysis of qualitative data. *The Qualitative Report, 11*(2), 374-392.

Gordon, K. (2003). The impermanence of being: Toward a psychology of uncertainty. *Journal of Humanistic Psychology, 43*, 96-117.

Graham, P. M. (2001). Political incorporation and re-incorporation: Simultaneity in the Dominican migrant experience. In H. R. Cordero-Guzmán, R. C. Smith, & R. Grosfoguel (Eds.), *Migration, transnationalization & race in a changing New York* (pp. 87-108). Philadelphia, PA: Temple University Press.

Grasmuck, S., & Pessar, P. (1991). *Between two islands: Dominican international migration*. Berkeley, CA: University of California Press.

Greene, M. (2001). *Variations on a blue guitar: The Lincoln Center Institute lectures on aesthetic education*. New York, NY: Teachers College Press.

Grieco, E. M., Acosta, Y. D., de la Cruz, P., Gambino, C., Gryn, T., Larsen, L. J., Trevelyan, E.N. & Walters, N. P. (2012). *The Foreign-Born Population in the United States: 2010* (No. ACS-

19). Washington, D.C.: U.S. CensusBureau. Retrieved from http://www.census.gov/prod/2012pubs/acs-19.pdf

Guarnizo, L. E., & Díaz, L. M. (1999). Transnational migration: A view from Colombia. *Ethnic and Racial Studies*, *22*(2), 397-421.

Guarnizo, L. E., Sanchez, A. I., & Roach, E. M. (1999). Mistrust, fragmented solidarity and transnational migration: Colombians in New York City and Los Angeles. *Ethnic and Racial Studies*, *22*(2), 367-396.

Gutierrez, K., Rymes, B., & Larson, J. (1995). Script, counterscript, and underlife in the classroom: James Brown v. board of education. *Harvard Educational Review*, *65*, 441-471.

Hart, S. N., & Lindegger, G. C. (2002). Self and culture as revealed in career narratives. In *Self-concept research: Driving international research agendas*. Presented at the 2nd International Biennial, Sydney, Australia.

Hermans, H. J. (1999). Dialogical thinking and self-innovation. *Culture & Psychology*, *5*(1), 67-87. doi:10.1177/1354067X9951004

Hermans, H. J. (2001). The dialogical self: Toward a theory of personal and cultural positioning. *Culture & Psychology*, *7*(3), 243-281. doi:10.1177/1354067X0173001

Hermans, H. J., & Kempen, H. J. (1998). Moving cultures: The perilous problems of cultural dichotomies in a globalizing society. *American psychologist*, *53*(10), 1111–1120.

Hermans, H. J., Kempen, H. J., & Van Loon, R. J. (1992). The dialogical self: Beyond individualism and rationalism. *American Psychologist*, *47*, 23-33.

Hernández, R. (2002). *The mobility of workers under advanced capitalism*. New York, NY: Columbia University Press.

Hill, N. E., & Torres, K. (2010). Negotiating the American dream: The paradox of aspirations and achievement among Latino students and engagement between their families and schools. *Journal of Social Issues*, *66*(1), 95-112. doi:10.1111/j.1540-4560.2009.01635.x.

Hirabayashi, L. R. (2002). Reconsidering transculturation and power. *Amerasia Journal*, *28*(2), ix-xxii.

Hirsch, J. S. (2000). En el norte la mujer manda: Gender, generation, and geography in a Mexican transnational community. In N. Foner, R. G. Rumbaut, & S. J. Gold (Eds.), *Immigration research for a new century* (pp. 53-70). New York, NY: Russell Sage Foundation Publications.

Hoffman, A., & Escala, Z. (1999). The Colombian community in metropolitan New York: Who are we and where are we going? *Migration World Magazine*, *27*, 13-17.

Hoffman, E. (2003). P.S. In I. D. Courtivron (Ed.), *Lives in translation: Bilingual writers on identity and creativity* (1st ed., pp. 49-54). New York, NY: Palgrave Macmillan.

Holloway, J. (2002). *Change the world without taking power*. London: Pluto Press.

Hondagneu-Sotelo, P., & Avila, E. (1997). "I'm here, but I'm there". The meanings of Latina transnational motherhood. *Gender and Society*, *11*(5), 548-571.

Hondagneu-Sotelo, P., & Avila, E. (2003). "I'm here but I'm there": The meanings of Latina transnational motherhood. In *Gender and U.S. immigration*. Berkeley, CA: University of California Press.

Hong, Y., Benet-Martinez, V., Chiu, C., & Morris, M. W. (2003). Boundaries of cultural influence: construct activation as a mechanism for cultural differences in social perception. *Journal of Cross-Cultural Psychology*, *34*(4), 453-464.

Hong, Y., & Chiu, C. (2001). Toward a paradigm shift: From cross-cultural differences in social cognition to social-cognitive mediation of cultural differences. *Social Cognition*, *19*(3: Special issue), 181–196.

Hong, Y., Morris, M. W., Chiu, C., & Benet-Martinez, V. (2000). Multicultural minds: A dynamic constructivist approach to culture and cognition. *American Psychologist*, *55*(7), 709–720.

Hutnyk, J. (2005). Hybridity. *Ethnic & Racial Studies*, *28*(1), 79-102. doi:10.1080/0141987042000280021

Itzigsohn, J. (2004). The formation of Latino and Latina panethnic identities. In N. Foner & G. Fredrickson (Eds.), *Not just Black and White: Historical and contemporary perspectives on immigration, race, and ethnicity in the United States* (pp. 197-234). New York, NY: Russell Sage Foundation Publications.

Itzigsohn, J. (2005). The Dominican Immigration experience. *Centro Journal*, *17*(1), 270-283.

Itzigsohn, J. (2009). Immigration and American society. In *Encountering American faultlines: Race. class, and the Dominican experience in Providence* (pp. 3-21). New York, NY: Russell Sage Foundation Publications.

Itzigsohn, J., Giorguli, S., & Vazquez, O. (2005). Immigrant incorporation and racial identity: Racial self-identification among Dominican immigrants. *Ethnic and Racial Studies*, *28*, 50-78. doi:10.1080/0141984042000280012

Itzigsohn, J., & Giorguli-Saucedo, S. (2005). Incorporation, transnationalism, and gender: Immigrant incorporation and transnational participation as gendered processes. *International Migration Review*, *39*(4), 895-920. doi:10.1111/j.1747-7379.2005.tb00293.x

Jensen, L., Cohen, J. H., Toribio, A. J., Jong, G. F. D., & Rodríguez, L. (2006). Ethnic identities, language, and economic outcomes among Dominicans in a new destination. *Social Science Quarterly*, *87*(5), 1088-1099. doi:10.1111/j.1540-6237.2006.00417.x

Josselson, R. (1992). *The space between us: Exploring the dimensions of human relationships*. The Jossey-Bass Social and Behavioral Science. San Francisco, CA: Jossey-Bass Publishers.

Josselson, R. (2003). The space between in group psychotherapy: Application of a multidimensional model of relationship. *Group*, *27*(4), 203-219.

Kasinitz, P., Mollenkopf, J. H., & Waters, M. C. (2004). *Becoming New Yorkers: Ethnographies of the new second generation*. New York, NY: Russell Sage Foundation.

Kasinitz, P., Mollenkopf, J. H., Waters, M. C., & Holdaway, J. (2008). *Inheriting the city: The children of immigrants come of age*. New York: Russell Sage Foundation and Harvard University Press.

Kasinitz, P., Waters, M. C., Mollenkopf, J. H., & Anil, M. (2002). Transnationalism and the children of immigrants in contemporary New York. In P. Levitt & M. C. Waters (Eds.), *The changing face of home the transnational lives of the second generation.* (pp. 96-122). New York: Russell Sage Foundation.

Kibria, N. (2002). Of blood, belonging, and homeland trips: Transnationalism and identity among second-generation Chinese and Korean Americans. In P. Levitt & M. C. Waters (Eds.), *The changing face of home the transnational lives of the second generation* (pp. 295-311). New York, NY: Russell Sage Foundation.

Kristen, C. (2007). The educational attainment of the second generation in Germany: Social origin and gender inequality. *Ethnicities*, *7*(3), 343-366.

LaFromboise, T., Coleman, H. L. K., & Gerton, J. (1993).

Psychological impact of biculturalism: evidence and theory. *Psychological Bulletin, 114*(3), 395-412.

Lareau, A., & Weininger, E. (2008). Class and the transition to adulthood. In A. Lareau & D. Conley (Eds.), *Social class: How does it work?* (pp. 118-159). New York: Russell Sage Foundation.

Lee, E., & Burkam, D. (2002). *Inequality at the starting gate: Social background differences in achievements children begin school.* Washington, DC: Economic Policy Institute.

Levitt, P. (2000). Migrants participate across borders: Towards an understanding of forms and consequences. In N. Foner & R. G. Rumbaut (Eds.), *Immigration research for a new century* (pp. 459-479). New York, NY: Russell Sage Foundation.

Levitt, P. (2001a). Research. *Peggy Levitt faculty webpage*. Retrieved May 15, 2003, from http://www.peggylevitt.org/pages/research2.html

Levitt, P. (2001b). *The transnational villagers* (1st ed.). Berkeley, CA: University of California Press.

Levitt, P. (2002). The ties that change: Relations to the ancestral home over the life cycle. In P. Levitt & M. C. Waters (Eds.), *The changing face of home the transnational lives of the second generation* (pp. 123-144). New York, NY?: Russell Sage Foundation.

Levitt, P., DeWind, J., & Vertovec, S. (2003). International perspectives on transnational migration: An introduction. *International Migration Review, 37*(3), 565-575.

Levitt, P., & Glick-Schiller, N. (2004). Conceptualizing simultaneity: A transnational social field perspective on society. *International Migration Review, 38*(3), 1002-1039.

Levitt, P., & Waters, M. C. (Eds.). (2002). *The changing face of home: The transnational lives of the second generation.* New York, NY: Russell Sage Foundation.

Lewin, K. (1997). *Resolving social conflicts and field theory in social science.* Washington, DC: American Psychological Association.

Li, G. (2010). Social class, culture, and "good parenting": Voices of low-SES families. In M. Miller Marsh & T. Turner-Vorbeck (Eds.), *(Mis)understanding families: Learning from real families in our schools* (pp. 162-178). New York, NY: Teachers College Press.

López, N. (2002). *Hopeful girls, troubled boys: Race and gender*

disparity in urban education (1st ed.). New York, NY: Routledge.
López, N. (2004). Unraveling the race-gender gap in education: Second-generation Dominican men's high school experiences. In P. Kasinitz, J. H. Mollenkopf, & M. C. Waters (Eds.), *Becoming New Yorkers: Ethnographies of the new second generation* (pp. 28-56). New York, NY: Russell Sage Foundation.
López, N. (2006). Resistance to race and gender oppression: Dominican high school girls in New York City. In J. Denner & B. Guzman (Eds.), *Latina girls: Voices of adolescent strength in the U.S.* (illustrated edition.). New York, NY: New York University Press.
Lundquist, J. H., & Massey, D. S. (2005). Politics or economics? International migration during the Nicaraguan contra war. *Journal of Latin American Studies, 37*, 29-53.
Mahalingam, R. (2006). Cultural psychology of immigrants: An introduction. In R. Mahalingam (Ed.), *Cultural psychology of immigrants* (pp. 1-12). Mahwah, NJ: Lawrence Erlbaum Associates Publishers.
Mahalingam, R., Balan, S., & Haritatos, J. (2008). Engendering immigrant psychology: An intersectionality perspective. *Sex Roles, 59*(5), 326-336. doi:10.1007/s11199-008-9495-2
Mahalingam, R., & Haritatos, J. (2006). Cultural psychology of gender and immigration. In R. Mahalingam (Ed.), *Cultural psychology of immigrants* (pp. 259-273). Mahwah, NJ: Lawrence Erlbaum Associates Publishers.
Mahler, S. (2001). Suburban transnational migrants: Long Island's Salvadorians. In H. R. Cordero-Guzmán, R. C. Smith, & R. Grosfoguel (Eds.), *Migration, transnationalization & race in a changing New York* (pp. 109-130). Philadelphia, PA: Temple University Press.
Marrow, H. B. (2008). Hispanic immigration, black population size, and intergroup relations in rural, and intergroup relations in the rural and small-town south. In D. S. Massey (Ed.), *New faces in new places* (pp. 211-249). New York, NY: Russell Sage Foundation Publications.
Martin, J. L. (2003). What s field theory? *American Journal of Sociology, 109*(1), 1-49. doi:10.1086/375201
Martín-Baró, I., & Cañas, J. S. (1990). ¿Trabajador alegre o trabajador explotado? La identidad nacional del Salvadoreño. *Revista*

Interamericana de Psicología/ Interamerican Journal of Psychology, 24(1), 1-24.

Meyer, J., Charum, J., Bernal, D., Gaillard, J., Granes, J., Leon, J., Montenegro, A., et al. (1997). Turning brain drain into brain gain: The Colombian Experience of the diaspora option. *Science Technology and Society, 2*(2), 285-315. doi:10.1177/097172189700200205

Mignolo, W. (2000). *Local histories/global designs*. Princeton, NJ: Princeton University Press.

Miller, R. E., & Spellmeyer, K. (2008). Preface. In R. E. Miller & K. Spellmeyer (Eds.), *The new humanities reader* (3rd ed.). Florence, KY: Wadsworth Publishing.

Miller, S. C., Olson, M. A., & Fazio, R. H. (2004). Perceived reactions to interracial romantic relationships: When race is used as a cue to status. *Group Processes Intergroup Relations, 7*(4), 354-369. doi:10.1177/1368430204046143

Moraga, C., & Anzaldúa, G. (1984). *This bridge called my back: Writings by radical women of color* (Second edition.). New York, NY: Kitchen Table: Women of Color Press.

Murphy, E. J., & Mahalingam, R. (2004). Transnational ties and mental health of Caribbean immigrants. *Journal of Immigrant Health, 6*(4), 167–178.

Murphy, E. J. (2006). Transnational ties and mental health. In R. Mahalingam (Ed.), *Cultural psychology of immigrants* (pp. 79-92). Mahwah, NJ: Lawrence Erlbaum Associates Publishers.

Newman, J. (2003). *Narrating displacement: Oral histories of Sri Lankan women* (Working Paper No. 15). Refugee Studies Centre. Oxford, UK: International Development Centre, University of Oxford. Retrieved March 10, 2010 from www.rsc.ox.ac.uk/PDFs/workingpaper15.pdf

Nguyen, A. D., Huynh, Q., & Benet-Martinez, V. (2009). Bicultural identities in a diverse world. In *Diversity in mind and action: Multiple faces of identities*, Race and ethnicity in Psychology. Santa Barbara, CA: Praeger.

Nishino, Y., Ujiie, T., Ninomiya, K., Igarashi, A., Inoue, H., & Yamamoto, C. (2009). A longitudinal study of the trajectories of deviant behavior among junior high school students. *Japanese Journal of Psychology, 80*(1), 17-24.

Oboler, S. (1995). *Ethnic labels, Latino lives. Identity and the politics of (re)presentation in the United States.* Minneapolis, MN: University of Minnesota Press.

van Ours, J. C., & Veenman, J. (2001). *The educational attainment of second generation immigrants in the Netherlands* (No. 297). Discussion Paper. Boon, Germany: Institute for the Study of Labor. Retrieved March 9, 2010 from ftp://repec.iza.org/RePEc/Discussionpaper/dp297.pdf

Padilla, B., & Peixoto, J. (2007). *Latin American immigration to southern Europe* (Research Report). Migration information source. Washington, D.C.: Migration Policy Institute. Retrieved from http://www.migrationinformation.org/Feature/display.cfm?ID=609

Pearson, B. Z. (2008). *Raising a bilingual child: A step-by-step guide for parents.* Living language series. New York, NY: Random House, Inc.

Pedraza, S. (2006). Assimilation or transnationalism? Conceptual models of the immigrant experience in America. In R. Mahalingam (Ed.), *Cultural psychology of immigrants* (pp. 33-54). Mahwah, NJ: Lawrence Erlbaum Associates Publishers.

Pessach-Ramati, D., & Josselson, R. (2007). Vicissitudes of "holding" in the immigration experience: The case of Ethiopian Israeli adolescents. In R. Josselson, A. Lieblich, & D. P. McAdams (Eds.), *The meaning of others: Narrative studies of relationships*, The narrative study of lives series (pp. 143-163). Washington, D.C.: American Psychological Association (APA).

Pessar, P. (1987). The Dominicans: Women in the household and the garment industry. In N. Foner (Ed.), *New immigrants in New York.* New York, NY: Columbia University Press.

Pettigrew, T. F. (2006). A two-level approach to anti-immigrant prejudice and discrimination. In R. Mahalingam (Ed.), *Cultural psychology of immigrants* (pp. 95-112). Mahwah, NJ: Lawrence Erlbaum Associates Publishers.

Pew Hispanic Center. (2009, December 11) Between Two Worlds: How Young Latinos Come of Age in America. Washington, D.C. Retrieved from http://pewhispanic.org/reports/report.php?ReportID=117

Phinney, J. S. (2002). Ethnic identity and acculturation. In K. M. Chun, P. B. Organista, & G. Marin (Eds.), *Acculturation: Advances in theory, measurement, and applied research* (1st ed., pp. 63-81). Washington, DC: American Psychological Association.

Phinney, J. S., & Devich-Navarro, M. (1997). Variations in bicultural identification among African American and Mexican American adolescents. *Journal of Research on Adolescence*, *7*, 3-32.

Phinney, J. S., Horenczyk, G., Liebkind, K., & Vedder, P. (2001). Ethnic identity, immigration, and well-being: An interactional perspective. *Journal of Social Issues*, *57*(3), 493-510.

Portes, A. (1999). Conclusion: Towards a new world- the origins and effects of transnational activities. *Ethnic and Racial Studies*, *22*(2), 463-477.

Portes, A. (2003). Conclusion: Theoretical convergences and empirical evidence in the study of immigrant transnationalism. *International Migration Review*, *37*(3), 874-892.

Portes, A., Escobar, C., & Radford, A. (2007). Immigrant transnational organizations and development: A comparative study. *International Migration Review*, *37*(3), 874-892.

Portes, A., Fernandez-Kelly, P., & Haller, W. (2008). *The adaptation of the immigrant second generation in America: Theoretical overview and recent evidence* (Working Paper No. 08-02). Center for Migration and Development. Princeton, NJ: Princeton University. Retrieved March 5, 2010 from http://cmd.princeton.edu/papers/wp0802.pdf

Portes, A., Fernandez-Kelly, P., & Haller, W. (2009). The adaptation of the immigrant second generation in America: A theoretical overview and recent evidence. *Journal of Ethnic & Migration Studies*, *35*(7), 1077-1104. doi:10.1080/13691830903006127

Portes, A., Guarnizo, L. E., & Landolt, P. (1999). The study of transnationalism: Pitfalls and promise of an emergent research field. *Ethnic and Racial Studies*, *22*(2), 217-237.

Portes, A., & Rumbaut, R. G. (2001). *Legacies : the story of the immigrant second generation.* Berkeley, CA: University of California Press.

Portes, A., & Zhou, M. (1993). The new second generation: Segmented assimilation and its variants. *The ANNALS of the American Academy of Political and Social Science,*, 74 -96 vol. 530:

Pouliasi, K., & Verkuyten, M. (2007). Networks of meaning and the bicultural mind: A structural equation modeling approach. *Journal of Experimental Social Psychology*, *43*(6), 955-963.

Pratt, M. L. (1991). Arts of the contact zone. In *Profession 91* (pp. 33-40). New York NY: MLA.

Puzzanchera, C. (2000). What is truancy? The strength of the problem. *Psychopathology, 12*, 737–762.

Riaño-Alcalá, P., & Goldring, L. (2007). A Colombian diaspora? Characteristics, tensions and challenges in transnational engagements. In *After the Washington concensus: Collaborative scholarship for a new América*. Presented at the XXVII International Congress of Latin American Studies Association, Montréal, Canada.

Riccio, B. (2001). From 'ethnic group' to 'transnational community': Senegalese migrants' ambivalent experiences and multiple trajectories. *Journal of Ethnic and Migration Studies, 27*(4), 583-599.

Ricourt, M. (2002). *Dominicans in New York City*. New York, NY: Routledge.

Rivera Sánchez, L. (2008). Translocalidad y establecimiento: Lugares y espacios en la vida migrante. In D. Hiernaux & M. Zárate Vidal (Eds.), *Espacios y transnacionalismo*, Colección estudios transnacionales (pp. 195-233). Coyoácan, México: Casa Juan Pablos.

Robins, K., & Aksoy, A. (2001). From spaces of identity to mental spaces: lessons from Turkish-Cypriot cultural experience in Britain. *Journal of Ethnic and Migration Studies, 27*(4), 685. doi:10.1080/13691830120090458

Roth, W. (2004). Understanding race at home and abroad: The impact of migration on Dominican and Puerto Rican identities (p. 20). Presented at the Annual Meeting of the American Sociological Association, San Francisco, CA. Retrieved March 19, 2010 from http://www.allacademic.com/meta/p110500_index.html

Rothon, C., Heath, A., & Lessard-Phillips, L. (2009). The educational attainments of the "second generation": A comparative study of Britain, Canada, and the United States. *Teachers College Record, 111*(6), 1404-1443.

Ruiz, S. A., & Silverstein, M. (2007). Relationships with grandparents and the emotional well-being of late adolescent and young adult grandchildren. *Journal of Social Issues, 63*(4), 793-808. doi:10.1111/j.1540-4560.2007.00537.x

Rumbaut, R. G. (2002). Severed or sustained attachments? Language, identity, and imagined communities in the post-immigrant generation. In P. Levitt & M. C. Waters (Eds.), *The changing face of home the transnational lives of the second generation* (pp. 1-32). New York, NY: Russell Sage Foundation.

Rumbaut, R. G. (2008). The coming of the second generation: Immigration and ethnic mobility in southern California. *The ANNALS of the American Academy of Political and Social Science, 620*(1), 196-236. doi:10.1177/0002716208322957

Salazar Parreñas, R. (2005). *Children of global migration: Transnational families and gendered woes*. Palo Alto, CA: Stanford University Press.

Sam, D. L., & Berry, J. W. (2006). *The Cambridge handbook of acculturation psychology* (1st ed.). Cambridge, MA: Cambridge University Press.

Scahill, J. H. (1993). Meaning-construction and habitus. *Philosophy of Education Society*. Retrieved March 5, 2010, from http://www.ed.uiuc.edu/eps/PES-Yearbook/93_docs/SCAHILL.HTM

Schmid, K., Hewstone, M., Tausch, N., Cairns, E., & Hughes, J. (2009). Antecedents and consequences of social identity complexity: Intergroup contact, distinctiveness threat, and outgroup attitudes. *Personality & Social Psychology Bulletin*. doi:10.1177/0146167209337037

Scott, J. (1992). *Domination and the arts of resistance: Hidden transcripts*. Cumberland, RI: Yale University Press.

Shih, M., Bonam, C., Sanchez, D., & Peck, C. (2007). The social construction of race: Biracial identity and vulnerability to stereotypes. *Cultural Diversity & Ethnic Minority Psychology, 13*(2), 125-133. doi:10.1037/1099-9809.13.2.125

Sirin, S. R., & Fine, M. (2007). Hyphenated selves: Muslim American youth negotiating identities on the fault lines of global conflict. *Applied Developmental Science, 11*(3), 151-163. doi:10.1080/10888690701454658

Smith, L. T. (1999). *Decolonizing methodologies: Research and indigenous peoples*. London: Zed Books.

Smith, R. C. (2002). Life course, generation, and social location as factors shaping second-generation transnational life. In P. Levitt & M. C. Waters (Eds.), *The changing face of home the transnational lives of the second generation* (pp. 145-167). New York: Russell Sage Foundation.

Smith, R. C. (2003). Diasporic memberships in historical perspective:

Comparative insights from the Mexican, Italian and Polish cases. *International Migration Review*, *37*(3), 724-759.

Sorensen, N. N. (1998). Narrating identity across Dominican worlds. In M. P. Smith & L. E. Guarnizo (Eds.), *Transnationalism from below* (pp. 241-269). New Brunswick, NJ: Transaction Publishers.

Sorensen, N. N. (2005). Transnational family life across the Atlantic: the experience of Colombian and Dominican migrants in Europe (p. 17). Presented at the International Conference on Migration and Domestic Work in a Global Perspective, Wassenar, The Netherlands.

Statistical portrait of Hispanics in the United States, 2008. (2010). . Washington, D.C.: Pew Hispanic Center.

Stepick, A., & Stepick, C. D. (2010). The complexities and confusions of segmented assimilation. *Ethnic & Racial Studies*, *33*(7), 1149-1167. doi:10.1080/01419871003599518

Stewart, A. J., & Healy, J. M. (1989). Linking individual development and social changes. *American Psychologist*, *44*(1), 30-42. doi:10.1037/0003-066X.44.1.30

Suárez-Orozco, C., Rhodes, J., & Milburn, M. (2009). Unraveling the immigrant paradox: Academic engagement and disengagement among recently arrived immigrant youth. *Youth Society*, *41*(2), 151-185. doi:10.1177/0044118X09333647

Suárez-Orozco, C., & Suárez-Orozco, M. M. (2001). *Children of immigration*. Cambridge, MA: Harvard University Press.

Suárez-Orozco, M. M. (2002). Everything you ever wanted to know about assimilation but were afraid to ask. In R. A. Shweder, M. Minow, & H. R. Markus (Eds.), *Engaging cultural differences: The multicultural challenge in liberal democracies* (pp. 19-42). New York, NY: Russell Sage Foundation.

Suro, R., & Passel, J. (2003). *The rise of the second-generation: Changing patterns in Hispanic population growth*. Washington, D.C.: Pew Hispanic Center. Retrieved March 9, 2010 from http://pewhispanic.org/files/reports/22.pdf

Tadmor, C. T., Tetlock, P. E., & Peng, K. (2009). Acculturation strategies and integrative complexity: The cognitive implications of biculturalism. *Journal of Cross-Cultural Psychology*, *40*(1), 105-139.

Tajfel, H. (1981). *Human groups and social categories: Studies in social psychology*. Cambridge, MA: Cambridge University Press.

Tappan, M. B. (2005). Domination, subordination and the dialogical self: identity development and the politics of 'ideological becoming'. *Culture & Psychology*, *11*(1), 47-75. doi:10.1177/1354067X05050743

Tormala, T. T., & Deaux, K. (2006). Black immigrants to the United States: Confronting and constructing ethnicity and race. In R. Mahalingam (Ed.), *Cultural psychology of immigrants* (pp. 131-150). New York, NY: Routledge.

Torre, M. E., & Ayala, J. (2009). Envisioning participatory action research entremundos. *Feminism & Psychology*, *19*(3), 387-393. doi:10.1177/0959353509105630

Triandafyllidou, A., & Wodak, R. (2003). Conceptual and methodological questions in the study of collective identities. *Journal of Language & Politics*, *2*(2), 205-223.

Trillo, A. (2004). Somewhere between Wall Street and El Barrio: Community college as a second chance for second-generation Latino students. In P. Kasinitz, J. H. Mollenkopf, & M. C. Waters (Eds.), *Becoming New Yorkers: Ethnographies of the new second generation* (pp. 57-78). New York, NY: Russell Sage Foundation.

Tudge, J. R. H., Mokrova, I., Hatfield, B. E., & Karnik, R. B. (2009). Uses and misuses of Bronfenbrenner's bioecological theory of human development. *Journal of Family Theory & Review*, *1*(4), 198-210. doi:10.1111/j.1756-2589.2009.00026.x

Tummala-Narra, P. (2009). The immigrants real and imagined return home. *Psychoanalysis, Culture & Society*, *14*(3), 237–252. doi:10.1057/pcs.2009.9

Turits, R. L. (2002). A world destroyed, a nation imposed: The 1937 Haitian massacre in the Dominican Republic. *Hispanic American Historical Review*, *82*(3), 589-635.

Umana-Taylor, A. J., & Guimond, A. B. (2010). A longitudinal examination of parenting behaviors and perceived discrimination predicting Latino adolescents' ethnic identity. *Developmental Psychology*, *46*(3), 636–650.

Upegui-Hérnandez, D. (2009). Double-consciousness: A journey through the multiplicity of personal and social selves in the context of migration. In *Diversity in mind and action: multiple faces of identities*, Race and ethnicity in psychology series (Vols. 1-3, Vol. 1, pp. 129-148). Santa Barbara, CA: Praeger.

U.S. Census Bureau, American Community Survey. (2009a). *2006-2008 American Community Survey 3-year estimates*. Washington, D.C. Retrieved from http://www.census.gov/acs/www/index.html

U.S. Census Bureau, American Community Survey. (2009b). *2008 American Community Survey 1-year estimates*. Washington, D.C.

U.S. Census Bureau, Current Population Survey. (2011). *Characteristics of the Foreign-Born by Generation* (p. Table 4.1). Retrieved from http://www.census.gov/population/foreign/files/cps2011/2011T4.pdf

Valentine, D. E. (2006). The dialectic of recognition and displacement in a globalized world. In R. Mahalingam (Ed.), *Cultural psychology of immigrants* (pp. 33-54). Mahwah, NJ: Lawrence Erlbaum Associates Publishers.

Van Gennep, A. (1977). *The rites of passage*. New York: Routledge.

Verkuyten, M. (2005a). *The social psychology of ethnic identity*. Hove, UK and New York, NY: Psychology Press.

Verkuyten, M. (2005b). Ethnic group identification and group evaluation among minority and majority groups: Testing the multiculturalism hypothesis. *Journal of Social Personality and Social Psychology*, *88*, 121-138.

Verkuyten, M., & deWolf, A. (2002). Being, feeling and doing: Discourses and ethnic self-definitions among minority group members. *Culture Psychology*, *8*(4), 371-399. doi:10.1177/1354067X0284001

Vertovec, S. (1999). Conceiving and researching transnationalism. *Ethnic and Racial Studies*, *22*(2), 447-462.

Vertovec, S. (2004). Migrant transnationalism and modes of transformation. *International Migration Review*, *38*(3), 970-999.

Vertovec, S. (2009). *Transnationalism*. New York, NY: Routledge.

Vickerman, M. (2002). Second-generation West Indian transnationalilsm. In P. Levitt & M. C. Waters (Eds.), *The changing face of home the transnational lives of the second generation* (pp. 341-366). New York, NY: Russell Sage Foundation.

Waldinger, R. (2004). Will the second generation experiencc 'downward assimilation'? Segmented assimilation re-assessed. *Ethnic and Racial Studies*, *27*(2), 376-402.

Waters, M. C., & Kasinitz, P. (2010). Discrimination, race relations, and the second generation. *Social Research: An International Quarterly*, *77*(1), 101–132.

Waters, M. C. (1994). Ethnic and racial identities of second-generation Black immigrants in New York City. *International Migration Review*, *28*(4), 795-820.

Waters, M. C., Tran, V. C., Kasinitz, P., & Mollenkopf, J. H. (2010). Segmented assimilation revisited: types of acculturation and socioeconomic mobility in young adulthood. *Ethnic & Racial Studies*, *33*(7), 1168-1193. doi:10.1080/01419871003624076

Webster, T., & Ayala, E. (2006, June 18). Hiding in plain sight: Some students say cutting class is easy, especially if they don't try to leave campus. *Red Orbit*. News, . Retrieved March 9, 2010, from http://www.redorbit.com/news/education/541764/hiding_in_plain_sight_some_students_say_cutting_class_is/index.html

Weininger, E., & Lareau, A. (2007). Cultural capital. In G. Ritzer (Ed.), *Encyclopedia of sociology* (p. 5). Oxford, UK: Blackwell.

Wiley, S. (2005). *"Proving yourself in both worlds": A study of bicultural identification with Mexican and Dominican immigrants* . (Unpublished Dissertation). New York, NY: The CUNY Graduate Center.

Wiley, S., & Deaux, K. (2010) The bicultural identity performance of immigrants. In A. Azzi, B. Chryssochoou, B. Klandermans, & Simon (Eds.), *Identity and participation in culturally diverse societies: A multidisciplinary perspective*. Oxford: Blackwell Wiley.

Wimmer, A. (2007). *How (not) to think about ethnicity in immigrant societies: A boundary making perspective* (Working Paper). ESRC Centre on Migration, Policy and Society. Retrieved March 9, 2010 from http://www.compas.ox.ac.uk/fileadmin/files/pdfs/WP0744-Wimmer.pdf

Wimmer, A., & Glick-Schiller, N. (2003). Methodological nationalism, the social sciences, and the study of migration: An essay on historical epistemology. *International Migration Review*, *37*(Fall), 576-610.

Wolf, D. L. (2002). There's no place like "home": Emotional transnationalism and the struggles of second-generation Filipinos. In P. Levitt & M. C. Waters (Eds.), *The changing face of home the transnational lives of the second generation* (pp. 255-294). New York: Russell Sage Foundation.

Zaal, M., Salah, T., & Fine, M. (2007). The weight of the hyphen: Freedom, fusion and responsibility embodied by young Muslim American women during a time of surveillance. *Applied Developmental Science, 11*(3), 164-177.

Zentella, A. C. (2005). Premises, promises, and pitfalls of language socialization research in Latino families and communities. In A. C. Zentella (Ed.), *Building on strengths: Language and literacy in Latino families and communities*, Language and Literacy (pp. 13-30). New YorkNY: Teachers College Press.

Zentella, A. C. (2008). Latin@ languages and identities. In M. Suarez-Orozco & M. Páez (Eds.), *Latinos: Remaking America*. Berkeley, CA: University of California Press.

Index

CPSIA information can be obtained at www.ICGtesting.com
Printed in the USA
BVOW05*0825030614

354798BV00002B/3/P